CASS SERIES: BRITISH POLITICS AND SOCIETY
Series Editor: Peter Catterall
ISSN: 1467-1441

Social change impacts not just upon voting behaviour and party identity but also the formulation of policy. But how do social changes and political developments interact? Which shapes which? Reflecting a belief that social and political structures cannot be understood either in isolation from each other or from the historical processes which form them, this series will examine the forces that have shaped British society. Cross-disciplinary approaches will be encouraged. In the process, the series will aim to make a contribution to existing fields, such as politics, sociology and media studies, as well as opening out new and hitherto-neglected fields.

Peter Catterall (ed.), *The Making of Channel 4*

Brock Millman, *Managing Domestic Dissent in First World War Britain*

Peter Catterall, Wolfram Kaiser and Ulrike Walton-Jordan (eds), *Reforming the Constitution: Debates in Twenty-Century Britain*

Brock Millman, *Pessimism and British War Policy, 1916–1918*

Adrian Smith and Dilwyn Porter (eds), *Amateurs and Professionals in Post-war British Sport*

Archie Hunter, *A Life of Sir John Eldon Gorst: Disraeli's Awkward Disciple*

Harry Defries, *Conservative Party Attitudes to Jews, 1900–1950*

Virginia Berridge and Stuart Blume (eds), *Poor Health: Social Inequality before and after the Black Report*

Stuart Ball and Ian Holliday (eds), *Mass Conservatism: The Conservatives and the Public since the 1880s*

Rieko Karatani, *Defining British Citizenship: Empire, Commonwealth and Modern Britain*

MASS CONSERVATISM

The Conservatives and the Public since the 1880s

Editors

Stuart Ball
University of Leicester

Ian Holliday
City University of Hong Kong

With a Foreword by
Rt Hon. William Hague MP

FRANK CASS
LONDON • PORTLAND, OR

First published in 2002 in Great Britain by
FRANK CASS PUBLISHERS
Crown House, 47 Chase Side, Southgate
London N14 5BP

and in the United States of America by
FRANK CASS PUBLISHERS
c/o ISBS, 5824 N.E. Hassalo Street
Portland, Oregon, 97213-3644

Website: www.frankcass.com

British Library Cataloguing in Publication Data

Mass conservatism: the Conservatives and the public since
the 1880s. – (Cass series. British politics and society)
1. Conservative Party – History – 19th century
2. Conservative Party – History – 20th century
3. Conservatism – Great Britain – History – 19th century
4. Conservatism – Great Britain – History – 20th century
5. Great Britain – Politics and government – 1837–1901
6. Great Britain – Politics and government – 20th century
I. Ball, Stuart, 1956– II. Holliday, Ian
324.2'4104'09034

ISBN 0-7146-5223-7 (cloth)
ISBN 0-7146-8208-X (paper)
ISSN 1467-1441

Library of Congress Cataloging-in-Publication Data

Mass conservatism: the Conservatives and the public since the 1880s/
edited by Stuart Ball and Ian Holliday: with a foreword by William
Hague
   p. cm. – (Cass series – British politics and society, ISSN 1467-1441)
Includes bibliographical references and index.
   ISBN 0-7146-5223-7 (cloth) – ISBN 0-7146-8208-X (paper)
1. Great Britain – Politics and government – 20th century. 2.
Conservatism – Great Britain – History – 20th century. 3.
Conservatism – Great Britain – History – 19th century. 4. Great
Britain – Politics and government – 1837–1901. 5. Conservative Party
(Great Britain) – History. 6. Popular culture – Great Britain – History
7. Public opinion – Great Britain – History. I. Ball, Stuart, 1956– II.
Holliday, Ian. III. Series.
   DA566.7 .M375
   324.24104'09'04–dc21

2002073524

Typeset in 11/12½ Palatino by Frank Cass Publishers
Printed in Great Britain by MPG Books Ltd, Bodmin, Cornwall

Contents

Tables

Foreword

Over the past century the Conservative Party has been the dominant political force in British politics. During this time the party has undergone many changes. It has had long periods in government but has also, at times, been both divided and defeated. It has shaped many aspects of British life and has always remained relevant. However, seeking to define what has made it so attractive to so many people has proven more difficult.

The first reason for this is that, unlike the parties of the left, the Conservative Party has always been suspicious of strict ideology and abstract doctrine. Consequently, throughout its history, the party has favoured a more pragmatic approach and has continually adapted its core values to fit the prevailing political conditions of the time. Although conservatism has consistently upheld the values of freedom, individual responsibility and open economy, the Conservative Party has always sought to adapt these values to fit policies and programmes that appeal to the mainstream majority of British people. How else could a party that supposedly had so much to lose from the extension of the franchise maintain its appeal and increase its supporter base, and how could a party that once relied on landowners and the privileged be able to command significant support from all classes?

Secondly, although essentially a practical party, the Conservative Party has always respected the power of ideas in shaping political debate. Throughout its history it has been the party of great political thinkers such as Edmund Burke and Keith Joseph, but when there has been a need for ideological flexibility the party has sought to meet this challenge while remaining true to its basic values. It is this ability to generate ideas but never become a slave to them that has appealed to so many people over the years. I am proud of the history and traditions of the Conservative Party and I am proud of the principles that have been the bedrock of Conservatism for generations.

The essays in this volume chart the successes and failures of the Conservative Party to communicate its policies to its membership and to society at large over the past 120 years. They represent a variety of viewpoints, both critical and sympathetic towards the party. Together, they demonstrate that for supporters and opponents alike the resilience of mass Conservatism is one of the keys to understanding modern British history.

Rt Hon. William Hague MP
April 2002

Series Editor's Preface

At least until the 1950s, and arguably until the 1980s, many on the left remained convinced that they were the natural vehicle of popular political aspirations, if only the people would realise it! Conservative success was to be explained in sub-Gramscian terms as the inculcation of false consciousness amongst the masses. Successive Conservative victories in the 1950s, for instance, were ascribed to a base appeal to consumerism. And at the end of another run of Conservative success, in 1992, the left were equally apt to find the explanation in the alleged creation of a satisfied, and Tory, coalition of 'haves' determined to exclude the 'have-nots' from the enjoyment of power.

Superficially, such crude psephological perspectives may seem to have an ally in Lord Salisbury. He famously observed that the coalition in defence of established order is constantly being augmented by new allies with more to lose than gain by change. But these allies do not need to be 'haves'. The social goods they are defending can be cultural as well as material. And such defence may also be linked to a distrust or incredulity about the claims made by the Conservatives' opponents. As is pointed out in this collection, one of the key assets of the Conservative Party throughout the twentieth century was a reputation for governmental competence, exemplified by the way the word 'trust' was used in the 1992 election. This reputation, however, once lost in the aftermath of that election, has proved painfully difficult to recover.

Furthermore, of course, the charges of materialism that the left have always enjoyed throwing at the Conservatives can just as readily be flung back in their faces. At various times throughout the twentieth century accusations that the left represented the 'politics of envy', that its policies favoured the 'undeserving' over the 'deserving' poor, that its attitudes towards crime or defence would leave society insufficiently protected against internal or external enemies or that it is addicted to unproductive bureaucratic waste have spoken to a Conservative constituency that extends far beyond the boundaries of the middle classes. Indeed, if the Conservatives had ever simply been content to appeal to these supposed core supporters – the Margot Leadbetters of the 1970s situation-comedy *The Good Life* – it could hardly have hoped for the degree of electoral success it enjoyed for a century or so after 1885 under Lord Salisbury and his successors. And, as many of the essays in this collection show, these successes have come, not through sharing to some extent their opponents' assumptions that 'natural' supporters will come out to vote, but through organisation, hard work in identifying Conservatives on the doorsteps and, not least, carefully positioning the message and identity of the party so as to maximise its appeal. One example is the way in which the language of opportunity, as was eventually acknowledged by their political opponents, proved so potent in appealing to the aspirant working classes in the 1980s.

Understanding such phenomena has not always been aided by the processes of psephology. Founded in the 1950s, an unusual moment of two party dominance when a class-based model perhaps seemed peculiarly apt for describing twentieth-century electoral behaviour, this discipline has tended to privilege social class as an explanatory means. From this perspective popular Conservatism has been seen as aberrant, in much the same way as it has been seen by the left (though it might tell us something about the *a priori* assumptions of too many of these researchers to observe that middle-class Labour-voting does not seem to have been similarly treated as a problem to be explained). And working-class Conservatives have either been seen, patronisingly, as 'deferential', or as pocketbook voters momentarily lulled by promises of affluence into voting Conservative.

There are a number of problems with such a crude approach. Not least, 'working class' is rather a blanket term. A number of the essays here offer a more nuanced analysis of social class and its fit with political identities. This, of course, reflects the approach the Conservative Party, of necessity, has itself taken. Furthermore, as is also pointed out in this collection, the relationship between affluence and Conservative-voting has proved, in any case, to be rather more complex than was too readily assumed in the 1950s.

At the same time, the term 'deferential' is also problematic. It has generally been used to suggest simply an acceptance of existing elite structures. I would like suggest that it contains a more complex range of meanings. Firstly, as is shown here with reference to inter-war farm workers, it can indicate a broader attachment to a whole social order and set of social relationships and institutions. That social order can be regarded as beneficial, or at least as beneficial as any likely to be erected in its place by the Conservatives' opponents. In other words, 'deferential' voting is not an effect of false consciousness, but entirely rational behaviour.

Secondly, the somewhat cynical cast of the Conservative mind, regardless of social class, is more likely than most to subscribe to the truism that there will always be elites. Marx found it impossible to describe a society in which elites had ceased to exist, so why should Conservatives be any different? A healthy scepticism about all political promises can reinforce a rational resistance to change, and a preference for the devil you know as opposed to the unknown quantity of new masters.

Thirdly, 'deference' can be seen as indicating an attachment to a particular set of social values and order. This involves respect, certainly, for material goods in the form of property rights. But it also involves more general notions of respect in social relations: for elders from their children and from unruly youth; for teachers from their pupils; for society in general from disruptive elements within it. 'There isn't any respect any more' is a common lament from working-class Conservatives. Conservative defence of existing social order could thus appeal to deep-rooted social values held by their core supporters, whatever their social class.

Party allegiance is more complex than the traditional focus on social class allows. Consider the way in which the two main parties have historically been seen as 'better' at handling different issues – Labour generally enjoying a poll lead on social welfare matters and the Conservatives, at least until the 1990s, a similar advantage in areas such as public order, defence or the economy. Insofar as the twentieth was indeed a 'Conservative century', it was because the Conservative Party for most of that time was better able at manipulating the fit between its own identity, the issues of the day (perhaps the classic example being the 'Winter of Discontent' of 1978–79) and the attitudes and values of the public. In Britain electoral success is usually determined by building a successful electoral coalition, and the Conservatives have been not only relatively good at creating such coalitions, but have also generally been more successful than their opponents at keeping such coalitions, once established, in being. Their experience at the end of the twentieth century, however, illustrates that success is by no means guaranteed. Popular Conservatism, as this collection effectively demonstrates, depends upon the establishment and maintenance of a positive association between the party and public issues and values. It can hardly be expected to thrive when the party allows its opponents to define, negatively, the identity of the

Conservative Party, nor can it be expected to revive until the Conservative Party reclaims that identity and again imbues it with positive connotations in tune with public aspirations.

Peter Catterall
London

Acknowledgements

Most of the essays in this volume were delivered in preliminary form at the conference 'Mass Conservatism: The Tories and the People, 1867–1997', held at the National Museum of Labour History, Manchester, on 25–26 September 1998. The conference was accompanied by a National Museum of Labour History exhibition, opened by the then Conservative Party leader, the Right Honourable William Hague MP; the exhibition ran from 25 September 1998 to 17 January 1999. A third event was a brief film season, held at Manchester's Cornerhouse cinema on 25–27 September 1998. The principal sponsors of these linked events were the National Museum of Labour History, the University of Manchester and the journal *Party Politics*; we pay tribute to them here. Mr Hague has also kindly written a foreword for this volume, for which we are most grateful.

The editors would like to thank Andrew Taylor for his assistance in planning the conference and chairing some of the sessions. We are grateful to Peter Catterall, the series editor, and to Andrew Humphrys of Frank Cass for their support of the project, and their patience with the sometimes slow process of reshaping it into book form. The editors would also like to thank the contributors for their commitment to the project and their positive responses to our editorial suggestions. Jill Spellman, archivist at the Conservative Party Archive, Bodleian Library, kindly assisted with source material and queries about references.

Abbreviations

ACPPE	Advisory Committee on Policy and Political Education
BIPO	British Institute of Public Opinion
BHL	British Housewives League
CAD	Community Affairs Department
CCO	Conservative Central Office
CPF	Conservative Policy Forum
CPC	Conservative Political Centre
CPV	Colman, Prentis and Varley
CRD	Conservative Research Department
CTU	Conservative Trade Unionists
CUFA	Conservative and Unionist Film Association
E&NSLUA	East and North of Scotland Liberal Unionist Association
ERM	European exchange rate mechanism
FCS	Federation of Conservative Students
ILP	Independent Labour Party
LCC	London County Council
MO	Mass-Observation
NEDC	National Economic Development Council
NFU	National Farmers Union
NFWI	National Federation of Women's Institutes
NOP	National Opinion Polls Ltd
NUAW	National Union of Agricultural Workers
NUCAS	National Union of Conservative Associations for Scotland
NUR	National Union of Railwaymen
NUS	National Union of Students
PORD	Public Opinion Research Department
TUC	Trades Union Congress
VC	Vermin Club
WI	Women's Institute
WSLUA	West of Scotland Liberal Unionist Association
WU	Workers' Union
WVS	Women's Voluntary Service
YCs	Young Conservatives

Mass Conservatism:
An Introduction

STUART BALL and IAN HOLLIDAY

There are two aspects to the significance of the Conservative Party in modern British history. The first and most obvious is its electoral success. From the widening of the franchise in the 1880s to the end of the twentieth century, the Conservatives have been one of the most successful parties known to modern Western democracy. During the second half of the nineteenth century, the Conservative Party progressed from having minority status to being a powerful and dominant force under Lord Salisbury's leadership. It was the governing party for almost all of the period between the two world wars, and recovered from defeat in 1945 to hold power for a further 13 years from 1951 to 1964. After a difficult interval, the Conservatives returned to centre stage under Mrs Thatcher in 1979 and held office until 1997. Although they have ended it in an unusual atmosphere of public rejection, taken as a whole the twentieth century was indeed the Conservative century.[1]

The second aspect follows from this, for such longevity in power has meant that Britain's society and economy have been substantially shaped in the Conservative image. This has been crucial in the roles permitted to the state in areas such as economic management, fiscal strategy, social regulation and environmental control, in both war and peace. The process is a complex one, for Conservative success has been based upon absorbing key elements of the accepted values and attitudes of the British public. At the same time, those social and cultural assumptions have been reflected back and so further reinforced. In this way the Conservative Party became aligned with 'conventional wisdom'; for the mass of the population it seemed obvious that 'the facts of life are Tory'.[2] This was not a matter of conscious manipulation, for it derived from the party's core constituency of support. Middle-class culture became ever more pervasive from the mid-nineteenth century onwards, until by the last decades of the twentieth century it encompassed much of the former working class – at least in outlook and aspiration. The Conservatives seemed to be the 'natural party of government' for more than just tenure of office and executive competence. They have defined the norm from which others differ; this explains their continuing relevance as a political force, and has been the foundation for their resilience in defeat.

The link between the Conservatives' electoral record and social significance has been their role as a mass party. The ability to relate to wide and varied sections of British society and the capacity to mobilise an extensive body of supporters have been consistent features of the Conservative Party's performance since the 1880s. This made the advent of democracy an opportunity rather than a peril: the Conservatives defied pessimistic assumptions – including their own – and prospered with the extensions of the franchise in 1885 and 1918. They have not been undermined by the erosion of rigid class differences and the waning of deference since the First World War, and especially since the 1960s. During the twentieth century, the Conservatives evolved an identity that did not tie them down to any particular issue or vested interest. Above all, they sustained the position of a 'mass' party rather than just a 'class' party. By the second half of the century, the broad popular basis of Conservative support had become an unquestioned part of the political landscape and an integral part of the party's own identity and self-image.

The roots, ethos and image of modern Conservatism are aspects which historians and political scientists are still beginning to explore. Before the late 1970s the central questions in modern British politics appeared to revolve around the decline of the Liberals and the rise of Labour; the Conservatives were comparatively neglected. This began to change in the 1980s, partly under the impact of Margaret Thatcher's radical and populist agenda and the successive Conservative electoral victories. However, although the Conservative Party has received more extensive and sophisticated attention during the last two decades of the twentieth century, much remains to be investigated about the relationships between the party and civil society.[3] In part this reflects the Conservative Party's origins as an elite institution which started to build downwards into society in the second half of the nineteenth century. Unlike the Labour Party, its major challenger for most of the twentieth century, the Conservative Party can in no sense trace its initial development to widespread civil mobilisation. As a result, the party's social foundations, though often significant, have never attracted the attention paid to Labour's roots in the trade union movement, socialist societies, working men's clubs and so on. Instead, the Conservatives have been viewed from the top down, with a particular emphasis on the power and importance of the party leader.[4] This perspective channelled attention towards the personalities and manoeuvres of the elite and the evolution of policy, rather than the underlying purpose of connecting the party with the mass of the British people. Biographies far outweigh – in every sense – all other commentary on the Conservatives.

Discussions of Conservative politics have taken one of two main forms. The 'historical' approach is chronologically based and leans towards a narrative shaped by leading figures and periodic crises; these elements mainly determine the party's electoral fortunes, which are essentially reactive and thus a subordinate theme.[5] The 'political science' approach superficially appears more analytical but has operated within confining assumptions and parameters, concentrating upon the party's policy making and institutional development.[6] Analyses that have directly engaged with the party's support and public have been few and far between. In the 1950s and 1960s a number of local case-studies by political scientists interested in voting behaviour gave some contemporary glimpses of the Conservatives' roots.[7] Methodology from the nascent disciplines of sociology and political science was employed in three pioneering studies of working-class Conservatism which appeared almost simultaneously in the late 1960s.[8] This was a false dawn; apart from Andrew Gamble's more general survey, *The Conservative Nation*, published in 1974, the topic was then neglected.[9]

The resounding silence was compounded by the fact that neither the local nor the sociological approach was adopted as a model by historians (in notable contrast to the Nuffield general election studies). There was a considerable interval before the first historical work to take a broader view – Martin Pugh's examination of the Primrose League, *The Tories and the People 1880–1935*, appeared in 1985.[10] Even so, this and subsequent works deal mainly with specific parts of the Conservatives' organisation and campaigning.[11] It is hard to find studies that address the party's relationship with the British public over a long period of time and from a variety of angles, thereby enabling broad lessons to be drawn.[12] The only recent significant work of this nature can be found in two edited collections: *Conservative Century: The Conservative Party since 1900*, and *The Conservatives and British Society 1880–1990*.[13] The first of these is a thematic analysis of the Conservative Party in the twentieth century, in which several essays engage with aspects of its popular support. The second volume was inspired by the 'linguistic turn' and seeks to supplement – and even supplant – traditional class-based perspectives on Conservative Party development; the essays it contains are 'informed by recent developments in cultural theory and historical methodology'.[14] The present volume examines a similar period, from the emergence of an identifiably 'mass' dimension to British Conservatism in the 1880s to the increasingly difficult decade of the 1990s. In this instance, however, no particular methodology or theory has been prescribed, and the link between the essays is provided by the topic rather than the approach.

The studies in this volume seek to explore the phenomenon of 'mass Conservatism' in different periods and from varied perspectives, and to fill some of the many gaps that continue to exist. They have in common a concern with the relationship between the Conservative Party and the public, and an awareness of the complexities present in both parts of that equation. Each of the chapters has its intrinsic interest and relevance, while collectively they illuminate the two interwoven strands of 'mass Conservatism'. The first of these could be termed 'the Conservatives and the masses', and concerns the party's relationship with its members and supporters. It takes the party as its focus, and considers issues such as the role of party activists in shaping policy, the way in which the party has sought to manage its dealings with key elements of civil society, and the contribution of specialised party organisations to the party's links with the British people. The second strand, 'the Conservatism of the masses', looks at the relationship between party and society from an exterior perspective. It addresses, for example, the penetration of Toryism in particular classes and regions of Britain, the party's standing in public opinion, and the ways in which it has been regarded and responded to by various sections of society. Neither of these strands is self-contained, and many chapters have elements that relate to both. Although the order of the chapters is chronologically based, it is not our intention to offer a narrative survey of the whole period. Instead, the range of the chapters in time and theme should be taken to indicate the wide parameters and varied approaches which are needed in this field.

The first era in which the Conservative Party consciously faced the challenge of survival and success in a mass political system was after the Third Reform Act of 1884–85. Although contemporaries used the term 'democracy' to describe this, from our present perspective it would more accurately be described as a 'popular' and 'mass' electorate. Women were still excluded from the franchise and there was a bias in the registration system that worked against younger and single men and in favour of a 'householder' qualification. Even so, approximately two-thirds of adult males had the vote in a system in which the introduction of the secret ballot and the restriction of candidates' expenses had removed many of the constraints of bribery and intimidation. The electorate dwarfed that of previous eras, and in every constituency – rural, urban and even suburban – there was a majority of working-class voters. From this time onwards the Conservative Party operated in a mass environment, in which success could only be achieved through a wide-ranging appeal which crossed class, religious, regional and ethnic divisions.

The first chapter in the volume explores how this challenge was managed in Scotland, where Conservatism has experienced significantly changed identities and vastly differing fortunes over the years. In 'The Making of Scottish Unionism, 1886–1914', Burness analyses the alliance with Liberal Unionism which opened a comparatively successful episode in the history of Scottish Conservatism. Her argument is that Liberal Unionism altered the development of Scottish Toryism and enhanced its mass appeal by giving it a new identity and helping it to overcome historic anti-Conservative sentiment north of the border. Drawing lessons for the party in the difficult circumstances that it faces in Scotland at the beginning of the twenty-first century, she notes that a Unionist appeal may no longer be strong in a climate of devolution, but that organisational successes registered a century ago could perhaps be repeated.

The second chapter moves forward to the immediate wake of the First World War, an uneasy period in which the combination of a further massive extension of the franchise at home and the

collapse of many European states into chaos and revolution
aroused fear in the propertied classes. The economic and social
strains that resulted from the war and its impact upon the development of trade unionism and the rise of the Labour Party have
normally been explored from an urban perspective. However, the
war shook many certainties, and unsettled customary relationships in all parts of the nation. A neglected aspect is explored in
Mansfield's study of farm workers and local Conservatism in
south-west Shropshire in the period 1916–23. Although the
Conservative Party had been strong in this part of Britain, where it
was supported by structural factors that were often becoming
rather enervated elsewhere, its political domination could not be
taken for granted. Here, as in other regions, this period witnessed
a substantial increase in rural trade unionism and socialism.
Mansfield seeks to explain how the left-wing challenge was eventually overcome by local Conservatives. After assessing a range of
factors, he develops the argument that cultural factors were critical
to the maintenance of Conservative hegemony. In so doing, he
provides a wealth of evidence about the local social and political
scene. The considerable dynamism of Conservatism in rural
Britain that is revealed was an important element in the party's
electoral dominance in the inter-war era.

The inter-war period was the second of the four extended spells
of Conservative dominance during the period covered in this
book. The Conservatives entered the period still troubled by the
legacy of their divisive and barren period in opposition between
1906 and 1914. The war had restored their position as the patriotic
party, but at first they feared that only the continuation of the
broad appeal of the Coalition with Lloyd George's Liberals could
contain the challenges of militant trade unionism and the socialism
of the Labour Party. It was only after the failure and rejection of the
Coalition strategy and a sweeping change of leadership in 1922
that the Conservatives stood alone. The success they achieved
after this was the result of several factors, but important elements
were the inclusive appeal they projected, the aspirations and
needs they fostered, the organisational and campaigning innovations they embraced, and the effectiveness with which they
mobilised the largest element of new voters – women.

The next group of chapters explores new ground in relation to
these aspects. Housing was a central issue in the mass politics of
the inter-war years from Lloyd George's 'homes for heroes'
promise of 1918 onwards, and Morgan explores the Conservative
approach towards this key area. Chapter 4 illuminates the way in

which the imagery of the home represented distinctly Conservative terrain. However, Morgan's central concern is to make clear the complexities of party policy in this sphere. To do so, he looks at the different elements of private homes, public housing and building technology, demonstrating that no simple bipolar model can be used to capture Conservative housing policies in the inter-war period. He also provides a detailed account of one aspect of party strategy in making and remaking a Conservative majority in apparently unpromising times.

In 'Speaking to Democracy: The Conservative Party and Mass Opinion from the 1920s to the 1950s', Taylor traces Conservative attempts to influence the public by focusing on three distinct episodes. The first – the projection of an image of Stanley Baldwin through radio speeches and film in the 1920s and 1930s – provides further evidence of how the Conservatives managed to build an electoral hegemony in the inter-war years. However, the second is a story of failure: the inability of the *Industrial Charter*, launched with considerable fanfare in 1947, to penetrate mass opinion. Taylor ascribes this failure to the *Charter*'s complexity, which made it very nearly impossible to get a clear message across to a mass electorate. The third episode returns to the theme of success: the party's use of opinion-poll data in the 1950s to reinforce an image of governing competence. In this section, Taylor also indicates the extent to which party policy was shaped by information about the electorate gathered through polling, arguing that such information helped to prompt the Conservatives' embrace of modernisation in the 1960s.

The importance of Conservative support among women since their enfranchisement in 1918 has received some attention from historians, but they have mainly been considered as either voters or party members.[15] The topic is approached from a fresh angle in Hinton's examination of the associational life of middle-class and upper-class women in English provincial towns in the late 1930s and 1940s, focusing particularly on the Women's Voluntary Service, formed in 1938. He shows that voluntary associations provided publicly active middle-class women with a forum within which to exercise social leadership even in the formally non-partisan circumstances of the Second World War. He notes that there were pluses and minuses in this for the Conservative Party: the advantages came in the form of opportunities for recruitment to the party, while the disadvantages were the ways in which activists were drawn away from party work by their commitments to voluntary associations. Tensions of this kind were particularly

great when partisan activity formally recommenced at the end of
the war. However, Hinton shows that many women declined to
choose between party political activity and social leadership
through voluntary associations, preferring to remain active in both
spheres. He thereby demonstrates that in the middle years of the
twentieth century a rich associational life underpinned
Conservative politics in conditions of both war and peace.

The remaining chapters cover aspects of the period since 1945.
The first of these also explores the role of groups outside the
Conservative Party structure, although in this case they were both
more political and more ephemeral than the major voluntary
movements. In 'Echoes in the Wilderness: British Popular
Conservatism, 1945–51', Martin analyses the way in which some
popular opposition to the Attlee Labour government was channelled and led by the British Housewives League (BHL) and the
Vermin Club (VC). The former, apparently non-party, was founded
upon popular resentment of the continuing shortages of the
austerity era. However, it promoted traditionalist – even reactionary – conceptions of women's role in society, and had an
actively Conservative element in its leadership. This was even
truer of the Vermin Club, which stemmed from similar wells of
popular frustration, especially among the middle classes. It was
sparked by a vituperative phrase uttered by the left-wing Labour
Minister of Health, Aneurin Bevan, in a speech in 1948. Martin
shows that both organisations were formally unconnected with
the Conservative Party, emerging in largely spontaneous reaction
to the first majority Labour government. Indeed, he argues, each
was often as much of an embarrassment to the Conservative Party
as it was an irritant to Labour, and the party formally distanced
itself from the BHL while remaining slightly more ambivalent
about the VC. At a time when the party itself was on the defensive,
and when many Conservative values appeared to be under
sustained attack, these organisations used what Martin calls 'street
politics and populist hysteria' to take the anti-Labour fight on to
terrain that the Conservative Party itself was unwilling to occupy.

From these passionate and bitter debates, we then move
forward into the 1950s and 1960s – the era often identified with the
development of a 'consensus' between the main parties over the
parameters for state interventionism, economic planning, welfare
provision and the role of trade unionism. The relationship
between the party and the trade union movement is a core theme
of mass Conservatism. In 'Industrial Relations as "Human
Relations": Conservatism and Trade Unionism, 1945–64', Dorey

discusses how the Tories sought to manage this relationship in the period in which they were seeking to recover from their landslide defeat of 1945 and to re-establish their credentials as a party of government which could reflect and balance the interests of all classes. The first aspect of this was enshrined in the *Industrial Charter*, previously considered by Taylor from another perspective. Dorey argues that the *Charter* played an important role in developing a more conciliatory Tory approach to the trade unions, and selling it to party members. He holds that the new Conservative philosophy had four main elements: voluntarism, a socio-psychological critique of industrial conflict, advocacy of industrial partnership as an integral part of a 'human relations' approach, and ministerial exhortation that wage bargaining be 'responsible'. However, there were always intra-party tensions, which became increasingly prominent in the late 1950s and early 1960s. In the closing years of Macmillan's premiership, the modernisation strategy that Taylor holds to have been shaped, in part, by opinion-poll returns prompted a more interventionist Conservative policy towards the trade unions. At the same time, Conservatives continued to extol the virtues of free collective bargaining, making party policy in the run-up to the 1964 general election rather incoherent. At the close of Dorey's period, then, the party did not have a clear line on how to relate to organised labour, although it was to move towards more abrasive approaches in the following decades.

In more recent years attention has been drawn to the limits of the post-war 'consensus', and the value of the term itself has been questioned.[16] One of these disruptive aspects was the emerging tensions over racial issues in the wake of increasing non-white immigration into working-class urban areas that were already suffering economic decline. The issue of how to respond to this and manage Commonwealth immigration became an increasingly important – and explosive – issue for mass Conservatism in the 1950s and 1960s. However, whereas existing analyses tend to focus uniquely on the question of control, Crowson's chapter, 'Conservative Party Activists and Immigration Policy from the late 1940s to the mid-1970s', takes a greater interest in the ways in which the party sought to respond to the challenge of an emergent immigrant electorate. The chapter has three main themes. First, it looks at Conservative reaction to the social consequences of immigration, notably in the spheres of unemployment, housing and education. Second, it examines the means by which the party sought to court the immigrant vote. Third, it tackles the matter of immigration control, which can never be entirely overlooked. The divisions which are found run from the very top to the base of the party, reinforcing existing analyses of the great difficulty Conservatives experienced in seeking to manage mass opinion in this sphere.

The next two chapters focus on specific structures created within the Conservative Party's central organisation in the post-war era. Both were the product of fears that the party was losing contact with important elements of British society, and both were created against a background of electoral defeat and uncertainty about the social foundations of Conservative support. The first of these, the Conservative Political Centre (CPC), was established after the defeat of 1945. Although its institutional role was linked to the party's voluntary membership at local level, its purpose of developing political education also had a wider public remit. In a period when Conservatism was widely discredited and on the defensive, the aim of the CPC was to achieve 'victory in the battle of ideas'.[17] Norton identifies four main aspects to this function: facilitating dialogue between leaders and members; educating party members; influencing the intellectual climate; and providing a platform for party leaders. His verdict is that the CPC played a key role in reaching out beyond the party, and spreading Conservative ideas. He holds it to have been particularly import-ant in enabling party leaders to speak beyond the party to the nation as a whole. In this respect, it can be seen as a significant element in the party's post-war strategy for engaging with, and shaping, mass opinion. Although it was formally superseded by the Conservative Policy Forum in 1998, the new body has largely continued with the same functions and format.

The second organisational initiative had a much briefer existence, and was more directly concerned with the party's rela-tionship with external social groups. Between 1975 and 1979 the Community Affairs Department (CAD) was a key part of the struc-ture of Conservative Central Office, and represented a striking initiative in response to changes in society and public attitudes to party politics. This chapter has one crucial difference from the others in this collection: it is written from the inside, by someone at the heart of the events – Rowe was director of the CAD for almost all of its existence. As he notes, this was a critical period for the Conservative Party. In the 1960s, a great deal of political mobil-isation had taken place outside party structures, in voluntary organisations and single-issue pressure groups operating locally as well as nationally. This generated a challenge for all the major parties to reconnect with political activists, and was all the more pressing for the Conservatives in the wake of their defeats in 1974 and declining trends in elements of the party's support over the previous decade. In seeking to reach out to the mass of the British people the CAD faced internal as well as external problems, such as the formal autonomy of constituency associations, the low calibre of many agents and straightforward resistance to change. This chapter connects with the concerns of two previous ones, and provides further information about the party's attempts to forge links with ethnic minorities and trade union members.

The final chapter deals with the fourth and most recent period of Conservative governing dominance, the Thatcher and Major era of 1979 to 1997. In 'Thatcherism and the British People', Evans explodes a widespread myth of late twentieth-century mass Conservatism. Focusing upon the emblematic constituency of Basildon, home to 'Essex man', he analyses the extent to which Thatcherism succeeded in creating a populist hegemony in the years from Thatcher's election as party leader in February 1975 to sterling's ejection from the European exchange rate mechanism (ERM) on 'Black Wednesday' in September 1992. His argument is that such hegemony was never fully established, and that successive Conservative general election victories from 1979 to 1992 were the product of luck and manipulation of the electoral cycle rather than of any deeper shift in popular values. In so doing, he reinforces accounts of partisan dealignment and electoral volatility that move the focus of electoral analysis away from party identification towards images of governing competence. As such, Evans raises important questions about the extent to which mass Conservatism retains a vitality in the contemporary age. Recent analyses have documented the party's limited capacity for renewal, which is handicapped by the ageing nature of the local membership.[18] In the decade which followed Black Wednesday, the Conservative Party signally failed to reconnect with the British public, losing the 1997 and the 2001 general elections to Labour in an unprecedented double landslide.

The historical perspectives collected in this volume are not intended to provide explicit lessons for the Conservative elite as it seeks to re-establish its credentials with the British public, but they will enrich and encourage the growing debate about the nature of mass Conservatism in modern Britain. Taken together, they suggest a number of themes about the ethos of the Conservative Party and its relationship with the public. The first of these is the

tension between the concepts of 'mass' and 'class'. Initially fearful
of change and of being washed away on a tide of envy and ignorance after the franchise extensions of both 1884–85 and 1918,
the Conservatives' faith in mass politics evolved in the wake of
their electoral and governing success. With the wisdom of hind-
sight, Disraeli's mantra of 'trust the people' – previously a radical
slogan – became the foresight of a prophet, establishing with it the
Disraelian principles of concern for the condition of the ordinary
people and the 'one nation' tradition of unity through benev-
olence. 'Mass' gradually shed its dangerous connotations, and
instead became the party's counterweight to the rise of class-based
politics from the late nineteenth century onwards. The masses
embraced more than one class, and cut across both the sectional
appeals of Gladstonian Liberals and the class foundation of socialism and the emerging Labour Party. An appeal to mass opinion (or,
in the vocabulary more generally used in the twentieth century, to
the general public) was thus an inclusive and unifying stance. By
the 1920s, the Conservatives were entirely credible in putting their
trust in the decency and moderation of the masses; they no longer
feared the people, but only that they might be led astray by
extremists and agitators. Although the Conservatives had to work
with reality and so acknowledged the existence and nature of class
distinctions, they disliked thinking in these terms. At the same
time, they wanted and needed the endorsement of the majority
and the legitimacy and security which that conferred, and so
developed their party organisation, campaigning, imagery and
rhetoric to become a mass movement. Country and people became
one concept, and the patriotic party was thus also the national
party.

The second underlying theme is the role of the Conservative
Party membership as the bridge between the executive and
governing political heights and the general public. The active
members have relationships both upwards through the party's
institutions and still more through the parliamentary party,[19] and
outwards to the social and economic environment of their locality.
They are responsive to these external stimuli, and this produces
the essentially reactive agenda of local Conservatism. This can
manifest itself in issues which may appear unconnected, but it is
the task of the historian to map the submerged strata which link
the volcanic peaks, and which determine whether they are
erupting, simmering or – seemingly – exhausted.

A third theme is that the Conservative outlook reflects its times
and circumstances, and so rests more adaptably upon the shifting

currents of a mass political system. And the mass of Conservative supporters – party members or just voters – do not have a systematic view of the future. If there is a Conservative utopianism, it is based upon the past. This may be mythical, with every generation stretching out for a 'golden age' of social certainty which has somehow since evaporated, but it more easily evokes a consensus while placing fewer constraints or expectations upon Conservative governments in practice. Conservatism has been seen as 'common sense', from Salisburian practicality to Baldwin's plain truths and Thatcher's 'housewife economics'. Realism is linked to limited expectations, anti-intellectualism and instinctive suspicion of grand plans and panaceas. The Conservatives instead have offered the opportunity to get on with ordinary life, with concerns focused on the here and now.

This has also contributed to a fourth aspect of the Conservatives as a mass party: their greater national reach than any of their competitors, notwithstanding the decline in the Celtic regions in recent years. The similarities of Conservative support across different regions, economic sectors, and urban or rural environments is striking, and has time and again proven stronger than the opposite pulls of different interests and experiences. Conservative disunity has been a matter of rivalries and factions, visible in the leadership and the parliamentary party, but it does not shatter the party at mass level. It has been the role of the party organisation to knit the strands together, especially at regional and national levels. The organisation may have shed numbers steadily since the 1950s in response to changes in society and greater diversity in leisure activities, but it has not lost its stability and cohesiveness. For all of these reasons, even in the wake of the heavy defeats of 1997 and 2001, there is a presumption that the Conservative Party will survive and continue in more or less its present form. The day when it may return to government is unpredictable but not impossible, for underlying this is the expectation that mass Conservatism in all its forms will continue to be a feature of the British political landscape in the twenty-first century.

NOTES

1. A. Seldon and S. Ball (eds), *Conservative Century: The Conservative Party since 1900* (Oxford, 1994). This also contains a full bibliographic survey: S. Ball, 'The Conservative Party since 1900: A Bibliography', 727–72.
2. R. McKibbin, 'Class and Conventional Wisdom: The Conservative Party and the "Public" in Inter-war Britain', in R. McKibbin, *The Ideologies of Class* (Oxford, 1990), 259–93; also discussion in S. Ball, *The Conservative Party and British Politics 1902–1951* (Harlow, 1995), 35, 120–3.

3. See the reviews of the literature in S. Ball, *The Conservative Party since 1945* (Manchester, 1998), 4–11, and M. Francis and I. Zweiniger-Bargielowska, 'Introduction', in M. Francis and I. Zweiniger-Bargielowska (eds), *The Conservatives and British Society 1880–1990* (Cardiff, 1996), 1–16; also Ball, 'The Conservative Party since 1900: A Bibliography', 729–39.

4. For a rare early view from below, see M. Wilson, 'Grass-roots Conservatism: Motions to the Party Conference', in N. Nugent and R. King (eds), *The British Right: Conservative and Right-wing Politics in Britain* (Farnborough, 1977), 64–98.

5. This has been approach of the standard history by R. Blake, *The Conservative Party from Peel to Churchill* (London, 1970, and subsequent eds); T. F. Lindsay and M. Harrington, *The Conservative Party 1918–79* (London, 1979); J. Charmley, *A History of Conservative Politics 1900–1996* (Basingstoke, 1996); J. Ramsden, *An Appetite for Power: A History of the Conservative Party since 1830* (London, 1998); and, despite their titles, of A. J. Davies, *We, the Nation: The Conservative Party and the Pursuit of Power* (London, 1995), and A. Clark, *The Tories: Conservatives and the Nation State 1922–1997* (London, 1998). There has been a greater focus on organisational development in the volumes in the Longman history of the Conservative Party, in particular J. Ramsden, *The Age of Balfour and Baldwin 1902–1940* (London, 1978). Some wider issues were raised in B. Coleman, *Conservatism and the Conservative Party in Nineteenth-century Britain* (London, 1988).

6. S. H. Beer, 'The Conservative Party of Great Britain', *Journal of Politics*, 14 (1952), 41–71; I. Bulmer-Thomas, 'How Conservative Policy is Formed', *Political Quarterly*, 24 (1953), 190–203; R. T. McKenzie, *British Political Parties* (London, 1955); J. Cornford, 'The Adoption of Mass Organisation by the British Conservative Party', in E. Allardt and Y. Littunen (eds), *Cleavages, Ideologies and Party Systems* (Helsinki, Westermarck Society Transactions, 1964), 400–24; J. D. Lees and R. Kimber (eds), *Political Parties in Modern Britain: An Organisational and Functional Guide* (London, 1972); M. Pinto-Duschinsky, 'Central Office and "Power" in the Conservative Party', *Political Studies*, 20 (1972), 1–16; N. Harris, *Competition and the Corporate Society: British Conservatives, the State and Industry 1945–1964* (London, 1972); Z. Layton-Henry, 'The Young Conservatives 1945–1970', *Journal of Contemporary History*, 8 (1973), 143–56; A. Beichman, 'The Conservative Research Department', *Journal of British Studies*, 13 (1974), 92–113; D. H. Close, 'The Growth of Backbench Organisation in the Conservative Party', *Parliamentary Affairs*, 27 (1974), 371–83; D. J. Wilson, *Power and Party Bureaucracy in Britain: Regional Organisation in the Conservative and Labour Parties* (Farnborough, 1975); P. Seyd, 'Democracy within the Conservative Party?', *Government and Opposition*, 10 (1975), 219–40; Z. Layton-Henry (ed.), *Conservative Party Politics* (London, 1980); P. Norton and A. Aughey, *Conservatives and Conservatism* (London, 1981); R. Kelly, *Conservative Party Conferences* (Manchester, 1989); C. Knight, *The Making of Tory Education Policy in Post-war Britain 1950–1986* (London, 1990). Seldon and Ball (eds), *Conservative Century*, drew authors from both disciplines and sought to merge the two approaches.

7. M. Benney, A. P. Gray and R. H. Pear, *How People Vote: A Study of Electoral Behaviour in Greenwich* (London, 1956); J. Blondel, 'The Conservative Association and the Labour Party in Reading', *Political Studies*, 6 (1958), 101–19; A. H. Birch, *Small Town Politics: A Study of Political Life in Glossop* (Oxford, 1959); M. Stacey, *Tradition and Change: A Study of Banbury* (London, 1960); F. Bealey, J. Blondel and W. P. McCann, *Constituency Politics: A Study of Newcastle-under-Lyme* (London, 1965); R. T. Holt and J. E. Turner, *Political Parties in Action:The Battle of Barons Court* (New York, 1968); D. Berry, *The Sociology of Grass-roots Politics* (London, 1970).

8. R. T. McKenzie and A. Silver, *Angels in Marble: Working-class Conservatives in Urban England* (London, 1968); E. A. Nordlinger, *The Working-class Tories* (London, 1967); F. Parkin, 'Working-class Conservatives', *British Journal of Sociology*, 18 (1967), 278–90.

9. A. Gamble, *The Conservative Nation* (London, 1974).

10. M. Pugh, *The Tories and the People 1880–1935* (Oxford, 1985).

11. B. Campbell, *The Iron Ladies: Why do Women Vote Tory?* (London, 1987); P. Dorey, *The Conservative Party and the Trade Unions* (London, 1995); N. McCrillis, *The British Conservative Party in the Age of Universal Suffrage: Popular Conservatism 1918–1929* (Columbus, 1998); G. Maguire, *Conservative Women: A History of Women and the Conservative Party 1874–1997* (Basingstoke, 1998).

12. An example which used regional electoral data is M. Pugh, 'Popular Conservatism in

Britain: Continuity and Change 1880–1987', *Journal of British Studies*, 27 (1988), 254–82.

13. R. Waller, 'Conservative Electoral Support and Social Class', and other essays including P. Catterall, 'The Party and Religion', and J. Lovenduski *et al.*, 'The Party and Women', in Seldon and Ball (eds), *Conservative Century*; Francis and Zweiniger-Bargielowska (eds), *The Conservatives and British Society 1880–1990*.

14. Francis and Zweiniger-Bargielowska (eds), *The Conservatives and British Society 1880–1990*, 1.

15. Campbell, *Iron Ladies*; Maguire, *Conservative Women*; J. Lovenduski *et al.*, 'The Party and Women'; D. Jarvis, 'Mrs Maggs and Betty: The Conservative Appeal to Women Voters in the 1920s', *20th Century British History*, 5, 2 (1994), 129–52; D. Jarvis, 'The Conservative Party and the Politics of Gender 1900–1939', and I. Zweiniger-Bargielowska, 'Explaining the Gender Gap: The Conservative Party and the Women's Vote 1945–1964', in Francis and Zweiniger-Bargielowska (eds), *The Conservatives and British Society 1880–1990*.

16. A. Seldon, 'Consensus: A Debate Too Long?', *Parliamentary Affairs*, 47 (1994); H. Jones and M. Kandiah (eds), *The Myth of Consensus: New Views on British History 1945–1964* (London, 1996); B. Harrison, 'The Rise, Fall and Rise of Political Consensus in Britain since 1940', *History*, 84 (1999).

17. *CPC in Action* (London, Conservative Political Centre, 1972), 6.

18. P. Whiteley, P. Seyd and J. Richardson, *True Blues: The Politics of Conservative Party Membership* (Oxford, 1994).

19. This is argued in S. Ball, 'The National and Regional Party Structure', in Seldon and Ball (eds), *Conservative Century*, 214–20.

2

The Making of Scottish Unionism, 1886–1914

CATRIONA BURNESS

'Mass Conservatism' and Scotland seem to be unlikely partners, particularly in the context of contemporary political developments. At the 1997 general election the Conservatives suffered their worst defeat since 1832, and Scotland and Wales became 'Tory-free' zones. The Labour Party won an overwhelming victory, returning to office after 18 wilderness years with a landslide majority of 179. Since 1997, thanks to limited successes in the elections to the Scottish and European Parliaments, and the election of one Scottish Conservative MP at the 2001 general election, reports of total Tory wipe-out north of the border have proved exaggerated but the party remains marginalised and ostracised. The scale of present Conservative woes remains unparalleled against even the party's gloomy electoral record in Scotland. There is nothing new in Tory unpopularity in Scotland: its weakness in nineteenth-century Scotland was the butt of many jokes. A gamekeeper would call an errant dog 'Tory', and during the 1860s it was jested that all the Conservative members for Scotland could travel from Edinburgh to London in one first-class railway carriage (seating six)! This was not quite true because Conservative representation actually ranged from 15 to eight MPs over the decade, but the joke reflected a perception of the Conservatives as marginal to the Scottish political scene.

The post-1832 weakness of the party in Scotland for many years ensured its neglect as a topic for study.[1] Neglect of Conservatism has extended to analysis of more successful stages in the party's history. This chapter focuses on a key period and a relatively successful phase in the development of modern Scottish Conservatism, the making of Scottish Unionism from 1886 to 1912.[2] It touches on the two interwoven strands of 'mass Conservatism' identified by the volume editors. The period 1886–1914 predates the era of universal suffrage, but aspects of how the Conservatives responded to a widening electorate from 1884 in which around two-thirds of adult males had the vote are considered. This fits in with the first of the themes of mass Conservatism, that is 'Conservatism and the masses'. However, the chapter also examines the position of Conservatism in Scotland, its public standing, and the ways in which it has been regarded and responded to in Scotland, linking into the second strand, the 'Conservatism of the masses'. While the historic contribution of Unionism to the appeal of Conservatism in Scotland has often been acknowledged, an arguably novel feature of this chapter is its focus on the significance of Liberal Unionism in Scotland and its assessment of the Liberal Unionist contribution to the making of modern Scottish Unionism.

The Scottish Unionist Association was created in 1912 by the fusion of the Conservative and Liberal Unionist parties in Scotland, a year after merger had taken place in England and Wales. The amalgamation of the two parties was a quiet affair, attracting little press comment, in comparison with the furore that marked the emergence of Liberal Unionism in 1886. The *Dundee Advertiser*, however, could not resist one last dig: 'We must wish all happiness to the contracting parties so soon to be made one. It is impossible to believe any bickerings can mar their happy union … We wonder indeed why they have waited all this time.'[3] The *Scotsman* questioned the benefit of the change, maintaining that 'a certain risk is taken when historic distinctions are abandoned'.[4] The merger took place in the aftermath of three successive general election defeats. An anonymous scrawl on the agenda of the twenty-seventh and last West of Scotland Liberal Unionist AGM questioned whether the amalgamation would prove 'a birth, a marriage or a funeral'.[5] The Glasgow Conservatives, however, welcomed fusion with the Liberal Unionists, asserting that 'as no change in principles or policy is thus involved, the only alteration which is thought to be necessary in the Rules and Constitution of this Association is the substitution of the name "Unionist" for "Conservative"'.[6] So, did Liberal Unionism in Scotland amount to a distinction without a difference as the Liberals had taunted since

1886? Did the merger simply spell a limp ending to a negative and unsuccessful campaign to halt home rule for Ireland? Would the Conservatives' 'unrivalled faculty for political organisation' have improved Tory standing in Scotland anyway?[7] This chapter will argue that Liberal Unionism was 'a distinction' that made a difference to the development of Scottish Conservatism and its aspirations to mass appeal.

GREATER EXPECTATIONS

From 1832 the Conservative Party in Scotland was profoundly unpopular. The 1832 Reform Act overthrew a system of political management that had allowed the Tories to monopolise Scotland's limited political representation. In 1832 only ten of Scotland's 53 MPs were Conservative and thereafter the Conservatives took a lower proportion of seats in Scotland than in Britain at every election from 1832. The Liberals actually won uncontested majorities in Scotland in 1859 and 1865. In this context the election of 19 Scottish Conservative MPs at the 1874 general election, including a Conservative MP for Glasgow, was a major boost. It encouraged Conservative platform speakers to voice the most jubilant of expectations. The *Scotsman* ridiculed these in 1885: 'They are always sure they are going to win. They are confident that the bright days of Conservatism in Scotland have not only dawned, but have got almost to noontide splendour. No past experience modifies this tone.'[8] However, although the elections of 1880 and 1885 returned only seven and ten Scottish Conservatives respectively, some aspects were encouraging and significant for the future.

For example, the Conservatives swiftly met the new electoral conditions created by the 1867–68 Reform Acts and the Secret Ballot Act of 1872 by reforming their party organisation. After the 1868 election John Gorst was appointed as principal agent and, according to Robert Blake, 'virtually created the Conservative Central Office, which ... was performing by 1874 nearly all the tasks that it does today'.[9] Developments in Scotland mirrored the founding of central organisations in England when the Scottish National Constitutional Association was founded in 1867. Initially, the national structure existed more on paper than in reality, but its foundation stimulated Scottish Conservative organisation in the late 1860s, as did the interest of the party leader, Disraeli. Although, in 1866, Disraeli told his secretary, Montagu Corry, that 'the Scotch shall have no more favours from me until they return more Tory members to the House of Commons', he showed more interest in the difficulties of Scottish Conservatism than any other Conservative leader since 1832.[10] In 1867 Sir Graham Montgomery, the Scottish Conservative Whip, briefed him on Tory prospects in Scotland. His assessment was bleak, describing the burghs as 'hopeless', although he thought that the counties were more promising.[11] Undaunted, Disraeli made a successful visit to Scotland in 1868, addressing a great Conservative banquet and a large audience of working men in the Music Hall in Edinburgh. The 'warmth' of his reception so 'delighted' Disraeli that he and his wife 'actually danced a jig (or was it a hornpipe?) in our bedroom'![12]

Following Disraeli's visit to Scotland, Conservative associations were founded in Glasgow and Dundee.[13] As the *Scotsman* commented, 'Since the election of 1874, more particularly, Conservative Clubs and Working Men's Conservative Associations have sprung up like mushrooms in all parts of the country.'[14] It was claimed that up to 500 attended meetings of the Glasgow Conservative Association, while on the eve of the general election in 1874 the number of ordinary members was put at 2,800.[15] The membership of the Glasgow association grew from 1,800 in 1880 to 6,854 in 1884, the last set of figures to be issued before the 1885 election.[16] These membership figures were high in comparison with those from other areas. In Dundee, for example, the Conservative organisation founded in 1869 apparently lapsed and was revived in 1882–83. In April 1883 the Dundee Tories – at a meeting 'with a good audience, including a few ladies' – congratulated themselves on raising their membership from 'less than half a score' to 'nearly one hundred'.[17] Yet, although lip service had been paid to the idea of a national organisation since 1867, the creation of the National Union of Conservative Associations for Scotland (NUCAS) in 1882 and the appointment of Reginald Macleod as full-time secretary ushered in more effective organisation.[18] NUCAS immediately showed its determination to co-ordinate Conservative activity in Scotland, devising a questionnaire to establish the state of organisation, funds and candidates in every constituency.[19] In some constituencies, however, these exhortations were to no avail; for example, not a single Highland constituency replied to the questionnaire.[20]

Some Liberal optimists predicted that the Conservatives would win only two, or at most four, Scottish seats in 1885.[21] Liberal self-confidence far outdid that of the Conservatives, and the election results showed this to be justified. Given the record number of instance in which Liberal candidates competed against each other in 1885, the returns were a tribute to the strength of Liberalism in Scotland. Disputes over Scottish church disestablishment and land policy (especially in the Highlands) had led to anticipation of Whig–Liberal defections and loss of seats, but Scotland returned only ten Conservative MPs. Fifty-seven official Liberal candidates were elected, along with five Crofter MPs, effectively giving the Liberals 62 Scottish votes. With a very high turnout of 81.4 per cent, Glasgow returned seven Liberal MPs and the jubilant Liberal association wired Gladstone: 'We are seven.'

Within 12 months Gladstone's historic measure on Irish home rule faced the Liberals with a danger quantitatively and qualitatively different from the threat posed, for example, by church disestablishment. The 1886 revolt was not a simple matter of 'the passing of the Whigs' from the Liberal Party. A coterie of Scottish Liberal landowners and MPs did leave but many Scottish Whig and right-of-centre and centre politicians remained within the Liberal Party, among them three future Liberal prime ministers: Rosebery, Campbell-Bannerman and Asquith.[22] The Whigs included Rosebery, Elgin, Dalhousie, Aberdeen, Reay, Breadalbane, Munro-Ferguson, Gibson Carmichael, the Master of Elibank, Sir Charles Tennant, J. G. C. Hamilton of Dalzell, and Maxtone Graham of Cultoquhey. Others on the centre and centre-right of the party who supported Gladstone's measure included Campbell-Bannerman, Haldane, C. S. Parker (member for Perth and 'the most outrageously Whiggish of all Scottish MPs'), Bryce, R. W. Duff, R. T. Reid, Dr Farquharson and P. McLagan.[23]

In England the 'advanced' Liberal Joseph Chamberlain broke with Gladstone, taking with him most of the Birmingham Liberal caucus. In Scotland 12 of the 23 MPs who voted against Gladstone's bill were Radicals. They included the Crofter MP, Charles Fraser-Macintosh (Inverness-shire), and J. B. Kinnear (East Fife) – 'whose election in 1885 was looked upon by the Whigs as tantamount to the implementation of the Communist Manifesto'.[24] Other Radicals were Alexander Cross, Walter MacFarlane and the temperance campaigner, A. C. Corbett, in Glasgow. In Edinburgh Thomas Raleigh and the prominent disestablisher Professor Calderwood left, along with Duncan McLaren, a former Edinburgh MP (1865–81), and a leading Scottish Radical over the previous 50 years.[25] The *Glasgow Herald* remarked:

For the moment all ordinary political conditions are changed and while Mr Chamberlain is thrown over by the caucuses, Lord Hartington is forced to rise against Mr Gladstone. What will ultimately come out of these strange associations and ruptures time alone can tell.[26]

The defeat of Gladstone's Irish Home Rule Bill by 343 votes to 313 in June 1886 heralded a general election fought on the lines of home ruler versus Unionist rather than Liberal versus Conservative, a contest described by the *Inverness Courier* as resembling 'in many places, on a small scale, the outbreak of civil war'.[27] Ninety-three Liberal MPs voted against Gladstone's Home Rule Bill. The revolt was proportionately greatest in Scotland where 23 out of 62 Liberal MPs opposed the bill.[28] The home rule split also accomplished the detachment of leading Scottish newspapers from the Liberal Party, notably the *Glasgow Herald* and the *Scotsman*. This removed one of the major disadvantages faced by Scottish Tories before 1886, although from 1903 the *Glasgow Herald* was deeply sceptical of the merits of tariff reform.

TABLE 2.1: ELECTION RESULTS IN SCOTLAND, 1885–1910 (72 SEATS)

	1885	1886	1892	1895	1900	1906	Jan. 1910	Dec. 1910
Conservative	10	12	11	20	21	7	–	–
Labour	–	–	–	–	–	2	2	3
Liberal	57	43	50	39	34	58	58	58
Liberal Unionist	–	17	11	13	17	5	–	–
Unionist	–	–	–	–	–	–	11	11
Others	5	–	–	–	–	–	1	–

Source: McCalmont's *Parliamentary Poll Book of All Elections 1832–1918* (Brighton, 1971), 273.

Scotland rapidly emerged as a key area of Liberal Unionist strength. Throughout Britain the Liberal Unionists put up 153 candidates; 46 Liberal Unionist candidates stood in Scotland and only 19 Conservative candidates.[29] In 1886 Scotland returned 43 Liberals, 'a disloyal and separatist majority', according to the *Scottish News*. Twelve Conservatives and 17 Liberal Unionists were elected (see Table 2.1).[30] The Liberal Unionists accounted for nearly one-quarter of Scottish MPs, and just over one in five (21.8 per cent) of the total number of Liberal Unionist MPs. The Conservatives and Liberal Unionists still expressed disappointment at the Scottish results. Yet, while Scotland remained more Liberal than the rest of Britain in the period 1886–1912, and while the pact was undermined by fiscal divisions by 1906, it offered the first major challenge to the Liberal ascendancy established in 1832.

A DISTINCTIVE LIBERAL UNIONIST APPEAL?

Defence of the Union with Ireland was the political cry that cracked Scottish Liberal hegemony. In 1885 the Radical push for church (Kirk) disestablishment had given Conservatism a Scottish cause which began to detach disillusioned churchmen from the Liberal Party. The raising of home rule in 1886 completed and widened the fissures of 1885, leading to the emergence of Liberal Unionism. The 1886 campaign established the main strands of the Unionist appeal. These were the constitutional question related to the supremacy of the Westminster Parliament, the implications of the Home Rule Scheme for the Empire, the cost of the scheme to the British taxpayer and, especially in Glasgow and the surrounding counties, the religious loyalties raised by the position of Protestant Ulster. The Irish dimension in the population and the proximity of Ireland itself gave the home rule question a sharp edge in the NUCAS region known as the West of Scotland.[31]

Over the period 1886–1912 the West of Scotland returned the overwhelming majority of Conservative and Liberal Unionist MPs. Glasgow, an unbroken Liberal stronghold until 1874, provides a striking example of the effect of the electoral pact. The return of seven Unionists in 1900 was particularly stunning. However, the NUCAS region known as the East of Scotland was less promising. The Liberals won every contest in Aberdeen and Dundee from 1886 to 1912, apart from Labour's breakthrough in Dundee in 1906. The picture was more encouraging for Unionism in Edinburgh, although far less so than in Glasgow.

In 1900 the Unionists presented their appeal for a fresh mandate to handle the settlement in South Africa as consolidating the security of the Empire, an extension of their defence of it since 1886 in resisting home rule. In 1906, however, the presentation of tariff reform as a further extension of imperial politics, involving closer union with the colonies on a commercial and preferential basis, failed to appeal to Scottish electors. Defence of free trade shouldered home rule aside at the polls and brought out voters in

TABLE 2.2: GLASGOW ELECTION RESULTS, 1885–DECEMBER 1910 (7 SEATS)

	1885	1886	1892	1895	1900	1906	Jan. 1910	Dec. 1910
Conservative	–	1	1	3	4	–	–	–
Labour	–	–	–	–	–	1	1	1
Liberal	7	4	4	2	–	4	4*	4
Liberal Unionist	–	2	2	2	3	2	–	–
Unionist	–	–	–	–	–	–	2	2

Note: *Includes Cameron Corbett as an Independent Liberal.

Source: McCalmont's *Parliamentary Poll Book of All Elections 1832–1918* (Brighton, 1971), *passim*.

TABLE 2.3: EDINBURGH ELECTION RESULTS, 1885–DECEMBER 1910 (4 SEATS)

	1885	1886	1892	1895	1900	1906	Jan. 1910	Dec. 1910
Conservative	–	–	–	1	–	–	–	–
Liberal	4	3	3	2	2	3	3	3
Liberal Unionist	–	1	1	1	2	1	–	–
Unionist	–	–	–	–	–	–	1	1

Source: McCalmont's *Parliamentary Poll Book of All Elections 1832–1918* (Brighton, 1971), *passim*.

overwhelming numbers. Tariff reform also fundamentally undermined Liberal Unionism, creating new lines of political division and making it impossible for Liberal Unionism to contain all those Liberals who were Unionist.

The 1906 election, however, did not simply turn back the clock. For example, the Liberals regained only four of Glasgow's seven constituencies (see Table 2.2). Free Food Liberal Unionists hung on in Tradeston and Camlachie while George Barnes took Blackfriars for Labour. The Labour breakthrough in Blackfriars hinged on the transfer of Irish support to Labour in preference to the Liberals. However, the general loyalty shown by the Nationalists to the Liberals over most of the period, despite an interest in and desire for Labour reforms, lends credence to the view that the protracted home rule crisis delayed a serious electoral challenge from Labour until after the First World War. The extension of the franchise in 1918 was a prerequisite for such a challenge. Labour intervention before 1918 was limited by the small number of candidates put up by the party, but probably damaged the Liberals most. Labour candidates, for example, contributed to Liberal Unionist gains in Govan and North West Lanark against the national and local trends in 1906, and prevented the Liberals from taking Camlachie at the same election. However, there are indications that the Unionists also lost votes to Labour, for example when Bonar Law, a future Conservative Party leader and Prime Minister, lost Glasgow Blackfriars to Labour's George Barnes in 1906. Labour and labour questions were important over the period. In 1892 and 1895 the Irish question was presented as a working man's question while the Liberal Unionists were active in developing a programme of social reforms to accompany the Unionist cry. The 1906 election touched on the living conditions of ordinary people to a hitherto unparalleled extent. After 1906, the Conservatives and Liberal Unionists, always inclined to take an apocalyptic view of Liberalism splintering into its moderate and radical parts, clearly perceived socialism as a threat now to be countered.

However, while strongly anti-socialist, the Liberal Unionists attempted to inject a constructive element into the Unionist appeal. Apart from the pressure exerted by national leaders like Chamberlain on social questions and Irish land reform, the West of Scotland Association took a lead in raising Scottish concerns and pressing them upon Unionist leaders. Issues taken up by the association ranged from education to private bill procedure to land reform. One of the most striking transformations in Conservative policy brought about by Liberal Unionist pressure was the abandonment of the position that emigration was the best solution to the Highland land problem, although this achievement won little electoral reward.[32] The defeat of politicians such as Charles Fraser-Mackintosh in 1892 undermined the capacity for radical Scottish Liberal Unionism to make a lasting impact. Other Radicals such as the Glasgow MP, James Caldwell, contributed to the development of Highland land policy up to 1889 but returned to the Liberals by 1892. Throughout its existence Liberal Unionism haemorrhaged members to both the left and right of the political spectrum. The original premise of Liberal Unionists – that they were Unionists who had not ceased to be Liberals – made a constructive programme essential, as the *Dundee Advertiser* pointed out:

> For the necessities of their existence Unionists must show a Liberal face to the country, however half-hearted or positively reactionary their doings. Thus the historic Liberal Party

is confronted by a quasi-Liberal Party dating from 1886, a party driven for very life to compete with it in professions of eagerness to promote social reform. In performance the competition is not serious; but that is another matter.[33]

The distinctive and constructive aspect of Liberal Unionism was most apparent up to the mid-1890s. The Conservatives certainly proved less susceptible to Liberal Unionist influence after 1895 when they had an independent parliamentary majority even if they had leaned upon the Liberal Unionist crutch to take it. However, the Liberal Unionists seemed more active in promoting 'constructive' programmes in opposition in 1892–95 and 1906–12 than in government. The failure to introduce an old age pensions scheme, in particular, left the Liberals to set the agenda on social reform. The Scottish Liberal Unionists (especially in the West) took care to present themselves as a group distinct from the Tories. While in England a pattern of fairly harmonious Liberal Unionist–Conservative co-operation rapidly emerged, in Scotland, as Lord Wolmer noted, 'it does not do for a Lib. Ust. to go on a Conserv. platform. – In England nobody minds.'[34] From 1900, although successful at the polls, the Khaki factor linked to the Boer War blurred the lines of distinction between Liberal Unionists and Conservatives. The peace settlement in 1902 ushered in a Liberal Unionist identity crisis due to the realisation that Liberal Unionism was thought to be part and parcel of the Conservative Party, particularly by young men. Given the roots of Liberal Unionism in the home rule crisis of 1886 and the related 'strange associations and ruptures', its continued separate identity was likely to be questioned as time wore on.[35]

To an extent Liberal Unionism might be regarded as a Unionist pressure group rather than a political party because it existed only within the framework of the anti-home rule pact. As Bird, the Liberal Unionist secretary, pointed out in 1892, 'in the West of Scotland, they [the Liberal Unionists] can never rival in organisation, the two great parties in the state, but that in weight and numbers, they are quite sufficient to turn many a scale'.[36] Its Liberal dimension was a crucial part of its appeal. The intervention of the tariff question from 1903, however, prevented an attempt to reassert this aspect, and particularly divided and depleted Liberal Unionism. Ironically enough, the constructive aspects of Liberal Unionism, although designed to underline their distinct position, improved the standing of the Scottish Tories. The Unionist appeal might well have been entirely negative had it not been for the input of Liberal Unionism, acknowledged in the West as 'often the driving force behind the alliance'.

AN 'UNRIVALLED FACULTY FOR POLITICAL ORGANISATION'?

The Conservatives, however, took the lead in evolving modern, efficient party organisation, and by 1892 had made some striking advances. Nationally for the Tories, this was the beginning of the era of the 'Middleton machine'. 'Captain' Middleton became principal agent for the Conservatives just before Salisbury became Prime Minister. He was part of the 'Kentish gang', a group of Conservative organisers led by Lord Abergavenny and including Akers-Douglas, Conservative Chief Whip from 1885 to 1895. Middleton's appointment completed the reconstruction of party headquarters after the 1880 electoral disaster. He brought professionalism into party organisation, spreading a network of full-time agents to collect detailed information on the constituencies, the candidates, the rival parties and the state of the electoral register. Scotland, however, was a separate sphere of party organisation although the principal agent for Scotland, Lieutenant-Colonel Haig, was a London appointee. NUCAS ran offices for the East and North of Scotland from Edinburgh (E&NSLUA) and opened a West of Scotland base in Glasgow in March 1890 (WSLUA).[37] This reflected the growth of the national union from its formation in 1882; 60 organisations were affiliated in 1883, and 340 by 1892.[38]

The main thrust of the Conservative organisational efforts, however, revolved around full-time organising secretaries. For example, by May 1900 'approved' organising secretaries were at work in the seven Glasgow constituencies and Partick & Govan.[39] This kind of activity explains why, as Urwin observes, Glasgow and Lanarkshire had 'come to be regarded as models of Conservative organisation' in Scotland.[40] The Eastern Divisional Council covered 17 constituencies, including the Edinburgh and St Andrews Universities seat, and it was reported in 1899 that 12 employed organising secretaries.[41] Ten Tory organisers had been employed in 1897, suggesting an effort to maintain organisation and activity between elections.[42]

Another new departure for the Conservatives over 1886–92 was the introduction of social events, such as soirées and musical evenings, and the founding of cards and draught clubs. This development was probably stimulated by the enormous success of the Primrose League. The league presented Conservative propaganda 'disguised with a coating of popular entertainment, or was so surreptitiously introduced into the evening's gaiety as to be almost unnoticed'.[43] The social events drew more women into political surroundings and probably stimulated the creation of women's party organisations. However, the Conservatives lagged behind the Liberal Unionists in this last area. As in the East of Scotland, a Women's Liberal Unionist Association for the West of Scotland was formed in 1888–89; the first Conservative Women's League in Glasgow was set up in the College division in 1894.[44]

Liberal Unionist organisation and activity was more effective in the West of Scotland than in the East and North. By October 1894 there were 15 organisers, canvassers and clerks in the employ of the WSLUA, putting it on a comparable footing with the Conservatives.[45] The *Glasgow Herald* applauded what it saw as timely reorganisation:

> New life was put into the association last May. ... The war-chest replenished, active canvassing is being carried on, and due attention has been paid to registration, with excellent results. We may look forward with confidence to the result of these labours, which will appear at the coming general election. Time has already proved the wisdom of the policy of avoiding complete fusion between the two wings of the Unionist Party ... Liberal Unionism is still a creed ... It has its own field, and as has been shown, is tilling it industriously.[46]

In the period 1895–1900 the Liberal Unionists could take comfort in some positive features such as the canvassing returns supplied by the organisers. These indicated that the Conservatives needed the Liberal Unionist 'crutch' to match the Liberals although the number of 'undecided' voters underlines the shifting state of politics. Table 2.4 shows some of the canvassing returns supplied by the organisers.

Voter registration figures were also encouraging. For example, although the Glasgow Conservatives retained their spectacular lead in registration activities, and the Liberal Unionists registered the lowest total of voters, their figures were certainly respectable in comparison with the Liberal figures. The Liberal Unionists were keeping their end up in registration, and the combined Unionist registration totals should have alarmed the Liberals, even allowing for what the Glasgow Conservative Association reckoned to be a 25 per cent turnover in the lodger vote.[47] The Liberal Unionists also made a significant contribution to Unionist political education through the series of lantern lectures given all over the West of

TABLE 2.4: CANVASSING RETURNS, 1896–99

Area and date of canvass		Conservative	Liberal Unionist	Liberal	Undecided
Kilmarnock	17 April 1896	1,037	488	2,020	816
Govanhill	19 May 1899	64	232	221	250
N.W. Lanark	19 May 1899	422	254	697	234
Possilpark	7 July 1899	194	322	556	142
Maryhill	7 July 1899	219	207	328	243
Coatbridge	7 July 1899	850	305	1,217	369

Source: West of Scotland Liberal Unionist Association, Vol. 2, dates as given in table, National Library of Scotland, Acc. 10424/20.

TABLE 2.5: WEST OF SCOTLAND LECTURES, 1895–1900

Season	No. of lectures	Total attendance	Average attendance
1895/96	49	9,353	191
1896/97	40	7,315	183
1897/98	72	15,710	218
1898/99	91	24,045	264
1899/1900	104	30,440	292

Source: West of Scotland Liberal Unionist Association, Vol. 2, 5 May 1899 and 8 June 1900, National Library of Scotland, Acc. 10424/20.

Scotland by two of their organisers, Hurst and McCulloch. The figures for 1895–1900 lectures show the build-up of this activity prior to the 1900 election (see Table 2.5).

Meanwhile the members of the WSLUA retained their ability to raise election funds. Subscriptions promised to the special election fund stood at £7,375 in August 1900 although the remarkably generous contributions of some leading Liberal Unionists should be acknowledged. Sir John Muir contributed £2,000; Matthew Arthur, and James and Archibald Coats gave £1,000 each.[48] This enabled the Liberal Unionists to put up candidates for North West and North East Lanark in 1900 chiefly for the benefit of the Unionist candidates in the other Lanarkshire seats. The Scottish Conservative agent, Colonel Haig, and George Robb of the Glasgow Tories expressed gratitude to the Liberal Unionists for providing candidates for these two unpromising constituencies.[49] Finding candidates had been difficult for the Conservatives in the past. It remained so for both Unionist parties, perhaps because of the marked preference of all the political associations for running local candidates. However, this difficulty was combined in the Liberal Unionist case with the problem of maintaining and building its own position as highlighted in an organiser's report in April 1899:

> In almost all the branches there are vacancies in the principal offices, and it is very difficult to induce anyone to take up the work. Deaths and other causes have removed many of our best men in these and other districts, and our ranks have also been weakened by numbers of our members being induced to join the Conservatives, especially in places where there are Conservative clubs. At the same time, there are no evidences of accessions to our ranks from the Gladstonians, such as took place prior to the last election. The result is to make the work of Liberal Unionist organisation increasingly difficult in the smaller districts where our numbers were never great.[50]

Overall, however, despite inherent difficulties of maintaining its position, the WSLUA remained effective into the early 1900s. On policy, the national consensus on imperial and foreign affairs prevailed locally; the Liberal Unionists tried to maintain a distinctive position on domestic policy. Successive annual general meetings confirmed the fresh significance of foreign policy and the effort to maintain some kind of distinctive Liberal Unionist approach to both Ireland and social questions.

Liberal Unionism in the East and North of Scotland faced more difficult prospects than in the West; most of the seats in its area of operation remained loyal to Liberalism after 1886. The E&NSLUA seemed less active in promoting resolutions than the WSLUA although in 1896 it passed resolutions applauding the government's foreign policy and expressing its regret that 'no bill has yet been introduced for the transference to Scotland, of Scottish private bill legislation'.[51] As in the West, however, there was great faith in what might be accomplished by the appointment of organising secretaries and the development of clubs. Pioneering action approved in 1897 included the grant of £40 to the East and North of Scotland Women's Liberal Unionist Association towards the salary and expenses of a lady organiser.[52] Another article of faith was the view that 'no enthusiasm can be created in any constituency if there is neither a Unionist member or a Unionist candidate, and all enthusiasm will be useless if not supported by the votes of duly registered electors'.[53]

Yet, at the 1900 election, the Conservatives put up more candidates in the East and North than the Liberal Unionists, and actually contested six of the seats the Liberal Unionists had identified as their 'key seats'. This reflected the gathering effacement of Liberal Unionism in the East and North of Scotland. In the Highland area (excluding Argyll) where the Liberal Unionists had fought all seven seats in 1886, the Conservatives fought five seats in 1900, and the Liberal Unionists only two. This development does not seem to have led to stormy executives and harsh exchanges of words between the Liberal Unionists and the Conservatives. Nor did it lead to the issuing of guidelines for constituency organisation such as those issued by the WSLUA in its efforts to keep a grip on organisational developments in constituencies.

Developments were apparently pushed by local initiatives. The E&NSLUA occasionally had difficulty in establishing what was going on in constituencies. As early as 1889 the Dundee Liberal Unionist Association insisted on maintaining 'a position of absolute independence ... on the understanding that representation on the national councils of the party [was] unaffected'.[54] Meanwhile, in May 1899, the secretary was instructed to find out whether or not Mr Sinclair had 'ceased to act as organising secretary in Dumfriesshire, and, if so, to offer the services of Captain Munro or Mr Rae with the view to procuring a successor and to assist in the meantime'.[55] This led to the information that a meeting was about to take place to form a joint Unionist association.[56] This was full amalgamation but the association recorded no discussion or comment on the development. There were also instances of assertive Liberal Unionist organisation, particularly in Leith Burghs. However, the widespread use of the term 'Unionist' rather than 'Conservative' or 'Liberal Unionist' during the 1910 elections by Unionists and their opponents alike foreshadowed the eventual formal amalgamation of the two Unionist parties in 1912.

The Conservatives were undoubtedly deeply frustrated by the outcome of the 1910 elections, as they had been in 1880 and 1885 when organisational efforts did not lead to electoral success. However, the strength of the Conservative Party machine survived the period and left the Unionists, while reduced to a rump in Scotland from 1906 to 1918, with at least an organisational base on which to build. The new name, 'Unionist' drew on the Liberal Unionist legacy, being more closely associated with Liberal Unionism than Conservatism.

THE STRENGTHS AND WEAKNESSES OF LIBERAL UNIONISM

So, how might we assess the impact of Liberal Unionism? It clearly failed in its founding objective of 'maintaining the legislative union between Great Britain and Ireland'. Irish nationalism was stronger and more determined at the end of the period than in 1886. In 1910 it was estimated that there was an Irish nationalist vote (ranging from 1 per cent in Arygll to 24 per cent in West Fife) in 46 of Scotland's 72 constituencies.[57] The anti-home rule cry did win support in the West of Scotland but on a more limited scale than some anticipated. Linkage between the Orange Order and the Conservatives is well known; historians of the Orange movement in Scotland, however, emphasise 'the fundamentally *conditional* nature of the relationship' between the Orange Order and the Conservative Party.[58] Many Tory grandees preferred not to have public links with the order; the Liberal Unionists later observed a greater distance.[59] The Orange Order lay on the outer fringes of respectability; its working-class base 'was both its great strength and its great weakness'.[60] Iain Hutchison nevertheless argues that by the 1880s fusion between the Orange Order and the Tories grew apace, and by 1893 the Orange Order had a place within the Western Divisional Council of the Conservative Party.[61] However, by 1904 disillusionment with the Tory party led the order to pass a resolution supporting the efforts of the Grand Lodge of Scotland to form 'a political organisation unfettered by any party ties and free to act with or against any party in the interests of Protestantism'.[62] Orange influence was also limited. According to Marshall, 'The Orange vote only existed in the sense that there was a number of constituencies in the West Central Scotland which contained a sizeable Orange presence', in particular, West Renfrewshire.[63] Although the existence of anti-Catholic and anti-Irish sentiment in Victorian and Edwardian Scotland is undeniable, there were limits to sectarianism in the West of Scotland. Glasgow and the West of Scotland were more than cultural extensions of Ulster.

While unsuccessful as a Unionist pressure group, the Unionist pact and eventual merger gave a new identity to the Conservative Party. There are some references in the inter-war years to the Liberal Unionists having been 'swallowed whole' by the Conservatives.[64] There is an element of truth in this but it is not the whole story, especially in Scotland. By 1906 Liberal Unionism as such was fighting a battle for survival. The Conservatives provided the majority of candidates and the pace of local mergers of the Conservative and Liberal Unionist parties quickened. Increasing use of the term 'Unionist' as a shorthand expression for both parties pointed to the future. Yet the Conservative Party did not simply reappear in 1912. In 1922 it was fiercely observed that 'reverting to the designation "Conservative" is, as you will readily believe, repugnant to the great body of Unionists in Scotland'.[65] In Scotland the party fought elections as 'Unionists' until the 1960s, retaining the name decades after it was dropped in favour of 'Conservative' in England and Wales. This acknowledged the need for a distinctive appeal in Scotland and historic anti-Conservative feeling.

CONCLUSION

The period 1886 to 1912 marked a relatively successful phase in the development of the Scottish Conservative Party. Considerable improvements in party organisation took place as the party came to terms with 'mass politics' and changing electoral conditions. The electoral pact with the Liberal Unionists made a significant contribution to better Conservative election results in Scotland after 1886; and the Conservatives became increasingly dominant within the coalition from 1900. The merged Unionists also proved a significant force in Scottish politics after 1912 as a brief review of subsequent developments shows.

Although the Unionist merger in 1912 took place at a nadir of Conservative and Liberal Unionist electoral fortunes, by 1924 the electoral landscape had changed radically. The once mighty Scottish Liberal Party was reduced to a rump of eight seats, squeezed between the emerging Labour Party (26) and the Unionists who took a majority of the Scottish seats (36). The Labour Party first took a majority of the Scottish seats in 1929, but as partners in the coalition governments of 1918, 1931 and 1935 the Unionists were the most dominant of the Scottish parties. They also regained ground in Glasgow, and as late as the 1950s held seven of the 15 city constituencies, while taking a majority of the Scottish seats in 1955. Historic patterns and recent developments have ensured that these Unionist successes are widely regarded as 'not the norm but the lucky tactical exceptions. ... The Unionists of the 1920s and 1930s benefited both from strong anti-Catholicism and from the Labour split at the time of the National Government.'[66]

The reasons for the Conservatives' subsequent decline remain under-investigated. It is generally agreed that 'the party has lost its ability to appeal to certain symbols of Scottish culture and suffered from a leftward drift among the Scots electorate'. Curtice and Seawright further argued that the economic experience of the Scots over the last 40 years was an equally crucial factor in failing party fortunes.[67] In 1990, in his study of Conservative Party attitudes to Scotland, James Mitchell remarked: 'Few Conservative politicians have articulated their political philosophy in a Scottish context.'[68] The irony, often remarked on, is that opposition to Irish home rule gave the Conservatives an important rallying cry in Scotland but the initial 'Unionist' reference point was Ireland not Scotland. The party has persistently suffered from the perception that it is 'English and anti-Scottish', as an internal party report concluded in 1987.[69] Yet Mitchell referred to 'the myth ... that the Scots are anti-Conservative', pointing out that 'the only party ever to achieve a clear majority of the popular vote in Scotland this century was the Unionist Party in 1955'.[70] It is certainly true that the Conservatives and/or Unionists have enjoyed greater success in Scotland than might be popularly supposed but it is equally true that the party has often endured minority status in Scotland while successful in England.

The change in the party's name in 1965 did not in itself precipitate Conservative decline but the Unionists fared better at the polls than the Conservatives. Since re-entering the political field as Conservatives, the best performances for the Scottish Tories came at elections which returned the Conservatives to government – 1970 (23 seats) and 1979 (22 seats). Since 1979 the party's representation fell to 21 in 1983, ten in 1987, 11 in 1992, nil in 1997 and one in 2001. After devastating results at the 1997 and 2001 general elections the Scottish Tories now face their greatest struggle yet for survival and revival. Some have suggested that the party might return to its former name in the hope of regaining past success because 'In recent years political opponents have succeeded in making a "boo" word of "Conservative" in Scotland.'[71] We may yet see Scottish 'Unionists' fighting for seats in the devolved Scottish Parliament or perhaps 'Scottish New Unionists' or 'New Scottish Unionists'. If so, this would say a great deal for the staying power of the Unionist legacy in Scotland although it is debatable whether 'Unionist' would prove to be a 'hurrah' word in the post-devolution Scottish political scene. A renewed focus on and 'prodigious faith' in organisation is more likely to be crucial for Conservative revival in Scotland.

NOTES

1. Studies made include B. Crapster, 'Scotland and the Conservative Party in 1876', *Journal of Modern History*, 29 (1957); D. W. Urwin, 'The Development of Conservative Party Organisation in Scotland until 1912', *Scottish Historical Review*, 44 (1965); J. T. Ward, *The First Century: A History of Scottish Tory Organisation 1882–1982* (Edinburgh, 1982); G. Warner, *The Scottish Tory Party* (London, 1988); M. Fry, *Patronage and Principle: A Political History of Modern Scotland* (Aberdeen, 1987); I. G. C. Hutchison, *A Political History of Scotland 1832–1924* (Edinburgh, 1986); T. Gallacher, *Glasgow: The Uneasy Peace* (Manchester, 1987); E. W. McFarland, *Protestants First: Orangeism in Nineteenth-century Scotland* (Edinburgh, 1990); and G. Walker, *Intimate Strangers: Political and Cultural Interaction between Scotland and Ulster in Modern Time* (Edinburgh, 1995).
2. This is discussed further in my forthcoming monograph, *Strange Associations: The Irish Question and the Making of Scottish Unionism 1886–1918* (Edinburgh, 2002), on which this chapter is based.
3. *Dundee Advertiser*, 6 December 1912.
4. *Scotsman*, 6 December 1912.
5. West of Scotland Liberal Unionist Association (WSLUA), Vol. 4, 27th AGM, 5 December 1912, 104, National Library of Scotland (NLS), Acc. 10424/22.
6. Glasgow Conservation Association (GCA), 44th annual report, 27 January 1913, NLS, Acc. 10424/24.
7. *Glasgow News*, 10 April 1880.
8. *Scotsman*, 24 August 1885.
9. R. Blake, *Disraeli* (London, 1966), 556; see also A. Hunter, *A Life of Sir John Eldon Gorst: Disraeli's Awkward Disciple* (London, 2001).
10. 8 October 1866, Hughenden Papers, Box 95, B/XX/D/18, cited in Blake, *Disraeli*, 481.
11. Sir Graham Montgomery to Disraeli, 21 January 1867, Disraeli Papers, cited in H. J. Hanham, *Elections and Party Management* (London, 1959), 161.
12. Disraeli to John Skelton, cited in Ward, *First Century*, 9.
13. Glasgow Conservative Workingmen's Association (GCWMA), 5th annual report, 13 January 1874, NLS, Acc. 10424/23.
14. *Scotsman*, 26 September 1886.
15. GCWMA, 1st annual report, 25 January 1870, and 5th annual report, 13 January 1874.
16. GCA, annual reports, 1881–85, *passim*.
17. News cutting, probably from *Dundee Courier*, 23 April 1883, Dundee Public Library, Lamb Collection, 17/3.
18. Son of MacLeod of MacLeod of Dunvegan, Isle of Skye, and son-in-law of Tory leader Sir Stafford Northcote.
19. National Union of Conservative Associations of Scotland (NUCAS), Vol. 1, 4, Meeting of Council, 24 November 1882, NLS, Acc. 10424/72.
20. Ibid., 7–15; Meeting of Council, 12 February 1883.
21. *Glasgow Herald*, 28 October 1885.
22. These included the Marquis of Stafford (Sutherland), Arthur and Hugh Elliot (Roxburgh and Ayrshire North), Sir George Grant (Elgin & Nairn), Sir Robert Anstruther (St Andrews Burghs), Richard Campbell (Ayr Burghs) and 'the lawyer Craig Sellar (Lanarkshire Partick) whose father had been responsible for the Sutherland clearances'. M. Dyer, *Capable Citizens and Improvident Democrats: The Scottish Electoral System 1884–1929*, (Aberdeen, 1996), 49.
23. Hutchison, *Political History*, 163.
24. Ibid., 163.
25. Ibid.
26. *Glasgow Herald*, 15 May 1886.
27. *Inverness Courier*, 20 July 1886.
28. *Glasgow Herald*, 26 June 1886.
29. *McCalmont's Parliamentary Poll Book of All Elections 1832–1918* (Brighton, 1971), *passim*. These figures include the Scottish University seats and are drawn from the party listings given for each Scottish constituency by *McCalmont's*.
30. *Scottish News*, 14 July 1886, 4; see also Tables 2.1, 2.2 and 2.3.
31. In 1901 three-fifths of the Irish-born in Scotland lived in Lanarkshire alone, and more

than four-fifths were in Lanarkshire, Dunbartonshire, Renfrewshire and Ayrshire taken together: H. Pelling, *Social Geography of British Elections 1885–1910* (London, 1957), 400.

32. C. B. Robertson, 'Patterns of Political Behaviour in the North-west Highlands of Scotland 1880–1900' (Honours MA thesis, University of Dundee, 1978), *passim*.
33. *Dundee Advertiser*, 17 October 1900.
34. On England see P. Marsh, *The Discipline of Popular Government* (Hassocks, 1978); Lord Wolmer to Salisbury, 10 February 1889, Hatfield MSS, 3M/E, cited in Hutchison, *Political History*, 208.
35. *Glasgow Herald*, 15 May 1886.
36. WSLUA, Vol. 1, Bird to Organising Committee, 30 December 1892, opposite 216.
37. NUCAS, annual report for 1890, 1.
38. NUCAS, annual report for 1892, 2.
39. Papers of Glasgow Joint Executive Committee, 1894–1939, *passim*, Lewis Shedden MSS, G117, NLS, Acc. 10424.
40. D. W. Urwin, 'Politics and the Development of the Unionist Party in Scotland' (MA thesis, University of Manchester, 1963), 117.
41. NUCAS, Report of the Eastern Divisional Council, 1898/99.
42. NUCAS, Eastern Organising Committee, Vol. 3, Report by secretary, May 1897.
43. J. H. Robb, *The Primrose League, 1883–1906* (New York, 1942), 56 and 118.
44. WSLUA, 4th AGM, 3 December 1889, 114; GCA, 26th annual report, 14 January 1895.
45. WSLUA, Vol. 2, 15 October 1894, 14.
46. *Glasgow Herald*, 30 November 1893.
47. Papers of Glasgow Joint Executive Committee, 1894–1939, 1, Lewis Shedden MSS, G117.
48. WSLUA, Vol. 2, 8 August 1900, opp. 342.
49. WSLUA, Vol. 2, 28 September 1900, opp. 1–2 and 350; both seats remained Liberal in 1900.
50. WSLUA, Vol. 2, 21 April 1899, 2 and 284.
51. East and North of Scotland Liberal Unionist Association (E&NSLUA), Vol. 1, General Committee, 27 May 1886, 520, NLS, Acc. 10424/17–18.
52. E&NSLUA, Vol. 1, Executive Committee, 14 April 1897, 534.
53. E&NSLUA, Vol. 2, Organising Committee, 12 May 1899, 30.
54. E&NSLUA, Vol. 1, Executive Committee, 1 November 1889, 84–5.
55. E&NSLUA, Vol. 2, Organising Committee, 26 May 1899, 36.
56. E&NSLUA, Vol. 2, Organising Committee, 30 June 1899, 37.
57. *Scotsman*, 18 January 1910.
58. McFarland, *Protestants First*, 195.
59. Ibid., 195–6.
60. W. S. Marshall, *'Billy Boys'* (Edinburgh, 1996), 84.
61. Hutchison, *Political History*, 384.
62. *Glasgow Herald*, 11 July 1904, cited in Marshall, *'The Billy Boys'*, 96.
63. Marshall, *'The Billy Boys'*, 87.
64. Notes on Conservatism, 1916–24, from Maurice Cowling's boxes. Thanks to Dr Philip Williamson, University of Durham, for access to these files.
65. Notes on Conservatism, 1916–24, from Maurice Cowling's boxes. Thanks to Dr Philip Williamson, University of Durham, for access to these files.
66. A. Marr, *The Battle for Scotland* (London, 1992), 112. See also S. J. Brown, '"Outside the Covenant": The Scottish Presbyterian Churches and Irish Immigration 1922–1938', *The Innes Review*, 42 (1991); and T. Gallacher, 'Protestant Extremism in Urban Scotland 1930–1939: Its Growth and Contraction', *Scottish Historical Review*, 64 (1985).
67. See D. Seawright and J. Curtice, 'The Decline of the Scottish Conservative and Unionist Party 1950–92: Religion, Ideology or Economics?', *Contemporary Record*, 9 (1995), 319.
68. J. Mitchell, *Conservatives and the Union: A Study of Conservative Party Attitudes to Scotland* (Edinburgh, 1990), 1.
69. Cited in Mitchell, *Conservatives and the Union*, xiii.
70. Ibid., xiii.
71. See D. Seawright, 'The Scottish Unionist Party: What's in a Name?', *Scottish Affairs*, 23 (1996) 101.

3

Farmworkers and Local Conservatism in South-west Shropshire, 1916–23

NICHOLAS MANSFIELD

The Conservative Party's political domination in rural areas has often been taken for granted and it is assumed that, even after the arrival of mass democracy, this state of affairs has been unchanging. Until the wholesale mechanisation of British agriculture during and after the Second World War, the largest occupational group in the countryside was farmworkers and their families. Only a minority were involved in trade unionism, often workers with nonconformist backgrounds. In many parts of the country, after their enfranchisement in 1884, they tended to vote Liberal. This contributed to the return of farmworkers' leaders such as the Liberal Joseph Arch to the rural seat of North-west Norfolk in the 1880s. Many of the rural poor, working closely with their employers and often living alongside them, chose co-operation with the paternalism of farmers and gentry. While this probably meant voting Conservative, the phenomenon of working-class Conservatism has been little studied, especially when compared with the numerous accounts of agricultural trade unionism. This chapter attempts to address this imbalance, concentrating on an even bigger threat than nineteenth-century Liberalism to Tory political hegemony in the English countryside. In an account of the development of political culture in part of one English county, it describes how the changes brought about by the First World War caused a massive expansion of rural socialism and how this challenge was ultimately mastered by mass Conservatism. This chapter explains the defeat of the virulent radical challenge in the country-side by the forces of rural Conservatism. It will examine the strength of the Conservatism of the masses among both landed elites and the rural poor, the dynamism of cultural conservatism with its new post-war institutions and the ability of the local Conservative Party to build on its traditional success by skilfully adapting to modern electoral conditions.

Evidence is used mainly from Shropshire, and especially the south-west of the county, but the argument may be taken as typical of rural England in this period. Shropshire is a particularly rep-resentative area. The county was second in importance for the main farmworkers' union, the National Union of Agricultural Workers (NUAW), being eclipsed only by its Norfolk heartland. It was also the major seat of conflict between the NUAW and the Workers' Union (WU), which recruited farmworkers – a conflict that ultimate-ly weakened both organisations. Most importantly, the county retained a strong local character and its inhabitants had a pride in being from Shropshire – 'All friends around the Wrekin', as the toast eloquently puts it. The scarcity of records from farm-worker's unions locally means inevitably that there is a dependence on the local press in researching their history. However, Lydbury North – a large parish in south-west Shropshire – possesses an unusually complete set of parish records, strong on church, educa-tion and local charities, alongside records from friendly societies, chapels and the only existing papers from a Shropshire Conservative association. This makes it possible to explore the 'Conservatism of the masses' and the 'Conservatives and the masses' in one geographical area in the period after the First World War.[1]

THE RADICAL CHALLENGE

> Agricultural labourers in the Lydbury North district have decided to come out on strike and have handed in their notices. They demand 23 shillings per week … A number of farmers have expressed their willingness to comply with the demands of the men, but a few farmers reject their proposals and unless these alter their view a wholesale strike of labourers will take place in the district.[2]

Agricultural strikes in the early part of the last century were commoner than generally realised, but there are particularly remarkable things about this one. First, Lydbury North was a classic closed village with two estates: Walcot Hall, built by Clive of India (and the seat of his descendant, the Earl of Powis), and Plowden Hall, where the recusant Plowden family had been in residence since before the Norman Conquest. Yet, even with resident gentry, the Lydbury North branch of the NUAW had at this date 125 members – a clear majority of farmworkers in the parish. Second, the date of the strike, June 1916. This was just a few weeks away from the opening of the Battle of the Somme, when some of the close relations of the Lydbury strikers – younger farmworkers who had volunteered for the Kitchener battalions of the King's Shropshire Light Infantry – saw action for the first time. Although the shortage of rural labour put a premium on the skills of farmworkers above military age, there is no record that this strike was received with the sort of bitterness shown in other wartime industrial actions.[3]

Remote parts of south-west Shropshire were taking part in the phenomenal growth of agricultural trade unionism from the middle years of the First World War. Before 1914, the NUAW, with fewer than 5,000 members, was essentially a regional front organisation for the Liberal Party to harvest the working-class vote in East Anglia.[4] The growth in agricultural unionism must be considered in the context of the ambivalence to the war on the part of many of the rural poor. After the initial enthusiasm there was passive opposition to conscription, appeals to military tribunals and, as we have seen, strikes. Farmers, and their sons in particular, were widely criticised for avoiding military service and for profiteering. In a series of highly effective haysel or harvest strikes in villages where they had strong branches, the farmworkers' unions established higher wages throughout the county and rapidly increased the number and distribution of their members. Their position was further consolidated with the passing of the 1917 Corn Production Act which introduced state minimum wage machinery in the form of agricultural wages boards, on which the unions enjoyed equal representation with the employers.[5]

Such wartime ambivalence was further manifested by the activities of the now largely forgotten National Federation of Discharged and Demobilised Soldiers and Sailors. Formed in 1917 in opposition to government 'comb-outs' to recall wounded ex-servicemen, it soon developed a left-wing programme including the 'colonial' rate of pay for soldiers, full employment or £2 unemployed benefit and nationalisation of the land and the means of production. (This was before the last policy was adopted by the Labour Party.) The federation was particularly critical of the Conservative-sponsored and officer-led Comrades of the Great War and it would allow ex-officers to be members only if they had risen from the ranks. From the autumn of 1917, branches of the federation became active in the country towns and even villages of Shropshire, becoming a focus of the working-class search for 'homes fit for heroes'. In the words of the federation's Shropshire secretary, W. H. Edwards, a farmworkers' union organiser and ex-serviceman:

> They contended that the men who had 'done their bit' were entitled to preference in relation to employment and that they should be paid the trade union rate of wages for the district. It was important that they should secure representation on public bodies. They went out to fight Prussian autocracy and now they must get rid of Prussianism in their own country.[6]

As farmworkers were demobilised after the Armistice, many returned with the feeling that some positive changes, based on shared class solidarity, were necessary to justify the 'blood sacrifice':

> Through the curtain of shell fire he may have seen a Vision – a Vision of himself and his comrades working in common to create and not to destroy. It is all the same to him whether it is Yorkshire or Wales, Cambridge or Shropshire. He wants to till the land with his fellows, and keep the fruits of his labour. The future depends largely upon the temper in which these young men return from the war ... our soldier sons will no longer tolerate the land of England remaining in the hands of a privileged class, but will demand its restoration to the people, or they will feel that their sacrifices have been in vain.[7]

In a few short months either side of the Armistice, the federation worked closely with the farmworkers' unions and the National Union of Railwaymen (NUR) – itself largely consisting of ex-farmworkers – to create a rural labour movement. By the time of the 'Coupon election' of December 1918, these organisations had set up rudimentary constituency Labour parties in many rural areas. They were often joined by middle-class radicals, who deserted the Liberal Party, bringing with them their views on land reform. In Shropshire the Liberal Party had never been strong, so almost overnight the emerging Labour Party found itself the main opposition to the prevailing Conservative hegemony.

By the end of 1919, representatives of 80 Shropshire agricultural workers union branches met at Shrewsbury and heard the NUAW general secretary, R. B. Walker, 'in a rousing, eloquent and inspiring discourse explain that the union had now 250,000 members!'[8] This growth brought with it socialist ideology. In 1923, listeners at the fifth annual joint demonstration of the NUR and the NUAW held at Craven Arms, a railway junction five miles from Lydbury North, heard:

> rousing and inspiring addresses on the need for unity among all sections of wage workers … the day had arrived when the wage earning class would undoubtedly be powerful enough to be able to take office and control their own destiny, politically as well as, sooner or later, taking complete control of industry.[9]

THE RADICAL CHALLENGE DEFEATED

In the same year, a by-election occurred in the Ludlow parliamentary constituency, in which Lydbury North was situated. Although R. B. Walker, the NUAW general secretary, declined to stand, others in the Labour Party considered 'what better opportunity would we have both to rivet public attention on the injustices of the agricultural labourers and to win the landworkers to the cause of Socialism and Labour'.[10] According to the chief women's officer of the Labour Party, Marion Phillips: 'Nor should we forget that it is vain to hope that Labour can ever secure a clear majority in the House of Commons until it wins a large number of these backward rural districts … Through these dreaming Shropshire villages lies our road to power.'[11] But the socialists had completely overestimated their support, gaining only 1,300 votes. The Tory victor, Hon Robert Clive (son of the Earl of Powis), claimed with justification: 'Ludlow has emphatically shown it does not want to have anything to do with Socialism.'[12] 'Not since I was a lad', wrote Labour's agent, 'have I seen such "true blueism" displayed alike by farmers' lads, country squires and village tradesmen'.[13] Alongside rout at the polls that spring, Labour's industrial organisation had collapsed in the face of relentless agricultural depression, and a vain attempt to stage a countywide farmworkers' strike to prevent wage cuts had fizzled out.[14]

It is worth considering at this point the obvious reasons for this failure. Structural issues were certainly important. Upland

Shropshire farms tended to be small and pastoral, needing only a small workforce per holding – often with the survival of the 'living in' system creating close relationships between farmers and their men. While, in Britain as a whole, death duties and high wartime officer fatalities caused a break-up of landed estates, the Shropshire gentry showed a remarkable capacity for survival in this period. The county also contained over 7,000 well-established smallholders. Although they were mainly linked to upland squatter settlements and adjacent common land (the Tory-dominated local authority being remarkably slow at providing county council smallholdings), they did provide a niche for Shropshire farmworkers attempting to become producers, often in conjunction with part-time work in farms, quarries or coal mines. So, it is possible to argue a crude economic determinism. Agricultural trade unionism was linked to the price of wheat, more so perhaps when state intervention occurred with the agricultural wages boards. While these gave minimum wage protection during economic boom, they could not prevent the reduction in wages from 1921 in line with the drastic fall in agricultural prices.[15]

Such general economic explanations do not account for wide variations in the level of agricultural trade unionism in various locations throughout the country. The drastic agricultural depression from the end of 1920 applied to both Shropshire and Norfolk. In the former county the union became marginal; in the latter, within a generation, it dominated local and parliamentary politics. In the 1945 general election, in Shropshire Labour won the Wrekin, a semi-industrial seat; yet five out of six rural Norfolk MPs were Labour and sponsored by the NUAW.[16] In searching for explanations on the course of events in Shropshire, it becomes apparent that cultural factors, which contributed to an intensely conservative society – where local pride seems to have been more important than class differences – were crucial. The cultural factors that influenced farmworkers in south-west Shropshire are now explored, looking first at the more traditional ones, then at those new ones which came out of the upheavals of the war period. To conclude, the role of the Conservative Party in south-west Shropshire within these continuities and changes is examined.

'ALL FRIENDS AROUND THE WREKIN': SHROPSHIRE CULTURE

Shropshire had been involved in centuries of conflict with the Welsh. In the pre-modern period local people supported their gentry and the crown as protection from cross-border raiders. Martial spirit was encouraged – Shropshire for example, was a prime recruiting ground for the Royalist army during the Civil War – and this had a long resonance, its rhetoric still apparent in recruiting for the First World War.[17]

Shropshire's geographical remoteness means that its gentry's concerns were local rather than metropolitan. Polite county society wintered in Shrewsbury or Ludlow rather than London or Bath. Remoteness also caused the folk customs of the rural poor to survive into the twentieth century.[18] These were the source material for the popular bucolic novels of local author Mary Webb: 'Shropshire is a county where the dignity and beauty of ancient things lingers long, and I have been fortunate … in being born and brought up in its magical atmosphere.'[19] Webb was Stanley Baldwin's favourite author, and despite his own industrial origins he successfully incorporated the rural Englishness represented by her novels into his popular public image as a bluff farmer. Specifically, with gentry approval, folk events such as Oak Apple Day – the celebration of the restoration of Charles II – had a loyalist flavour.[20] An anti-Welsh outlook was also shared by farmworkers and their employers:

> Shropshire border people were always very wary of Welsh people you know … We didn't trust them somehow, I don't know why. There was something underhand about them. I'm only saying what the general feeling in Shropshire was. The Welsh will always look after themselves.[21]

In the nineteenth century, this threat from the west was matched by an eastern threat from the growth of the Birmingham conurbation. Shropshire's landowners and farmers, at least, attributed the agricultural trade unionism of the 1870s to outside agitators sponsored by Birmingham Radical MPs like Joseph Chamberlain. However, by the First World War, Chamberlain's Midlands urban Radicalism had transmogrified into demands for tariff reform and was soon to incorporate Stanley Baldwin's affected Tory ruralism.

Nonconformity was historically weak in Shropshire, so an alternative dissenting ideology was absent. Middle-class nonconformists emigrated when their industrial base in the Ironbridge Gorge collapsed. Methodism, which some historians have claimed was so important to the early farmworkers' unions, was in Shropshire a miners' and smallholders' movement; their rugged independence, if anything, was hostile to any sort of radicalism.

Mild Anglicanism, conservative in its theology as well as in its social relationships, was more typical of rural Shropshire.[22] All the factors outlined above bred a strong sense of place, rooted in history, shared by all classes in Marcher society.

LANDLORDS AND PATERNALISM: OLD RURAL INSTITUTIONS

Shropshire landed society was dominated by long-established gentry rather than aristocracy: 'there was a strikingly high proportion of ancient gentry families whose lineages ran unbroken from Norman or Plantagenet times'.[23] Their rent rolls supplied by pastoral agriculture, they bucked the national trend of the dispersal of large estates. By and large, the Shropshire gentry behaved in a paternalistic way to the rural poor until well into the twentieth century. In particular they played an active part in parish government and local charity administration. In Lydbury North, the Plowdens were successive chairmen of the parish council and trustees of the Poor's Estate Charity. In conjunction with R. H. Nevill (the Earl of Powis' estate agent) – who was also the Conservative Party secretary as well as being the returning officer – Poor's Estate was run as an adjunct to the needs of the two local big houses. To the 'deserving poor' it paid out private unemployment doles, which compared well to the working wage, as well as grants for apprenticeships and scholarships. It provided retirement pensions, cottage tenancies and even employed a parish nurse.[24]

Paternalism was also practised by the newer 'in-comer' gentry. Miss Jewell Allcroft of Stokesay Court, descended from a family of Worcester glovers, voiced paternalistic views at her coming-of-age party given for tenants, servants and farmworkers:

> It seemed very sad to her that so many of the big estates in that neighbourhood were being broken up. She thought that they at Stokesay should hang together and help each other as much as possible. Nobody who did not run an estate could form any idea of what it cost ... Rates and taxes were making it almost impossible for people to live on their land.[25]

Similar events – such as tenants' garden parties, servants' balls and suppers for beaters – seem to have been celebrated regularly and reported in the local press; they were undoubtedly very effective in binding farmworkers to their organic rural roots. The rural Labour movement had little to offer culturally as an alternative and even many of its activists were drawn into paternalism; for example, at least two village co-operative societies – Bourton and Burwarton (both affiliated to the Co-operative Wholesale Society and the Co-operative Union) – had been set up by and were supported by Shropshire landowners.[26]

Evidence of paternalism on the part of tenant farmers is very mixed. Retrospective oral histories, almost always from non-farmworkers, often paint a rosy picture: 'They were a team. There was none of those questions that the farmer was having goose and the workmen having bread and cheese and that sort of thing.'[27] 'Mother used to do a lot for the poor people of the village, giving them eggs and fruit.'[28] There is on one side, clear evidence of genuine concern for employees, reflected in extraordinary lengths of loyal service: 'Even in our periods of greatest distress I can't remember anyone ever suggesting that they should be sacked.'[29] 'I had a cowman, he was with me 27 years, which says a lot for me and him doesn't it?'[30] None the less, some Shropshire farmers could be as hard-nosed and unjust as any of those examined by other historians of the agricultural depression. One farmworker's union member was reduced to inarticulateness when he tried to explain his exploitation to an interviewer in the 1970s:

> No harvest supper, no just the three pounds for harvest – An all the blumin hours done, we done a lot of overtime with that yer know. Oh I can't tell yer how many hours we done for that … It's a job to get a job anywhere in them days you know. You get cused and blumin I don't know what it is you, yer couldna leave, nothing like it is now.[31]

Foxhunting was one of the institutions that reinforced paternalism. In remote Shropshire it was the premier winter entertainment for the resident gentry. The first Shropshire pack in 1753 was known as the True Blues, an indication perhaps of its members' political views.[32] Shropshire hounds accompanied the Duke of Wellington in the Peninsular War. In the view of an early Victorian sports writer: 'No other county showed more respect for the "noble science" or had more sportsmen and well wishers among the "higher orders" and the yeomen, the result being an "excellent feeling" between tenant and landlord.'[33] Here, as elsewhere in the country, there was an attempt to extend this 'excellent feeling' to rural workers, as 'spotters' (who built artificial earths and fed 'wild' foxes); and to publicans who victualled the hunters, gate-openers and hunt followers. Shropshire had more packs of hounds than Norfolk, with only half the population. The hunts put effort into maintaining goodwill throughout rural society with dinners for gamekeepers, garden parties for farmers and 'point to points' for everybody. Even at the height of the First World War, foxhunting was maintained, and exemption to conscription was given by local military tribunals to hunt servants.[34]

With so many foxhunting landlords, the usual tension between shooting and hunting was lessened. In addition, many farmers were foxhunters and did not resent such tenancy restrictions as the compulsory removal of barbed-wire fences by 1 November. According to one hunting farmer, 'It was a form of local entertainment, life wasn't so busy in winter. It was a way of doing business.'[35] In December 1928 the National Farmers Union (NFU) had devised a plan for farmers to produce lists to be distributed to hunt followers to protect vulnerable crops. The same month (at his coming of age) the tenants of Lord Acton of Aldenham Hall presented him with a hunting saddle and horn. Acton was one of the older gentry, the grandson of the famous Liberal historian, and his own father had briefly supported the Labour Party before his death. The young man became a member of his local Conservative association, and the gift seems to symbolise the harmony between gentry and farmers, and the strength and political influence of paternalism.[36]

Informally, foxhunting also gave politicians access to the nexus of powerful people at county and even national level. One aspiring Conservative MP found his political career was enhanced by becoming joint master of his local pack: 'The position of Master of Fox Hounds put me in contact with a great many well-established and influential Tories in the country, many of whom were either politicians themselves in local or national government, or took part in the country's social life.'[37]

The Shropshire Yeomanry consisted of the foxhunters in military uniform – tenant farmers sons, officered by young landowners. Its social events were the most important in the county. Originally formed as part-time cavalry during the French Revolutionary Wars, in the early nineteenth century – under the control of the Home Office – its role was the preservation of public order. Although pastoral Shropshire was little affected by the intermittent disturbances that characterised the corn-growing parts of southern England, the Yeomanry took an active part in dispersing political and industrial movements in the Shropshire coalfield and in neighbouring parts of Wales. It was revived as a serious military unit at the time of the Boer War, sending special companies – blessed by the county – to South Africa, and rode off to war in 1914.

Although part of the county establishment, the Yeomanry could also be part of the apparatus of state control. As late as the 1921 railway strike, a special unit – the Shropshire Dragoons – was raised from the Yeomanry as an aide to the civil power, commanded by a master of fox hounds.[38]

The friendly societies, although probably in decline, were also village institutions which reinforced rural paternalism in Shropshire. Although still relatively under-researched, some recent historians have concluded that they were highly independent working-class organisations, which trained their members in skills which were transferred to chapels or trade union branches. Although, in the late nineteenth century, locally based societies – often patronised by the gentry – had been eclipsed by branches of the large affiliated orders, this did not effect the social conservatism which both types displayed in their Edwardian heyday as key rural cultural institutions. The only surviving Oddfellows minute book – again from Lydbury North – details a yearly calendar of funeral processions, church parades, the hospital Sunday walk, the foundation dinner and anniversary sports. A financially prudent branch, critical of members 'so frequently in receipt of sick pay', its funds were invested in Madras railway securities and Manchester Corporation stock. Although membership was overwhelmingly working class – including many farmworkers – the lodge's officers and patrons were largely from the more substantial members of rural society. One example of a lodge trustee was Richard Kilvert, farmer, president of the South Shropshire Farmers' Association, parish councillor and officer of the Lydbury North Conservative Association. It was men like this who controlled south-west Shropshire for the Tory party.[39]

BRIGHTER VILLAGES: NEW RURAL INSTITUTIONS

Richard Kilvert was also a county committee member of the NFU. The first new rural institution to come out of the First World War, the NFU was significant in reinforcing Shropshire paternalism and Conservative political domination of the county. Although not formed until 1908, the county NFU rapidly established itself, claiming to represent small as well as large farmers. It moved from a pre-war preoccupation with particular problems of livestock husbandry to being the employers' negotiators for the wage-level settlement in the county's premier industry. It coolly and successfully countered the threat from organised labour during, for example, the wave of strikes in 1919:

> Referring to the strike of agricultural labourers which occurred in the middle of the corn harvest, and which affected several villages on the Shropshire border, the report stated that the machinery of the Union enabled members all over the county to keep in touch with each other and act in unity. Arrangements for mutual assistance were organised and as a result, members successfully weathered the stormy period.[40]

In the 'Coupon election' of 1918, the NFU ran candidates in Worcestershire and the neighbouring constituency of Leominster, with programmes focusing on the difficulties of tenant farmers. However, the NFU in Shropshire showed little conflict with landowners, ostracised those few farmers who expressed support for the emerging Labour Party and specifically voted to support the Conservative Party. Its authority as the voice of Shropshire's main industry grew more confident despite the recession. By 1922, in conjunction with the local press, it was sponsoring a 'Brighter Villages' campaign which was crucial in stemming rural depopulation and in maintaining a loyalist consensus in the countryside: 'The men have returned restless and more ambitious, and consequently they have set out to seek their fortunes in the big cities ... if they were to have a greater production of food from rural areas, they must endeavour to make the life of those working on the land more pleasant and agreeable.'[41]

The NFU was only one of the new institutions that were significant in this campaign. Ploughing matches had been used by nineteenth-century agricultural societies as a way of strengthening the pride and interest of the workforce, but they had died out in the late Victorian period. Now they were revived along with hedging competitions and sheepdog trials because 'Farmworkers welcomed the opportunity given of testing their skills with the champions of neighbouring villages.' Such competitions were linked to the growth of local agricultural shows and were rewarded with prizes and cups presented by the local gentry; they were publicised with features and photographs in the county press.[42] This combination of recreation and education may also be linked to the appearance – at the end of the 1920s – of the first Young Farmers Clubs, fostered by the NFU and seen deliberately as harmonising the interests of farmers and farmworkers.[43]

Originally developed in Canada, the Women's Institute (WI) first appeared in Shropshire in 1917, sponsored by government to

aid the war effort. Some historians see local WIs as feminist organisations that campaigned on important welfare issues.[44] However,
Shropshire evidence (again in a surviving minute book from
Lydbury North) show fairly mundane activities – fruit bottling and
folk dancing – with the wives of the gentry taking a lead. In the
ballot for Shropshire representatives on the National Executive
Committee in 1933, both candidates were titled. WI branches were
particularly involved in the spread of Empire Day festivities in the
villages, another new development that underpinned the rural
consensus:

> The highlight of the year was the tea party given by our local
> Women's Institute on Empire Day. All the children would line
> up in rows in front of the Union Jack and sing 'God Save the
> King', then they would march past and salute before going to
> the field nearby where they held all kinds of sports.
> Afterwards they would tidy themselves up and march up to
> the Hall where they were entertained to a marvellous tea.[45]

REMEMBRANCE: POST-WAR POLITICS AND EX-SERVICEMEN

The post-war challenge from radical ex-servicemen has already
been briefly discussed. The Conservative Party set up its own ex-
service organisation, incongruously named the Comrades of the
Great War, which was present in Shropshire from 1918. The
comrades were officially non-political: 'Party politics would have
nothing to do with the movement.'[46] None the less they successfully destabilised the radical National Federation of Discharged
and Demobilised Soldiers and Sailors, weakening its links with the
Labour movement through anti-socialist propaganda emphasising
the pacifist record of the Independent Labour Party (ILP).
Federation activists, like W. H. Edwards, the Workers' Union
organiser, were forced to acknowledge this weakness:

> They would recognise that the Trades and Labour Council
> had rendered valuable service to the cause of the movement.
> But there happened to be one section of the party, the ILP,
> which did not want to be Labour, but something more ...
> [they] could not do their work without being hampered by
> men of the Bolshevik type.[47]

In addition, the comrades' wealthier ex-officer members were able
to organise sponsorship for their social activities, club premises

and sometimes lavish entertainments at the country houses of rich members, which the poorer federation could not rival.[48]

By 1920, the government offered to put the profits of wartime canteens at the disposal of a united ex-service organisation and the National Federation of Discharged and Demobilised Soldiers and Sailors, and the Comrades of the Great War merged into the British Legion. Although non-political, village British Legion branches almost always chose ex-officer members of the gentry for their officials. In Leebotwood, a neighbouring village to Lydbury North, the 'squire' Major Trevor Corbett was elected chairman, a post he held concurrently with that of chairmanship of the Shropshire Agricultural Wages Board. By the end of the 1930s, it was claimed of the British Legion: 'They differ hardly in any respect from a collection of Conservative working men's clubs.' Its 'anti-Bolshevist' politics probably accounted for the fact that it attracted only 10 per cent of eligible ex-servicemen as members, although there is evidence that this proportion was higher in rural areas.[49]

The commemoration of the war dead became one function of the British Legion, but it predated its formation. The village war memorial movement was clearly a potent weapon in uniting all levels of rural society in a common bond of the grief, although its form and ceremony often retained the class tensions, which united sacrifice was meant to transcend. None the less the dedication of the village war memorial was often the opportunity for a community to patriotically redefine itself on a county or even national basis. In the words of the Lydbury unveiling programme, 'Lydbury North was similar to most English villages in its condition or life. Our knowledge of geography was not great, Britain to most of us meant little more than Lydbury North or at most Shropshire.'[50]

However, the connection between remembrance and military patriotism was initially not a foregone conclusion, indeed there was a decided move to commemorate the dead with utilitarian schemes, particularly village memorial halls. This notion was often opposed by an alliance of gentry and farmers, who favoured capital expenditure on a stone cross or brass tablet, rather than the ongoing cost of maintaining a hall; also, as the village arbiters of good taste, they might genuinely prefer a stylish cross or tablet to army-surplus village hall erected by enthusiastic amateurs. The solid, unfunctional memorial was usually supported by the Anglican clergy who wanted the local focus of public mourning to be within the curtilage of the established church, in order to consolidate their place in the potential uncertainties of village life. Nevertheless, local public opinion often ensured that village halls were erected. They became the focus of the mildly hedonistic culture:

> When the young boys returned from the war, and with some money from a 'canteen fund' for boys who had been in the forces, they decided they needed a village hall to meet instead of just 'Clayton's Corner'. They bought an old army hut and put it on a piece of land given them by a local farmer. With the help of other young people of the village, they held whist drives and dances to finish paying for it and for the upkeep, taking it in turns to light the stove to heat the hall and generally keep it clean.[51]

Generally, the halls, which were proving their worth in the re-establishment of post-war rural life, were run by committees on which the village elites were dominant. So, in Lydbury North, the village hall trustees were Captain Plowden of Plowden Hall, Major Whittaker of Totterton Hall, plus two farmers and the vicar.[52]

The formation of the British Legion coincided with the development of Armistice Day in a militaristic form.[53] Moreover, in Shropshire, 11 November was joined by a June event – Bligny Day. On mobilisation in 1914 the existing county territorial battalion was sent to the Far East on garrison duty. It retained its local identity, after the other volunteer 'Kitchener' battalions of the King's Shropshire Light Infantry had been virtually wiped out on the Western Front and filled up with conscripts drawn from all over the country. By 1918 the territorials were themselves posted to Flanders and, in their first battle at Bligny, the battalion stemmed the German advance, winning the unique award of the French *Croix de Guerre*. After the war, 6 June was celebrated by all battalions of the King's Shropshire Light Infantry and, by 1921, Bligny Day parades involving all ex-servicemen were established all over the county. By celebrating a particular identity of Shropshire and its military prowess, the phenomenon had the effect of welding ex-servicemen to an establishment and military perspective at a time when returning soldiers, as we have seen, had the potential to be subversive. In addition, Bligny Day was used by the local establishment to ensure that its own regiment survived the Geddes axe of central government, when the Territorial Army came to be re-established in the early 1920s.[54] So this and the other new village institutions – ploughing matches, Women's Institutes, Young Farmers' Clubs, Empire Day, the British Legion, war memorials and village halls – had the effect of strengthening the loyalist consensus.

CONSERVATIVES AND THE MASSES

In conclusion, the role of the Conservative Party itself in Shropshire society is examined, with specific reference to the impact on farmworkers of party activists. This will be contrasted with the relative weakness of the local Labour organisation. Historically, the Conservative Party did well in Shropshire. Even in the 1906 Liberal landslide, four Conservatives were returned and only one Liberal. This support was based on the gentry and farmers but, with the gradual extension of the franchise, there was a need to woo the rural poor. Before the war the Primrose League, which organised elaborate social events in the country houses of the gentry and was particularly geared to women's interests, was important in mobilising Tory consensus in the Shropshire villages. Potentially, the post-war political scene was transformed:

> The Representation of the People Act [1918] trebled the size of the electorate. New constituencies were created and the rural divisions were obliged to cover huge areas in order to incorporate the requisite numbers of new voters. Local Conservative associations were forced to expand in the drive to recruit more party workers and more Conservative voters.[55]

In Shropshire, however, the 'increasingly sophisticated propaganda techniques developed by Conservative Central Office' were still supplemented by old-fashioned paternalism on special occasions:

> The Wrekin Conservative Party at this time organised the Baldwin-Webb outings. Besides keeping the party in the news, they gave the constituents the chance to see parts of the country they would not have otherwise enjoyed. These outings were train excursions and people took advantage of them in their hundreds, flocking to their railway station to board the special excursion trains. One year they visited the Military Tattoo in London … One was to the Isle of Wight with a beautiful view of the Needles, and the other was to the British Empire Exhibition in Glasgow with a sail round the Kyles of Bute. Colonel Baldwin-Webb, with his sister and agent, travelled to Glasgow by aeroplane, so that they were there to welcome the Shropshire constituents when they arrived.[56]

These sort of accounts tend to confirm Simon Moore's findings that farmers, and especially farmworkers, were not themselves the activists in the rural Conservative associations, but were content to act as passive constituents and Tory voters in supporting the political status quo.[57]

On the other hand, there is evidence that intimidation was used by the Tories as a political weapon. One Shropshire resident recalled of her childhood:

> I can remember every child in the school had to wear a blue rosette … the agent said tell them they're Conservative or else, you know what I shall do? He came down to the house … Oh yes that's the gentry for yer. You don't know what this village was like.[58]

The Labour parliamentary candidate for Oswestry in 1924, inevitably perhaps, blamed his defeat on 'several glaring cases where people were almost afraid of being seen speaking to him. One man had told him that after the election he had lost his job. It takes real men and women to take their stand for Labour.'[59] The Labour Party also listed as a factor in the debacle of the Ludlow by-election 'tenants who dared not show the Labour colours, everywhere the chains of feudal oppression'.[60]

Tory political domination was reinforced by the Conservative local press. Labour activists found that the press 'did the Conservatives' work for them in rural areas … the local Conservative Party had very little contact with the general public but got unusual publicity for Conservative activities.'[61] The *Shrewsbury Chronicle,* the main weekly farmers' journal, was owned by Sir Beville Stanier, Tory MP for Ludlow until 1923. It was specifically anti-socialist after the war, even to the point of suggesting that the Labour Party had no place in the political process: 'Shrewsbury was not troubled with a Labour candidate, although Oswestry was.' Curiously it moved further to the right and between 1922 and 1929 it expressed support for the British fascists and continued to show sympathy for Mosley's British Union of Fascists in the 1930s.[62]

The surviving Conservative minute books from Lydbury North, dating from 1886 to 1924, when read in conjunction with the parish records, indicate the enmeshed network of gentry and farmer involvement in the party. One gentry family, the Plowdens, father followed by son, provided the association chairmen; R. H. Newill, the Earl of Powis' agent, was the secretary (with the Earl as a member); and a member of the NFU county committee was the canvasser. (Newill also acted as returning officer!) The local association was well organised with fetes, whist drives and the visits of a cinema van. The latter was especially potent in areas that did not yet have cinemas: 'For rural districts the phonofilm cinema van is by common consent the most powerful agency at the disposal of the party.'[63] A surviving set of canvass cards for the adjoining village of Edgton relating to the 1923 election shows an almost total Tory domination, with only two socialist votes and one Liberal. If, as seems likely, Tory organisation was as good in other villages, the Labour Party could offer little in opposition.[64]

Based on isolated rural groups of workers – typically railway-men, quarrymen or even organised farmworkers themselves – the Labour Party in Shropshire had practically no middle-class activists at all.[65] It therefore could not consolidate on the post-war potential for drastic change and let the initiative pass to the Tories. In addition, the relatively poor showing of the Liberal Party in Shropshire meant that there was little in the way of a Liberal rump vote, which, as Clare Griffiths points out, Labour successfully captured in other rural seats.[66]

The largest Labour event consisted of 100 people at a rally in Ludlow, and even this involved bussing in supporters from other constituencies. This was puny compared to the numbers mustered by the Conservatives: the Junior Imperial League welcomed 600 to its Empire Day dinner in Shrewsbury in 1924; in 1926 it claimed nearly 1,500 members. (Thousands of schoolchildren with flags were also mobilised in their school classes to attend the official Empire Day celebration in town.[67]) By its gentle handling of crises like the 1919 railway strike, the 1926 General Strike – when the chief constable could state: 'I feel I must express to all strikers my appreciation of their good behaviour during the strike'[68] – and county-wide strikes of farmworkers in 1917, 1919 and 1923, Shropshire Conservatism showed its political skill. Carrot and stick were a potent mix to secure farmworkers' votes and even though from 1918 most of the Shropshire rural poor had the opportunity to vote for Labour candidates – with the exception of the Wrekin in 1929 – most chose not to do so.[69]

Furthermore, many union activists, rather than undertake the thankless task of attempting to organise fellow farmworkers, migrated from the land either to work on the railways or into the cities. Once they had gone, the majority of farmworkers felt their interests were protected by choosing to vote Conservative, as they did in the Ludlow by-election of 1923 and consistently thereafter. Even the victory of 1945, the high tide of rural socialism, had little impact in Shropshire. Given the passage of time, the voice of the rural poor is muted, but one informant from the Shropshire WI's oral history project demonstrates the extent to which farmworkers were hostile to agricultural trade unionism, which in reality was relatively powerless:

> When Bert had his fourteenth birthday, the farmer was informed by the labour union that he should pay Bert three shillings and sixpence per week and that this would be increased every year. The farmer told Bert that he could not afford to pay such high wages, and he must give him the sack! Such was life in those days.[70]

Similar hostility of farmers towards trade unions is also recorded: 'There was a lot of pride in those farm cottagers, farmworkers and still is … that's why they can't get anyone to join the farmworkers' union, they'd rather be on better terms with their boss.'[71]

CONCLUSION

The cultural separateness of Shropshire and neighbouring English counties continued to foster traditional rural institutions and encouraged the persistence of paternalism in relationships between classes. Although widespread, the radical challenge had patchy roots within rural society and had few contacts with the new post-war village institutions, which tended to be culturally conservative. It can be concluded that the Conservative Party in south-west Shropshire was very skilled at using old and developing new institutions to reinforce the attitude of the rural poor illustrated above, to consolidate the Conservatism of the masses and to reinforce its political position within the masses.

The complete hegemony of the Conservative Party in this period, though, produced few favours for rural areas: 'It is concluded that between 1920 and 1929 agrarian Conservatives represented interests that were important to their party's electoral success … [but] failed to secure the main legislative measures most of them believed would help their industry'. Only such palliatives as 'Rate relief … help for farmers' mortages, improved quality controls on imports, marketing assistance and selected subsidies for promising agricultural entreprises such as the production of sugar beet and broccoli' were forthcoming.[72] Ironically, it was the failing rural Labour Party which advocated the state intervention which many in farming favoured. However, although 'in the 1920s the Conservative Party seems to have felt at liberty largely to ignore the demands of its agricultural supporters', culturally and politically, the farming community of south-west Shropshire could not bring itself to support Labour.[73]

NOTES

1. Some of this article derives from my PhD thesis, 'Agricultural Trades Unionism in Shropshire 1900–1930' (University of Wolverhampton, 1997). The relevant archives in Shropshire Record Office (SRO) are Parish records, St Michael and All Saints, Lydbury North, SRO P/177; Loyal Vale of Clun Lodge records, SRO 1927/1; Edgton Primitive Methodist Chapel records, SRO 4942/4/10/1–12; and Lydbury North Conservative Association records, SRO 552/114.
2. *Shrewsbury Chronicle*, 2 June 1916. The strike – expertly timed to coincide with the haysel (or hay) harvest, so important to pastoral Shropshire farming – is also mentioned in F. E. Green, *A History of the English Agricultural Labourer* (London, 1920), 246.
3. For agricultural strikes generally, see Reg Groves, *Sharpen the Sickle! The History of the Farm Workers' Union* (London, 1949) and Green, *English Agricultural Labourer*. The National Union of Agricultural Workers was known as the National Agricultural Labourers' and Rural Workers' Union between 1910 and 1918, but is referred to as the NUAW throughout this chapter. The archives of the union are held at the Rural History Centre (RHC) at Reading University; the strength of the Lydbury North branch is recorded in NUAW, BVIII. For rural recruitment in the First World War, see N. Mansfield, *English Farmworkers and Local Patriotism 1900–1930* (Aldershot, 2001), ch. 4.
4. The Norfolk origins of the NUAW are covered in Alun Howkins, *Poor Labouring Men: Rural Radicalism in Norfolk 1870–1923* (London, 1985).
5. This ambivalence is discussed in Mansfield, *English Farmworkers*, ch. 5. See also E. Dewey, *British Agriculture in the First World War* (London, 1989).
6. For the federation, see N. Mansfield, 'Class Conflict and Village War Memorials 1914–24', *Rural History*, 6 (1995), and Mansfield, *English Farmworkers*, 160–2; *Shrewsbury Chronicle*, 9 May 1919.
7. F. E. Green, *The Awakening of Rural England* (London, 1919), 338.
8. *Shrewsbury Chronicle*, 23 January 1920.
9. *Shrewsbury Chronicle*, 22 June 1923.
10. NUAW, Executive Committee minutes, 16 March 1923, RHC.
11. *New Leader*, 20 April 1923.
12. *Shrewsbury Chronicle*, 27 April 1923.
13. H. Drinkwater, 'The Problem of Rural Constituencies', *Labour Organiser*, October 1923.
14. See also Clare Griffiths, 'Labour and the Countryside: Rural Strands in the British Labour Movement 1900–1939' (DPhil thesis, University of Oxford, 1996). For the Shropshire farmworkers' strike, see Mansfield, *English Farmworkers*, 163–5.
15. For a discussion of these issues, see Mansfield, 'Agricultural Trades Unionism', ch. 6.
16. For Norfolk, see Howkins, *Poor Labouring Men*, and N. Mansfield, 'George Edwards and Norfolk and the First World War: Oral History in the Norfolk Museum Service', *Oral History*, 14, 2 (1986), 51–8.
17. For this section of the chapter, see Mansfield, 'Agricultural Trades Unionism', ch. 7.
18. For Shropshire customs, see Charlotte Burne, *Shropshire Folklore* (London, 1883) and Christina Hole, *A Dictionary of British Folk Customs* (London, 1978).
19. Quoted in Vincent Waite, *Shropshire Hill Country* (1970).
20. For a modern discussion of Oak Apple Day, see Bob Bushaway, *By Rite: Custom, Ceremony and Community in England* (London, 1982), 150–2.
21. Mr Edwards, farmworker of Worthen, and Maurice Alderson (1894–1987), farmer of Bishop's Castle, Shropshire Museums Service Oral History Collection (SMSOHC), nos. 48 and 95.
22. Mansfield, 'Agricultural Trades Unionism', 175–6, 185–9. For farmworkers and Methodism, see Howkins, *Poor Labouring Men*, and the work of Nigel Scotland, particularly *Methodism and the Revolt of the Field* (Stroud, 1981).
23. F. M. L. Thompson, *English Landed Society in the Nineteenth Century* (London, 1963), 124.

24. See parish of Lydbury North, minute books 1894–1936, SRO, CP 177/1/1/1; Poor's Estate Charity, minute books 1916–1935, SRO, CP 177/Q/2/1; and Returning Officers papers, SRO, CP 177/9/10/1.
25. *Shrewsbury Chronicle*, 29 September 1928. The Allcroft family features in Julian Critchley's autobiography, *A Bag of Boiled Sweets* (London, 1994).
26. See Mansfield, 'Agricultural Trades Unionism', 173–9; Co-operative Congress, annual reports.
27. Maurice Alderson, SMSOHC, no. 36.
28. Gwen Wycherley, farmer's wife of Beckbury, SMSOHC, no. 17.
29. Arthur Hollins, *The Farmer, the Plough and the Devil* (Bath, 1984), 20
30. Alderson, SMSOHC, no. 103.
31. Bill Glaze (b. 1903), farmworker of Norton, SMSOHC, no. 103. See also Alun Howkins, *Reshaping Rural England: A Social History 1850–1925* (London, 1991), ch. 11. Even in the large capital-intensive farms of Norfolk there is evidence that farmers deliberately did not introduce new technology in order to provide winter work for their employees; see Susanna Wade Martins and Tom Williamson, 'Labour Improvement: Agricultural Change in East Anglia c. 1750–1870', *Labour History Review*, 62, 3 (1997).
32. *Victoria County History of Shropshire, Vol. 2* (London, 1973), 166.
33. 'Nimrod', writing in 1843, quoted in Paul Stamper, *The Farmer Feeds Us All: A Short History of Shropshire Agriculture* (Shrewsbury, 1989), 43.
34. *Kelly's Directory of Shropshire* (1900), 14, and (1929), 6; *Kelly's Directory of Norfolk and Suffolk* (1922), 3 and 10. When the South Shropshire Hunt applied for exemption for conscription for its kennelman: 'Colonel Wolseley Jenkins said the military had no objection at all to the application. It was a recognised thing that hunting should be kept up.' *Shrewsbury Chronicle*, 2 June 1918.
35. John Foster (b. 1917), M. F. H. Wheatland Hunt, Bridgnorth, interview with author, 17 July 1995.
36. *Shrewsbury Chronicle*, 14 and 21 December 1928.
37. Ronald Tree, *When the Moon was High* (London, 1975), 32, quoted in Simon Moore, 'Reactions to Agricultural Depression: The Agrarian Conservative Party in England and Wales 1920–1929' (DPhil thesis, University of Oxford, 1988).
38. See the author's unpublished paper 'Yeomanry, Foxhunting and the Idea of "Country"', presented at the Oral History Society conference 1999 and E. W. Gladstone, *The Shropshire Yeomanry 1795–1945* (Manchester, 1953), 138.
39. Recent work from the Friendly Societies Research Group (Open University Department of Social Sciences), presented at its annual conference in October 1999, suggests that they did not begin to decline in terms of numbers of members until after 1947. Rural friendly societies are covered in David Neave, *Mutual Aid in the Victorian Countryside 1830–1914* (Hull, 1991). For Lydbury, see SRO 1927/1.
40. See Shropshire NFU records, SRO 4531; *Shrewsbury Chronicle*, 23 January 1920.
41. For the NFU generally in politics, see Malcolm Wanklyn, 'Agriculture and Agrarian Society in the West Midlands', unpublished paper, 15–16, and Moore, 'Reactions to Agricultural Depression', 69–70. For the NFU's politics in Shropshire, see *Shrewsbury Chronicle*, 12 and 29 November 1918. For the Brighter Villages campaign, see *Shrewsbury Chronicle*, 24 September 1921, 28 July 1922 and 13 March 1925. The quotation is from *Shrewsbury Chronicle*, 28 January 1919.
42. For ploughing matches, see *Shrewsbury Chronicle*, 28 October and 4 November 1927 (source of quote) and 5 October 1928.
43. For Young Farmers' Clubs, see *Shrewsbury Chronicle*, 26 April 1929, 31 January and 26 September 1930.
44. For modern interpretations of the WI, see Maggie Morgan, 'Jam, Jerusalem and Feminism', *Oral History*, 23, 1 (1995), and Howkins, *Reshaping Rural England*, 278–9.
45. Lydbury North WI, minute book 1931–39, Shropshire Federation of Women's Institutes, SRO, P 177/G4/1; *Shropshire Within Living Memory* (Newbury, 1992), 243.
46. *Shrewsbury Chronicle*, 6 December 1918.
47. *Shrewsbury Chronicle*, 26 September 1919.
48. For examples of the lavish social activities of the comrades, see *Shrewsbury Chronicle*, 21 March 1919, 31 January and 22 October 1920.
49. *Shrewsbury Chronicle*, 16 January, 6 February, 11 June 1920, 29 April 1921 and

23 April 1926. On the British Legion see J. A. Niall Barr, 'Service Not Self: The British Legion 1921–1939' (PhD thesis, University of St Andrew's, 1994); the quotation is from Duff Cooper. Barr discusses membership on pp. 91–3 and the interesting way the legion's county structure reflected that of the county regiments on pp. 41–3.

50. See Mansfield, 'Class Conflict and Village War Memorials'; Programme and War Record for Lydbury North War Memorial, 1919, SRO, CP 177.

51. Mansfield, 'Class Conflict and Village War Memorials'; *Shropshire Within Living Memory*, 37.

52. Village Hall Trustees, minute book, SRO, CP 177/16/1/1.

53. For the development of Armistice Day, see Adrian Gregory, *The Silence of Memory* (Oxford, 1995).

54. W. de B. Wood (ed.), *The History of the KSLI in the First World War 1914–18* (London, 1925), 318; *Shrewsbury Chronicle*, 10 July and 11 July 1921.

55. *Victoria County History of Shropshire, Vol. 3* (London, 1979), 344, and Moore, 'Reactions to Agricultural Depression', iv.

56. Ibid., v; *Shropshire Within Living Memory*, 231.

57. Moore, 'Reactions to Agricultural Depression', 59, 62.

58. Mrs Bray (b. 1900) of Ackleton, SMSOHC, no. 104.

59. *Shrewsbury Chronicle*, 7 November 1924.

60. *New Leader*, 20 April 1923.

61. Griffiths, 'Labour and the Countryside', 73.

62. For anti-socialism and fascism, see *Shrewsbury Chronicle*, 24 February and 15 December 1922, 30 November and 14 December 1923, 1 February, 17 and 31 December 1924, 8 June 1934.

63. Lydbury North Conservative Association, minute book 1886–1924, SRO, 552/114.

64. Ibid.; Moore, 'Reactions to Agricultural Depression', 81–2.

65. For the composition of local Shropshire Labour parties see Mansfield, 'Agricultural Trades Unionism', ch. 5.

66. Griffiths, 'Labour and the Countryside', 14, 76.

67. *Shrewsbury Chronicle*, 22 June 1923, 30 May 1924, 24 March 1926, 3 October 1919, 15 April 1921, 7 May 1926, 4 June 1926.

68. D. J. Elliot, *Policing Shropshire 1836–1967* (Shrewsbury, 1984), 164–5.

69. See F. W. S. Craig (ed.), *British Parliamentary Results 1918–1945* (Chichester, 1977).

70. *Shropshire Within Living Memory*, 158. The informant appears to be talking about her father from Bromfield.

71. Maurice Alderson (1894–1987), farmer of Bishop's Castle, SMSOHC, no. 39.

72. Moore, 'Reactions to Agricultural Depression', iv.

73. Griffiths, 'Labour and the Countryside', 284.

— 4 —

The Conservative Party and Mass Housing, 1918–39

KEVIN MORGAN

In recent years one of the most keenly debated questions in the literature on British Conservatism has been that of its resilience and renewed electoral hegemony following the franchise extensions of 1918 and 1928. Accounts have ranged widely, from high politics and questions of ideology to constituency organisation and innovations in campaigning methods. Dominating many of them, as he did the age itself, is the figure of Stanley Baldwin, at once elusive and reassuring, and the consummate exponent of Conservative values in an age of social and technological transformation. Against the contemporaneous 'rise of Labour', traditionally framed in terms of class, the Conservatives' durability suggests that there were powerful political crosscurrents irreducible to such categories, and that the configurations of class itself are complex and negotiable. 'Staying power' to Baldwin was the supreme English attribute, and in that much at least the Conservatives were truly the party of the flag.[1]

Housing was one of the key issues in the battle for the new mass electorate; it provides a fruitful if somewhat neglected way of exploring these questions. Following the wartime gap in building there was in the 1920s an estimated shortfall of some 800,000 homes, not finally overcome until the following decade, which engendered that broad acceptance of a government responsibility for housing immortalised in the promise of 'homes fit for heroes'.

Like the new Ministry of Health on which the responsibility fell, this may be regarded as one of the hallmarks of a more democratic age. Even Conservatives, while favouring the private sector and the language of enterprise, hailed the achievements of the speculative builder as among the fruits of constructive statesmanship. Indeed, under the second Baldwin government (1924–29) some two-thirds of *all* new housing, and half of that privately built, was directly state-subsidised, prompting a form of crude quantitative competition between the parties which was to resurface periodically into the Bevan–Macmillan era and beyond. Baulking at the idea of state provision, Conservatives were forced into having a housing policy simply in response to their opponents.[2]

Housing, though, was more than just another social commodity. In the ethos of Conservatism, it was not the house but the home – with its richer and sometimes suffocating connotations – which had a powerful symbolic value resting on a gendered familial ideology and the threatened integrity of the private sphere.[3] 'Socialism stands for class war, chaos and disruption, the break-up of family life and religion', ran Mrs Baldwin's message to women voters in 1929. 'Our lives would be supervised at all points by State Officials and the women and children would be the first to suffer from such a changed order of society.'[4] Martin Pugh has suggested that Labour's own evocations of the home offered little more than a 'mirror image' of the same motifs, although in Labour's appeals to the housewife there lingered not only a sense of the home as workplace – which can indeed be detected even in Conservative sources – but the view that this required not just individual improvements but communal amenities, 'municipal meals' and what Herbert Morrison called 'something like "TU" conditions'. Home as a purely private sphere, fortified by ownership as well as possession, was more distinctly the terrain of the Conservatives.[5]

These positive images of domesticity had an equally powerful negative corollary: the view of housing shortages as a catalyst of social unrest, not just because of a sense of grievance or deprivation but because the home itself provided an anchorage of private contentment and atomisation which negated the appeals of socialism. During the immediate post-war unrest the Conservative mind teemed with images of single young men, ex-soldiers or unemployed, driven into the streets and the clutches of the agitator. According to one Midlands MP, 'much of the Bolshevik and Socialist menace in this country might be attributed directly to the influence of the housing problem',[6] while the Tory *Birmingham Mail* struck a similar note upon the launch of the city's housing bonds in 1920:

> The seeds of revolt most easily take root among those who have no sound stake in the country, no decent habitation, no foundation on which to build up that family life which is the great stabiliser ... Given a decent home, a bit of garden, a wife and children and a wage sufficient to maintain them ... ninety men out of a hundred would have no traffic with the strife-mongers and revolution-makers.[7]

A decade later, Winston Churchill went so far as to recommend plural votes for householders, thus counteracting the influence of the country's 'more dependent and more volatile elements ... the lodgers of all kinds and both sexes'.[8] Though such concerns were generally somewhat assuaged by this time, the framework of subsidies and rent restriction to which they had so largely contributed was maintained in some form throughout the inter-war years. Moreover, the notion of the home as the bedrock of an ordered society remained as strong as ever.[9]

Establishing what Conservatism represented in the field of housing is nevertheless far from straightforward. Administratively, the responsibilities for public housing of local government, in many instances still resisting formal party affiliations, made for a diversity of local practices across some 1,700 housing authorities. Geographically and socially, that itself was a reflection of the heterogeneous coalition of interests or perceived interests which provided the Tories with their electoral base. And the character of Conservative leadership and organisation was not entirely conducive to consistency. Lacking an effective policy-making apparatus, the party's housing programmes reflected the shifting concerns of its successive health ministers, who did not always carry with them the party in the country. Baldwin himself, while taking scant interest in policy details, offered such varied signals to this wider public that Philip Williamson has aptly likened him to a coalition in his own right. A further accent was provided by the part-absorption of an attenuated Liberal tradition, and by the scope of welfare issues to buttress the dubiously inclusive credentials of the National Government of the 1930s. From cabinet to grass roots, tensions were exposed at the heart of Conservative philosophy, with paternalism delimiting the market and traditionalism confronted by the language of efficiency. Williamson also stresses the sheer diversity of the forms of Conservatism available in the 1920s, and this was nowhere truer than in the field of housing.[10]

DUNROAMIN

To capture something of this diversity within a short chapter, three brief excursions are proposed. Taking in the main housing types of the inter-war years, they are intended to provide a glimpse not only of competing government policies but of the wider political aspects of housing provision. Indeed, on alighting at the first of our destinations, any trace of government initiative seems to have been self-consciously obliterated. Passing through the urban peripheries we think of as middle England we behold that bewildering collage of mock timber, sunray windows, crazy paving and 'Please Shut the Gate' signs: the ubiquitous inter-war speculative 'semi'. Lately rivalling the dole queues as a stock image of the 1930s, 'Dunroamin', as it has been generically dubbed, is enjoying a strange cultural rehabilitation, and the individualism of its design values as well as forms of tenure has been strongly counterposed with the collectivist prescriptions of a demonised planning establishment.[11] Politically it was inevitably the Conservatives who found in Dunroamin their home territory and whose main housing policies presupposed its innate superiority. After the bold but expensive experiment in public housing under the 1919 Addison Act, Neville Chamberlain's subsidies of 1923 were intended primarily for the construction of private houses for sale, and over the seven years of their operation four-fifths of them were used for this purpose. For most of this period they were supplemented by the more generous subsidies to local authorities provided under the Labour government's 1924 Wheatley Act. However, in 1932, it was again a Tory Health Minister, Hilton Young, who announced the cessation of all subsidies except for slum clearance, and a return to that basic reliance on the private sector which had been Chamberlain's underlying aim. Pragmatically adjusted according to circumstance, this continuity of purpose was discernible in the strictly limited scope and duration laid down in all Conservative housing legislation. The unifying principle seemed to be that housing must so far as possible be privately financed, privately built and privately owned.[12]

This then is 'home' as one finds it depicted on Conservative Party literature of the period. '*Yours!* But not under Socialism', warned a leaflet portraying exactly such a property in 1924. 'When you are asked "Is it your own house?" how proud you are when you can say "YES!"' But, on the other hand, 'If the Socialists have their way, we shall all have to live in State or Council houses, paying rent all the time, and *never having a house of our own.'* Hardly one-tenth of the population could then have said 'yes', but the appeal was as much to future aspirations and a vicarious stake in the country as to existing realities. Exactly so, a leaflet on housing giving 'The Workers' Case Against Socialism' addressed itself to all those who had bought or merely 'hoped' to buy their own home, and reproached the socialists for their 'stern and watchful eye' on such forms of self-improvement.[13] Though the phrase was not popularised until much later, it was in 1924 that the Scottish MP Noel Skelton defined his party's goal as that of a 'property-owning democracy', while in the same year Chamberlain himself drafted an official statement of 'aims and values' which looked to the extension of home ownership for a solution to the housing problem.[14] 'We are building up a whole new class of good citizens', he observed of this phenomenon the following year, and the property instinct was thus invested with a sense of civic purpose and moral uplift more commonly associated with the left.[15]

If such appeals had a resonance, it was because they drew on a language and world-view that were widely and continuously propagated beyond the world of party politics. Entrenched in the very order of society, the Conservatives naturally enjoyed the comparative advantage of their association with the powerful, articulated by press and pulpit. More particularly, in identifying themselves with the market they were also tacit beneficiaries of the new scope and sophistication of its methods of publicity as well as its somewhat patchier delivery of actual material benefts. This was nowhere more significant than in the case of housing, where not only the level of supply but its character divided the parties, expressing in bricks and mortar their different social ideals. Particularly influential was that unequalled vehicle of mass Conservatism, the *Daily Mail*, and its staggeringly successful Ideal Homes exhibition. First held in 1908, by its 1930s heyday the exhibition was attracting nearly 700,000 visitors as well as exhaustive coverage in the *Daily Mail*'s national and provincial stablemates. Not the house but the home was its theme, including settings, fittings, lifestyles and an ever greater profusion of labour-saving devices. Amidst the trappings of royal patronage and national self-esteem, it represented the housing and related industries in all their ingenuity, subliminally attesting the Conservative values of private provision, and holding out a vision of the affluent society of the future. 'Yours!', the exhibitions promised, and the politician had only to add: 'But not under Socialism.'

The appeal of such spectacles was a self-consciously feminised one, insidiously corroborating the so-called gender gap that appeared to work to the Tories' electoral advantage. That the home itself was routinely identified as a women's issue both reflected and legitimised the domestic circumstances of most inter-war households, though what the phrase meant for women in practice was far less clear. To Thomas Sharp, a prolific populariser of planning ideals, the very forms in which the suburb were clothed betrayed the baleful influence of the 'Emancipated Woman', described by him as individualistic, given to display, distracted by 'small novelty' and aesthetically possessing 'few or none of the makings of the citizen'.[16] Paul Oliver in *Dunroamin* has more recently celebrated the same 'feminine forms', though again without establishing how far their overpowering maternalist associations – 'The woman's place was not only in the home; the home was a woman' – were actually shaped by women's own fantasies. The same ambiguity underlay the cultivation of the woman consumer by the Ideal Homes exhibition, at once perpetuating, as it promised to transform, the prescriptive role of the housewife.[17]

That did not preclude a more active definition of 'women's issues'. In 1930, following earlier press campaigns for the employment of women architects, the exhibition had as its central feature a competition, 'The House that Jill Built', fulfilling in a less passive way its aim of establishing contact between the housewife and designer. More convincingly, during the Second World War it produced a prospectus for the post-war home embodying a national survey of women's organisations and the depiction by a woman architect of their desiderata for the domestic environment. Its author, Mrs Pleydell-Bouverie, though adopting a robust tone towards the high-handed architect and demanding fuller women's representation on housing bodies, was nevertheless self-effacing in everything except what she called the 'woman's business' of the home. 'The bigger problems', she ceded winningly, 'women leave to their menfolk', and even the architect's plans depicted mother peeling the potatoes while father read the paper with a masculine enlargement of mind.[18] Nevertheless, the immediate appeal to women of claims to light, space, gardens and basic amenities was difficult to resist. This broad and pragmatic familial ideology, simultaneously attested by the spectacular growth of women's magazines, was central to Conservative claims to the mantle of the 'women's party', and embodied in a vibrant women's organisation which also accorded women a distinct but highly circumscribed sphere of responsibility while eschewing any suggestion of an equalitarian agenda. Aptly enough, its own magazine was entitled *Home and Politics*.[19]

Even critics acknowledged that the spread of suburbia represented a qualitative improvement in Britain's housing stock.
Conservatives like Chamberlain also made the case that, by a
process of filtering down, its benefits would be disseminated
throughout society. Nevertheless, however beguiling the prospect
of a property-owning democracy, the terms were as yet far from
coterminous, and their juxtaposition could be interpreted as a
delimitation of democracy as readily as a diffusion of property
(and it may be recalled that in 1928 the cabinet actually decided on
the withdrawal of the local government franchise from Poor Law
recipients).[20] Often strung out in the total disaggregation of ribbon
development, the speculative housing scheme provided a form of
overt spatial separation which seemed the antithesis of more solidaristic values. Concerns with status, intransitively expressed in
the forms and symbols of the suburb, also encouraged the active
exclusion and repudiation of the rejected city. The suburb was in
this sense an unrehearsed form of zoning, not just of avenues and
crescents from the smoke and clamour of industry, but of
respectable British householders from Churchill's volatile and
dependent 'mob'. Usually distance lent an informality to the
process, but occasionally close proximity gave rise to open antag-
onism. Notoriously in the 1930s these were encapsulated by the
Cutteslowe Wall in north Oxford, built six feet high across the road
to barricade a speculative estate and its local amenities from
adjacent council tenants. In *Dunroamin* the episode is preciously
described as a clash of 'environments' hostile to each other's 'value
implications'. In reality, not values but people were forced into
long circumnavigations to the bus stop or shops, and the only
hostile action of the council tenants was to live in their own homes.
The real clash of values was that expressed in campaigns to have
the wall demolished on grounds of common rights of citizenship,
and these were not organised by Conservatives.[21]

HOMES FOR HEROES

In widening home ownership, in one of the major social changes
of the inter-war years, one nevertheless sees a development largely
conducive to Conservative well-being. This alone, however, was
not the stuff of which majorities were made. Though filtering
down was not entirely a myth, most British households remained
doggedly dependent on a rented sector which, as Chamberlain
conceded, offered little attraction to the private developer and

whose only prospect of renewal and extension lay in public investment. As the party unambiguously committed to that objective, Labour also had a strong card in housing, and it played it with some skill in winning control of cities like Leeds and London in the early 1930s. 'Up with the houses, down with the slums', a party pamphlet of 1934 promised, and thoughtful Conservatives, whether for reasons of genuine paternalism, social insurance or mere electoral prudence, did not believe that they could leave such a prospect uncontested to their opponents. For Chamberlain, the most influential such figure, it was by the test of its social programme that a Conservative government would stand or fall.

It is to the other side of the Cutteslowe Wall that we therefore make our second excursion. The scene is the Weoley Castle estate on the outskirts of Birmingham, and the occasion the opening in 1933 of the city's forty thousandth council house – a record then surpassed only by London. As local boy turned good, Chamberlain was there as guest of honour, and struck a note very different from his frugal demeanour as the then Chancellor of the Exchequer. Invoking the sense of a contract with the war generation, what he offered, somewhat complacently, was a retrospective version of the 'homes for heroes' refrain with which he had embellished his own speeches as the city's wartime mayor:

> When I look back on the type of house which was all that the working-man could hope for before the War, those great long rows of houses with their deadly monotony, haphazard in their lay-out, without a garden, or a bathroom or electric light …when I compare these houses with those which have been built by the corporation, with everything that science and ingenuity can provide to make the occupants happy and comfortable, I feel … that we have gone a long way to carrying out those hopes which inspired us all during the War.

'No one', he added, with uncertain perspicacity, begrudged the small extra burden that meant their fellow citizens living lives 'of human beings and not of wild beasts!' The only inauspicious note came when he proved unable to open the door of the house, requiring not one but two council officials to bring to bear upon it their extra corporate weight.[22]

In both the address and the achievement it celebrated, a singular legacy was perpetuated: that of Chamberlain's father, 'Brummagem' Joe, and the Liberal Unionism he created, which in the Midlands retained its separate identity until as late as 1914. Scottish Unionism also maintained something of this inheritance,[23] but in England it was within the west Midlands, and above all in Birmingham, that the Chamberlain legacy ran deepest. A Conservative city whose motto was 'Forward', and whose main thoroughfare memorialised neither prince nor patron but the Corporation, Birmingham continued during these years to pioneer such municipal accomplishments as its town planning schemes, civic orchestra and Municipal Savings Bank – respectively the first, the best and the only ones of their kind in the country. The bank especially was very much Neville Chamberlain's brainchild, and its 60 or so branches came to embrace one-third of the city's house-holds, and a rather greater proportion of its 'artisan population'. If this was socialism, Chamberlain grandiloquently declared, then he at least was not to be frightened by a mere word. Here were Conservatives who frankly contested Labour's claim to be the party of social reform, and saw in the municipality the most effec-tive vehicle of their own programmes.[24]

With regard to housing, this was not necessarily synonymous with council estates, and in Birmingham as elsewhere some Conservatives positively discountenanced such an idea. A differ-ent demotic strain – that of 'every man his own landlord' – can thus be traced in periodic demands for council house sales and in the 13,000 mortgages provided up to 1935 by Birmingham's Municipal Bank.[25] Nevertheless, given the lack of any effective challenge to the Conservative stranglehold on the region, it is to the Tories' own distinctive outlook that one must primarily credit Birmingham's exceptional vigour in the matter of public housing. While complex local factors enter into such calculations, it is remarkable that five of the seven counties building more munici-pal than private houses in the decade 1921–31 fell within the Conservatives' Midland Union, and that three of these – the Chamberlain heartlands of Warwickshire, Worcestershire and Staffordshire – were almost the only ones in which council housing added more than 10 per cent to the housing stock.[26] Even political opponents acknowledged the scale of this achievement. When the Independent Labour Party (ILP) conference was held in Birmingham in 1928, W. H. Milner, a sometime local councillor and militant tenants' leader, virtually puffed up his chest at the city's 'inspiring record of the success and practicability of social owner-ship, even when administered by those who do not believe in it'.[27] Five years later, the architects of the radical and controversial Leeds Labour housing policy of the mid-1930s commended not only fashionable continental prototypes like Stuttgart and Vienna, but the 'magnificence' of Birmingham's Fox Hollies and Bush

Moor estates. Implausible as it may seem, this Tory citadel had become a byword for progressive housing policy.[28]

Through Chamberlain's influence something of Birmingham's housing policy had an impact on national policy. As early as 1913 Conservatives had boldly claimed that state responsibility for housing was an idea 'deeply embedded' in their own tradition. Sir Arthur Griffith-Boscawen, an MP from Chamberlain country and recent London County Council (LCC) housing chairman, even moved progressive parliamentary bills which in this respect gave the Tories the edge over the Liberals.[29] It was Chamberlain himself, however, whose tenure of the Ministry of Health provided the chance to develop a coherent Conservative social policy through an activist legislative programme. With eyes fixed on Labour, he consciously risked the ire of that 'middle class who read the *Daily Mail*' for the larger constituency whose expectations he believed would henceforth hold the keys to office. 'To go to the country purely on economy and anti-Socialism seems bad tactics to me', he observed in 1922, 'and I can't imagine that Father would have done it.'[30] Two years later, unlike many of his colleagues, he pointedly failed to vote against the Wheatley subsidies and, though privately saluting himself as a master tactician, found himself constrained to continue the subsidies when returned to office. Between Labour's reformers and himself there appeared to be, if not actual fellow feeling, a certain common cause against the diehards which occasionally belied Chamberlain's apparent superciliousness towards political opponents. In 1927 he visited Sheffield, a city just fallen to Labour, and to his surprise came away with a 'rather favourable impression' of its highly partisan but constructive administration. 'I fancy the old lot were very reactionary and obstructive', he wrote, seemingly emptied of party prejudice. 'The present lot are certainly not revolutionary and it did not appear to me that their programme contained anything that might not equally have figured in that of a progressive Conservative party.' There was no consensus, and other Labour authorities attracted Chamberlain's fierce disapproval. But nor were differences of political approach neatly arranged along party lines.[31]

Even under the National Government, intricacies of collation remain. In 1932 all general subsidies were withdrawn and the market was reinstalled as sole housing provider except in respect of slum clearance. Described by critics as a return to a Victorian 'sanitary policy', this did at least mean addressing the long-neglected problem of the slums, which with the easing of the

general shortage was emerging as one of the issues of the hour.[32]
By general consent subsidised housing on new estates had proved
both physically and financially beyond the reach of the slum
dweller and it was in the guise of social reformer that
Chamberlain's successor, Sir Hilton Young, came forward with
plans for compulsory slum clearance, the statutory prohibition of
overcrowding, and the development of high-density schemes on
inner-urban sites. Young himself had defected from the Liberals as
recently as 1926, and in phrases becoming any Edwardian progressive he excoriated the 'evil legacy' of the Victorian city and defied
its legatees among a bedrock Tory constituency of property
owners. In the best paternalist tradition he looked highmindedly
to posterity for the recognition his reforms deserved, but like
Chamberlain he was not above considerations of how best to
neutralise the impact of his present-day opponents. Assisted by
the speculative housing boom, his reforms so far succeeded in this
objective that for the first time in almost 20 years housing was very
largely taken out of national politics.[33]

Effective implementation of the reforms depended on housing
authorities of varied political colourings, and this could sometimes
provide a further twist to the entanglements of party. Birmingham
was again a case in point. In 1939, the year of its fifty thousandth
council house, the city began a five-year plan to build half as many
more again, four-fifths of them for slum clearance, and in the
syncretic vernacular of Chamberlainism proclaimed this 'the
greatest socialistic proposal ever launched in the city'.
Nevertheless the scheme met with active tenants' resistance
because of its association with the controversial device of differential rents. This again was an issue over which both conflict and
consensus had a surprisingly bipartisan character. Combining the
principle of economic rents with support for those unable to afford
them, differential schemes commended themselves to both paternalist Tories and constructive socialists, and the Labour and
Conservative parties both formally supported them. Nevertheless,
the anticipated objections of better-off tenants meant that for pragmatic reasons they had almost nowhere been implemented in any
comprehensive fashion. The one major exception was Leeds,
where under trenchantly socialist auspices the issue became identified with the vast and modernistic Quarry Hill development, at
once an echo of the Karl-Marx-Hof and a foretaste of the post-war
council flat. Despite this socialist provenance, it was to both
modern flats and Leeds' method of financing them that
Birmingham turned in imitation. If that again attests the possibil-

ity of cross-fertilisation across the party divide, or by the neutral medium of city housing officers like Birmingham's Herbert Manzoni, reactions to the schemes also had a paradoxical symmetry. In Leeds, introduced by socialists, the schemes provoked an electoral backlash and the return of the council to Conservative hands. In Birmingham, introduced by Conservatives, they prompted a successful rent strike, supported by many Labour councillors, and the formation of a combative tenants' association. The common denominator was differential rents, but the parties were seemingly ranged on opposite sides.[34]

At the heart of the case against such schemes, at least in Birmingham, was the indignity of the means test which they required. This itself was a perenially emotive issue and it reminds us how ambivalent Conservatives actually were about the incursions of the state official they so freely stigmatised as the curse of socialism. To a rooted belief that public subventions demanded oversight and accountability, always a formidable device for controlling the 'poor', they sometimes added paternalist concerns for improvement and good conduct such as guided estate management practices on both sides of the party divide. In Birmingham, certainly, it was a strict condition of tenancies that gardens be properly tended; the city was one of many authorities which employed women 'visitors' or 'housing managers' avowedly in the Octavia Hill tradition. Chamberlain himself was a firm believer in the professionalisation of housing management, and once averred on these grounds that the eradication of the slums was impossible except by 'replac[ing] ownership by small individual landlords with ownership by the community'.[35] This too was an authentic Conservative tradition, though it seems a far cry from the beleaguered hearth of Mrs Baldwin. Recent accounts have rightly stressed the ambiguity of Conservative thinking on the state, but ambiguity can conceal a familiar and deep-seated consistency: that Conservatives believed in very different things for different people.[36]

WEIR'S TIN CANS

This view is borne out by the last of our outings, not this time to one of the built environments of inter-war Britain, but to their largely unrealised extension by the adoption of new building technologies. In such schemes or anticipations the public–private division was overlain with a further tension, between tradition and modernity, which has sometimes been positioned along the same axis, as if complementary aspects of a single clash of values. Quarry Hill, for example, has seamlessly been described as representing the rejection of 'individualism and backwardness' for 'social order and technical advance'. In polemics both for and against architectural modernism, this coupling of social and constructional experimentation has become a cliché.[37]

Perhaps around the Bauhaus or constructivist Moscow, progressiveness was indeed indivisible. In Britain, the picture was more confused. At the Ideal Homes exhibition the 'house of the future' vied with 'Tudor village' for attention, and even the latter had oaken beams sprouting electric sockets and bathrooms glistening like sets from the film *Things to Come*.[38] As for blocks of flats, those interloping symbols of the new mass man, Hilton Young lent them not only his outspoken advocacy but the quiet emphasis of differential subsidies. Fittingly, Quarry Hill's 'miniature prototype' in Manchester was named after him – exactly as its most 'advanced' precursor of the 1920s, on the LCC's Ossulston estate, is Chamberlain House. In Baldwin himself, political epitome of bypass variegated, conservationist instincts combined with modernising pressures in ways that were never as artless as they seemed. Easily confused with mere eclecticism, conflicting design values and housing types were reconciled in the Conservative mind as befitting the different orders of a class society.[39]

It is in this light that one may view the curious and abortive episode of the Weir steel house, launched amid tremendous publicity in 1924 and buried for the foreseeable future just three years later. Its originator, Lord Weir of Cathcart, was a Clydeside industrialist well connected with leading Conservatives and invited by Baldwin to join his government in 1924. Despite earlier ministerial experience, Weir preferred to carry on what had become a relentless personal propaganda against the inadequacies of the building industry, which appeared to him to be sheltered from foreign competition, unwilling to innovate and oblivious to the public interest. Like many at that time, he particularly anathematised the building operative, whose alleged restrictions of both output and labour supply were widely regarded as the key to the housing problem. Labour's response, embodied in the Wheatley Act, was to work with and through the building industry on semi-corporatist lines, matching supply to demand over a guaranteed long-term programme. A less conciliatory, more widely preferred, approach was to bypass or supplement building labour by the use of new materials and construction methods. To this end, the *Daily*

Mail had commissioned an 'ideal village' of prefabricated cottages at Welwyn. Among the many local authorities thinking on similar lines, Birmingham was just one in which councillors boasted of concrete housing schemes undertaken in defiance of the building trades. Weir too began with flat-roofed concrete, but by 1924 had settled on his so-called steel house – actually timber-framed with steel cladding, but aptly named to underline its derivation from the Fordist production lines which were Weir's great passion. Factory-built as entirely standardised units, his houses were to be parked on the ground like just so many Model Ts. He envisaged half a million of them, in three basic designs.[40]

As propaganda by deed or technocratic panacea, the initiative met with a ready response in government. Indeed, it was at Bonar Law's invitation that Weir had originally turned his thoughts to housing and, when his scheme was made public as a counterblast to the Wheatley Act, it was with the active encouragement of Baldwin, Churchill, Chamberlain and Scottish Secretary Sir John Gilmour. Briefly in 1924–25 the scheme provided a cornerstone of Chamberlain's housing policy, but its operation was held up by the threat of the excluded building unions to block all housing projects of any participating authority.[41] The political symbolism was heightened by the scheme's special application to the socialist west of Scotland – 'a far more favourable battleground for the fight with the trade unions', observed Chamberlain[42] – and it was on visiting Glasgow as Weir's guest that in October 1925 Baldwin announced a supplementary Scottish subsidy of £40 specifically for such houses. When this inducement also proved ineffective, the government finally undertook to promote such schemes itself through the Scottish National Housing Association.

For Weir himself, however, the moment of opportunity had now passed and in 1927 he was even rebuffed in attempting to give away his housing factory to Glasgow city council. Fatally undermined by a sharp fall in building costs, only 3,000 of his 'tin cans' ended up being built between the wars. Nevertheless, there is an intriguing postscript. In 1944 a Labour Scottish Secretary, Thomas Johnston, approached Weir about a possible Weir House mark 2, and in belated recognition of his genius Glasgow alone was to build several thousand of these houses in its new-found enthusiasm for alternative technologies. Nationally, standardisation and the use of new materials were widely promoted as solutions to the new housing crisis, and Weir's steel houses of the 1920s were frequently illustrated in 1940s housing manuals. It is a curious lineage, less often recalled than that of Quarry Hill. Subverting our conventional habits of association, the maligned system building of the high-rise 1960s can trace at least one of its lines of descent from the unaccredited innovations of the Baldwin era.[43]

The Weir controversy was partly about efficiency but also about the quality of public housing. It was a stock Conservative rejoinder that the standards Labour required of public housing meant that rents were affordable only by the more affluent worker, and in favouring numbers over size and amenity Conservatives thus linked the careful husbandry of economic rents with the winning refrain of more extensive, accessible and better-targeted provision. It was on these grounds that Bonar Law had originally approached Weir, and it was why Chamberlain preferred his schemes to costlier attempts at prefabrication.[44] What Weir offered was a huge emergency building programme, explicitly aimed at the slum dweller, and initally proposed at prices which would obviate the need for subsidies. Very deliberately, it was a populist equation and directly counterposed the public as consumer with the narrow self-interest of industrial labour. 'Bad houses made Bolshevists and the slum bred Socialism', said Sir Kingsley Wood, Chamberlain's junior Minister of Health. 'The government were not prepared to condemn the slum dweller to his miserable hovel for another generation.'[45] Nevertheless, it was not only the building worker who believed that houses built on such foundations would themselves prove the hovels of their day. Even so constitutional an organ as *Country Life* railed against Weir's 'excrescences' as an offence to the cultivated eye and likely incubators of a sullen discontent. 'Is it possible to imagine anything more sordid and objectionable … ?', its editor asked, and predicted an 'increase in communism and socialism', not from the slums but from their replacements. 'The country has no right to put up this wretched class of building.'[46]

This was a case of rank ambiguity. It was the moment of Baldwin's paeans to 'England', and the year that intense concerns about soulless and intrusive housing developments encroaching on the countryside gave rise to the Council for the Preservation of Rural England. Baldwin himself was ever the toast of such circles, echoing their disapproval of 'abortions of red brick and slate' and calling instead on the shades of William Morris and the 'springs of craftsmanship'.[47] In 1927, with a shudder of distaste for their more recent neighbours, he issued an appeal on behalf of Britain's cottage homes, 'built with material ready to the hand of the craftsman … just as naturally as the oaks and elms under whose shade they stand'.[48] Though less mellifluous in his concerns, Chamberlain in his aldermanic way was also far from insensitive to issues of siting and amenity, and was regarded by town planners as a friend in high places. Nevertheless, with Corbusian abandon he now dismissed the opposition to Weir's bungalows as the coachman's reflex confronted with the railways, while Baldwin's speech writer described the homes as being sent 'so to speak … by post' to settings sylvan or otherwise.[49]

No doubt the objections of those latterday coachmen of the building trades were far from disinterested. Nevertheless, it was they who were left to make the case for traditional skills and materials, for the avoidance of segregated housing types 'likely to deepen the division of the classes' and for the rejection of 'experiments on the bodies and minds of our people'. 'Human beings are not suited to become clockwork images in mechanical contrivances', argued builders' leader Dick Coppock, and the sentiments seem almost Baldwinian.[50] As W. D. Rubinstein has observed, not disapprovingly, 'There is nothing whatever in any aspect of the history of the Conservative Party to suggest that it ever confused symbol with reality in any economic policy.'[51]

CONCLUSION: HOUSING AND THE CONSERVATIVE 'PUBLIC'

On such a whistle-stop tour, the rapid succession of images can obscure the underlying topography. To contemporary reformers, certainly, there was nothing especially complex about the inter-war housing scene. On the contrary, its ebb and flow seemed readily explicable as a 'ding-dong struggle' between the two major philosophies of state and their respective preferment of public and private enterprise. In the 1930s, some of these reformers invoked this see-saw of party politics, and consequent unevenness and discontinuity of policy, as an argument for a National Housing Board conceived on technocratic lines.[52] Historians have echoed such judgements, and Alison Ravetz is just one of those to have detected 'two irreconcilable philosophies' in the major housing controversies of the period. However, Ravetz also points out that the relationship between these philosophies and the parties which might have championed them was anything but clear-cut. Perceived epiphenomena of a class society, the two philosophies were in reality refracted through a host of tensions which belie any simple bipolar model. Conservatism could prosper because the 'natural' majority on which Labour counted was itself part of the argument and not the basis on which it took place.[53]

However, that also meant that there was nothing natural, or intrinsic to our climate, about a Conservative majority. This too needed making and remaking and, according to one of the most cogent accounts of this process by Ross McKibbin, the one constructed between the wars depended not only on the direct middle-class beneficiaries of Tory economic policies but on a large section of unorganised workers to whom the Labour movement was successfully depicted as hostile and threatening. McKibbin's emphasis is on the power of ideology to override objective inter-ests and, though relying rather heavily on national economic policy in determining these, his broad categories do seem readily transferable to the field of housing.[54] The first of them, stretching somewhat further than McKibbin's £500-a-year man, would approximate to those whose housing needs were satisfied by the market, and more particularly the growing class of owner-occupiers which by 1939 comprised perhaps one-fifth of all British householders. Here, Conservative allegiance seems intelligible in terms of economic rationality, though not necessarily reducible to such calculations. The same claim would not however be made by McKibbin for his second constituency, which, while overlapping with the first at its lower end, would also have included some of the casual and lower-paid workers who were the bane of Labour agents, and many of the housewives who made up Britain's largest group of unorganised workers.

McKibbin plausibly argues that only a powerful ideological conditioning can explain Conservative support in such circles. In a housing context his blunt counterposition of 'objective' and 'subjective' factors is nevertheless too schematic to be really helpful. Certainly the building worker of the 1920s exemplified the negative stereotype of organised labour, whose significance as defining other for Conservative Britain McKibbin rightly empha-sises. However, it was not just fear and contempt that the building worker provoked, nor immediate concern for the imperilled constitution, but impatience with the faltering housing supply and its excessive cost. This was the real threat to social order, through its impact on housing conditions; in meeting it Conservatives expressed concern for those falling below as well as above Labour's own core constituency – that of 'decent respectable working people receiving ordinary artisan's wages' – and the housing programmes which catered for its interests.[55] All of these were contested arguments and, if Labour was reproached with its union connections, it had a ready retort in the shape of the landlord and developer. Nevertheless, to the extent that

Conservatives did hold their own over the issue of housing, it was by articulating and to some extent advancing a consumer's viewpoint unconstrained by Labour's concerns with employment issues. McKibbin's 'public' was a consuming public and, whether real or imagined, material interests as well as status helped to define it.

That is partly, but only partly, a secular rather than deferential view of the working-class Conservative. Appeals were made to self-interest, but always within a limiting context of social hierarchy, adjusting expectations to the sliding scale of an unequal society and constantly reaffirming its basic tenets. Just as women's issues were defined within a framework of male prerogatives, so the different social orders were to find contentment in housing types, locations and forms of management befitting their status and economic capacity. Labour's rhetoric was honed on such double standards, but conceivably its greater coherence of programme and constituency set a limit to its support as well as consolidated it. If it was the logic of a mass electorate that irreconcilable philosophies had to be reconciled, even if only verbally, then perhaps it was by not speaking with a single voice that that larger reconciliation, of the party of privilege with a democratic franchise, was for the time being secured.

NOTES

1. Stanley Baldwin, 'England', in S. Baldwin, *On England and Other Addresses* (London, 1926), 4.
2. Figures in Marian Bowley, *Housing and the State 1919–1944* (London, 1945), 271.
3. Baldwin, *On England*, 8.
4. Conservative Party leaflets, nos 3022, 3025, May 1929, Bodleian Library, 22775 d.50.
5. Martin Pugh, *Women and the Women's Movement in Britain 1914–1959* (Basingstoke, 1992), 115; Herbert Morrison, *Better Times for the Housewife! Labour's Policy for the Home-maker* (London, 1923), 8–11. See also Lynn F. Pearson, *The Architectural and Social History of Co-operative Living* (London, 1988), chs 8–9.
6. Sir Percy Newson, *Coventry Herald*, 4 May 1923.
7. *Birmingham Mail*, 27 April 1920.
8. Churchill, in Robert Rhodes James, *Churchill: A Study in Failure 1900–1939* (London, 1990 edn), 302–3.
9. Mark Swenarton, *Homes Fit For Heroe: The Architecture and Planning of Early State Housing in Britain* (London, 1981), 78ff. for the influence on housing policy of the post-war unrest.
10. Philip Williamson, *Stanley Baldwin* (Cambridge, 1999), 150–1, 342–3.
11. Paul Oliver, Ian David and Ian Bentley, *Dunroamin: The Suburban Semi and its Enemies* (London, 1981); Anthony King, *The Bungalow: The Production of a Global Culture* (London, 1984).
12. See, for example, G. D. H. and M. I. Cole, *The Condition of Britain* (London, 1937), 141–86, for such an assessment.
13. Conservative Party leaflets, nos 2334 and 2662, 1924 and 1926, Bodleian Library, 22775 d.50.

14. Conservative Party, *Looking Ahead: A Restatement of Unionist Principles and Aims* (London, 1924), 9–10.
15. Neville Chamberlain, letter to his sister, 17 October 1925, in Robert Self (ed.), *The Neville Chamberlain Diary Letters, Vol. 2: The Reform Years 1921–1927* (Aldershot, 2000), 315–16.
16. Thomas Sharp, *English Panorama* (London, 1936), 83–4.
17. Paul Oliver in Oliver *et al.*, *Dunroamin*, 161.
18. M. Pleydell-Bouverie, *Daily Mail Book of Britain's Post-war Homes* (London, *c.* 1944), 10, 27, 133–59 and passim.
19. Conservative Party leaflet, no. 3021, May 1929, Bodleian Library, 22775 d.50; G. E. Maguire, *Conservative Women: A History of Women and the Conservative Party 1874–1997* (Basingstoke, 1998), 78–82, 90.
20. Williamson, *Baldwin*, 220.
21. Ian Bentley, 'Individualism or Community? Private Enterprise Housing and the Council Estate', in Oliver *et al.*, *Dunroamin*, 120–1.
22. Conservative Party Archive (CPA), *The Times* cutting, 24 October 1933, CRD 1/1/1.
23. James Kellas, 'The Party in Scotland', in Anthony Seldon and Stuart Ball (eds), *Conservative Century: The Conservative Party since 1900* (Oxford, 1994), 674–5.
24. Joseph Trevor Jones, *History of the Corporation of Birmingham, Vol. 5: 1915–1935* (Birmingham, 1940), 460–71; David Dilks, *Neville Chamberlain, Vol. 1: 1869–1929* (Cambridge, 1984), 182–3, 186.
25. *Building News*, 20 October 1922, 248; local election addresses including R. H. Thornton, Ladywood, 1923, Birmingham Central Library.
26. Figures in Bowley, *Housing and the State*, 64.
27. Milner in the ILP's 1930 Easter conference *Souvenir*, 49.
28. F. Barraclough, F. H. O'Donnell and C. Jenkinson, *Housing Policy in Leeds* (Leeds, 1933), 18.
29. Sir Arthur Griffith-Boscawen, *Memories* (London, 1925).
30. Neville Chamberlain, letter to his sisters, 22 March 1922, in Self, *Neville Chamberlain Diary Letters, Vol. 2*, 104.
31. Arthur M. Edwards, *The Design of Suburbia: A Critical Study in Environmental History* (London, 1981), 91–2; Neville Chamberlain, letters to his sisters, 4 October 1925 and 30 October 1927, in Self, *Neville Chamberlain Diary Letters, Vol. 2*, 311–12, 425.
32. See, for example, Harry Barnes, *The Slum: Its Story and Solution* (London, 1931); Sir E. D. Simon, *The Anti-slum Campaign* (London, 1933); H. V. Morton, *What I Saw in the Slums* (London, n.d. but 1933).
33. It is barely even mentioned in *Labour's Immediate Programme* (London, 1937) or the corresponding chapter in C. R. Attlee, *The Labour Party in Perspective* (London, 1937), 166–98. For Conservative policy see CPA, CRD 1/1/1–2, for cuttings and memoranda re 1933 Housing Act; memorandum on 'Overcrowding and the New Housing Bill', 21 November 1934, Cambridge University Library, Baldwin MSS, 25/36; Young in *House of Commons Debates*, 5th series, 297, col. 359ff., 30 January 1935.
34. *Birmingham Gazette*, 13 May 1939; for Quarry Hill, Alison Ravetz, *Model Estate: Planned Housing at Quarry Hill, Leeds* (London, 1974), 35–6 and passim.
35. Jones, *Corporation of Birmingham*, 323; Arthur Griffiths (Birmingham council tenant), interview with author, 23 November 1987; Neville Chamberlain cited in B. S. Townroe, *The Slum Problem* (London, 1928), ch. 18. See also Neville Chamberlain's letters to his sisters, 23 January 1925, 4 and 11 December 1927, in Self, *Neville Chamberlain Diary Letters, Vol. 2*, 267, 432, 435.
36. Martin Francis, '"Set the people free"? Conservatives and the State 1920–1960', in M. Francis and I. Zweiniger-Bargielowska (eds), *The Conservatives and British Society 1880–1990* (Cardiff, 1996), 58–77.
37. W. Houghton-Evans, introduction to Ravetz, *Model Estate*, ix.
38. Based on the novel by H. G. Wells, Alexander Korda's futuristic 1936 film, *Things to Come*, expressed a visionary faith in scientific planning for peaceful ends. See Jeffrey Richards, *The Age of the Dream Palace: Cinema and Society in Britain 1930–1939* (London, 1984), 279–83.
39. Ravetz, *Model Estate*, 48–9 for Kennet House (Young became Lord Kennet in 1935); *House of Commons Debates*, 5th series, 30 January 1935, for Young's advocacy of flats.
40. W. J. Reader, *Architect of Air Power: The Life of the First Viscount Weir of Eastwood 1877–1959*

(London, 1968), 121; *Building News*, 9 April and 11 June 1920; A. H. Wright, election leaflets, Small Heath, 1925, Birmingham Central Library. For this and the following paragraphs I draw on the extensive documentation in the University of Glasgow archives, Weir MSS, 96/11/8–9.

41. Keith Middlemas (ed.), *Thomas Jones: Whitehall Diary, Vol. 2: 1926–1930* (Oxford, 1969), 6–7; Neville Chamberlain's attitudes can be traced in Self, *Neville Chamberlain Diary Letters, Vol. 2*, e.g. 155, 260–4, 269–71.

42. Neville Chamberlain, letter to his sister, 23 Sept. 1925, in Self, *Neville Chamberlain Diary Letters, Volume 2*, 309.

43. Weir MSS, DC 96/11/3. See, for example, John Madge (ed.), *Tomorrow's Houses: New Building Methods, Structures and Materials* (London, 1946), 116–17, 148.

44. Dilks, *Neville Chamberlain*, 377; Weir to Baldwin with enclosure, 11 July 1924, Weir MSS, DC 96/11/8–9.

45. *Gloucester Citizen*, 22 June 1925.

46. N. L. Carrington, editor of *Country Life*, to Sir John Baird, 5 January 1925, Weir MSS, DC 96/11/9

47. Baldwin cited in *Daily Mail Ideal Homes Exhibition*, catalogue (London, 1927), 59.

48. Stanley Baldwin, *The Preservation of Ancient Cottages* (London, 1927).

49. Neville Chamberlain, letter to his sister, 14 February 1925, in Self, *Neville Chamberlain Diary Letters, Vol. 2*, 270–1; Middlemas, *Jones: Whitehall Diary, Vol. 2*, 6–7.

50. Minutes of Court of Enquiry into Erection of Steel Houses, 24 March 1925, Weir MSS, DC 96/11/2, 14–32.

51. W. D. Rubinstein, *Capitalism, Culture and Decline in Britain 1750–1990* (London, 1993), 77–8.

52. Gilbert and Elizabeth Glen McAllister, *Town and Country Planning: A Study of Physical Environment: The Prelude to Post-war Reconstruction* (London, 1941), 45; Unwin, 'Memorandum on a National Housing Board' (to Moyne Committee), 1933, CPA, CRD 1/1/3.

53. Ravetz, *Model Estate*, 31, 205.

54. Ross McKibbin, 'Class and Conventional Wisdom: The Conservative Party and the "Public" in Inter-war Britain', in Ross McKibbin, *The Ideologies of Class: Social Relations in Britain 1880–1950* (Oxford, 1991 edn), 259–93.

55. Arthur Greenwood (arguing against the Weir house), *House of Commons Debates*, 5th series, 180, cols 485–6, 12 February 1925.

5

Speaking to Democracy: The Conservative Party and Mass Opinion from the 1920s to the 1950s

ANDREW TAYLOR

Peter Lilley attributed the 1997 Conservative defeat to a breakdown in communication: 'We continued to focus on problems which people felt were largely solved and seemed not to listen to people's new concerns.'[1] The Conservative Party's history conveys an impression of effortless electoral supremacy partly derived from the assumption that, of all British parties, the Conservative Party communicates most effectively with the electorate. When com-munication breaks down the result is defeat but the Conservatives then recreate their links with the electorate, paving the way back to office. The Conservative Party has thought long and hard about mass politics with a degree of sophistication unmatched by any other British party and has been at the forefront of deploying inno-vative political communication techniques.[2]

This chapter focuses on the Conservative Party's relationship with society and how the party has sought to present itself to, and understand, the dynamics of mass opinion. It explores three episodes in Conservative political communication in the pre-television era: the projection of Baldwin; the *Industrial Charter's* failure to penetrate mass opinion;[3] and the adoption of opinion research in the 1950s. After 1918, with Britain seemingly on the verge of class war, traditional techniques of mass political commun-ication were inadequate. The Conservatives married two traditional appeals – One Nation and anti-socialism – and used radio and film to project Baldwin as the embodiment of the 'new Conservatism'. The *Industrial Charter* is invariably presented as signalling to the electorate Conservatism's transformation so paving the way for 13 years in government. Opinion research offered a window into the electorate's mind and with understanding would come, perhaps, an ability to predict and direct behaviour.

These three episodes illustrate the party's willingness to innovate, but also the limits of these innovations. Baldwin's media skills did not save the party from defeat in 1929 and the Conservatives would have won in 1931 and 1935 irrespective of these skills. The *Industrial Charter* was a major attempt at rebranding the party but it had remarkably few consequences for policy or image because of basic errors in presentation. Opinion research provided valuable insights into electoral behaviour but it could not predict behaviour nor could it reverse electoral decline. These episodes reveal what really determined Conservative success, the perception of Conservative governing competence.

PROJECTING BALDWIN

In January 1910 the (all-male) electorate numbered 7.6 million (27 per cent of the adult population); in 1918 it increased to 21.3 million (78 per cent of the adult population); then in 1929 to 28.8 million (90 per cent of the adult population). The nature of British politics was changed in 1918 with the creation of an electorate thought to be politically unacculturated and vulnerable to alien doctrines and demagogues. As Baldwin told Edward Wood in 1928, 'Democracy has arrived at a gallop in England and I feel all the time that it is a race for life; can we educate them before the crash comes?'[4]

The Conservatives were fortunate that the advent of mass democracy was accompanied by the emergence of new media suited to mass political communication, and in Baldwin they had a leader who appreciated the possibilities of the new technologies and who worked hard to master them. Basic to the Conservative appeal to the new electorate was 'educative propaganda of a non-party character'.[5] 'Before the war', Davidson (a confidant of Baldwin and party chairman 1926–30) told Baldwin, 'it was possible with a limited and highly expert electorate to put forward party programmes of a restricted and well defined character, but nowadays I am quite sure that while not departing from the principles of our party we must endeavour to gain the confidence not only of our own supporters but of the mugwump vote.'[6] The 13.7 million increase in voters occurred at a time when politics and society had been destabilised by the war; in 1918 the Labour Party was not only on the point of supplanting the Liberals but had adopted a socialist objective and, looming over all, was the Bolshevik Revolution. The electorate was larger and more complex with more young voters, now including women, and this called for a more sophisticated political communication strategy.[7] Many of Baldwin's speeches in the 1920s explored mass political education. At the Cambridge University Conservative Association, for example, Baldwin articulated the Conservative dilemma: 'Since 1918 this country has become a democracy. Millions of new voters were enfranchised in 1918, and for the moment there is a real risk that the status of our electorate has got a little bit ahead of its culture, and that is a very serious thing.' Consequently, 'the greatest work of all that lies before us is to make that democracy fit for its task'.[8]

The literature emphasises Baldwin's skills with the new media but the adaptation was not automatic. After a rally in Manchester, Baldwin told Davidson he 'hated speaking through the amplifier … I had to stand stock still and speak into a thing like a beehive. You can't look up or down, right or left, and you establish no personal contact with your audience nor do you know if they are gripped … I did not enjoy it.'[9] Baldwin's description conveys the falsity and sterility of rallies and their failure to establish personal contact with the audience; an ability to address vast audiences was of little value when the technology came between him and his audience. Rallies were politically sterile because they failed to establish personal contact and they were composed of the partisan. The voters Baldwin wanted to reach did not go to Conservative rallies and the skills of platform oratory (which Baldwin had) were not those of the new media or democracy. 'Wireless', Baldwin insisted, 'was a sad show up of the pretentious. Listeners got to the real man.'[10]

Modern electioneering requires that a successful party leader build up a relationship with voters based on an image that evokes trust. In Baldwin's case creating a relationship was vital because he had risen to prominence quickly. The 1920s saw public opinion come to regard the leader and party as synonymous, so the leaders' personalities were 'matters of public interest and inquiry'. The party's adoption of the new communication technologies was a logical extension of its experience with print propaganda and the Primrose League.[11] Baldwin was also drawn to radio and film because of the hostility of Beaverbrook's *Daily Express* and

Rothermere's *Daily Mail*, which 'attack us more frequently than they support us, while although *The Times* and the *Daily Telegraph* are admirable newspapers and give us their full support, their circulations are so small [and] their influence among the masses is almost negligible'. Anti-socialist newspapers were not necessarily pro-Baldwin.[12]

What was to be projected? A contemporary wrote of Baldwin, 'there was no nonsense about him' and commented on 'his extraordinary friendliness, candour, and liberality of mind'.[13] Another, seated in a working-class audience in a Wood Green cinema, reported that of the party leaders only Baldwin was applauded and as she left heard 'a working man say: "What I likes about Baldwin 'e don't sling no mud"'.[14] Even allowing for the charge that Baldwin's image was, to a large extent, manufactured and manipulated by a compliant pro-Conservative media, Williamson argues the enthusiasm Baldwin evoked in all sections of public opinion meant his image 'cannot just have been a propaganda construction. The medium was not the message.'[15] Baldwin's radio speeches addressed 'ordinary non-party people'; he avoided making exaggerated claims or open attacks on the opposing parties because 'Such speeches in the ordinary voter's mind reek of party politics and fail to carry weight on that account.' Other politicians' broadcasts were 'too formal. They sound like speeches delivered in a hall rather than talks to people sitting in their armchairs at home … the more personal, intimate and friendly these talks can be, the greater the influence they will exercise, and there is nobody who can deliver a talk of this kind better than yourself.'[16]

Baldwin was the first party leader to appreciate radio's power.[17] Between 1922 and 1939 radio licences increased from 36,000 to 8.9 million with ownership densest in London, the south-east and Midlands. About one-third of working-class households were without a radio in the late 1920s and radio penetration was greatest among the middle classes, but by the mid-1930s ownership was marked among the more affluent working class. On 16 October 1924 Baldwin made his first party election broadcast. Arriving early, Baldwin was briefed by John Reith, the BBC director-general, and then delivered an 'intimate, conversational, and seductively "non-party" speech which contrasted strongly with the broadcast of Macdonald's formal speech on 13 October'.[18] Speeches were often 'made with only a few notes on a postcard' and Baldwin recognised that working on a speech would not necessarily make it effective. A painstakingly prepared speech by

Churchill prompted Baldwin to comment that impact needed more 'than matter and more than brains [but] heart and feeling ...'.[19] By 1935 it was estimated one-third to one-half of the electorate listened to election broadcasts which was 'an unprecedented degree of contact between politicians and electors'.[20]

Baldwin asked Reith 'for information about the social classification of the audience, and he wanted to know whether working men listened at home or in clubs and pubs'.[21] Reith's response demonstrated how little anyone knew about radio's impact, but he confirmed what Baldwin had grasped intuitively, that he would be addressing 'a large proportion of working-class people, mostly in their homes, not in clubs or pubs. The workman and his wife will certainly be there, but so will the ordinary middle-class fellow and his wife, mostly at the fireside.'[22] Baldwin's style recognised that radio had a large but fragmented audience – the audience was listening at home, very many were not Conservatives or even interested in politics – and that the BBC carried great authority. The result was a conversational, intimate, non-political style, which corresponded to the Reithian ethos that the BBC existed to serve democracy but that democracy had to be educated. Baldwin's broadcasts and Conservative strategy reflected this doctrine but his speeches *were* partisan, their object was winning elections. Baldwin's Conservative Party and Reith's BBC were national, unifying and educative institutions – a culture that enabled Baldwin 'to deliver political messages subliminally'.[23] As Davidson wrote, 'He managed to convey the impression that honest chaps though the opposition might be they lacked tradition and experience in dealing with the larger problems of life at home and abroad, and with a sob in his voice suggested that in these anxious times it might be wise for the country to give the Government which he led another term.'[24] In 1935 Lloyd recommended that Baldwin, 'without being offensive in any way ... make a suitable reference to the weakness of the Opposition Labour in leaders and experience ...'.[25]

Politicians and strategists tend to overestimate the impact of any new media. In an uncharacteristic display of braggadocio Baldwin declared in retirement: 'Give me a wireless a week before a general election, and anybody can have the papers.'[26] By 1929 Baldwin was acknowledged as the best broadcaster in British politics, but this did not prevent the Conservatives losing the general election of that year. In 1931 Baldwin was the only broadcaster with, as the *Manchester Guardian* put it, 'his feet on our fender' but the National Government would have won without the broadcasts.[27] Surveying the 'radio war' in the 1930s, Stannage concludes that radio influenced the conduct of elections by influencing the agenda to which politicians and the media reacted. In this the BBC cannot be considered other 'than a weapon in the armoury of the forces aligned with the National Government against the Labour Party'.[28] Baldwin's speeches reached huge audiences and impressionistic evidence indicates their effectiveness with many voters. Lloyd told Baldwin:

> Last night I heard of a Labour family in Ladywood who were brought right over to our side by listening to you ... If you can put those simple issues across to the working man and his family as they sit by their firesides tonight all over provincial England, I believe you shall have a great victory.[29]

Nevertheless, estimating radio's political impact remained a matter of anecdotal evidence.[30]

Baldwin recognised the value of instant recognition in a democracy, which explains his willingness to provide photo opportunities and exploit film. Ball insisted: 'It is a psychological fact that a story told by the talking film is more easily understood and makes a more lasting impression upon the memory than the same story told either by the written or spoken word.'[31] The party was an early and heavy user of film and Conservative Central Office (CCO) had its own film unit, the Conservative and Unionist Film Association (CUFA) and, though generally good, relations with the five newsreel companies were not always smooth. Ball complained Movietone had more than once 'refused to include in its programme speeches by ministers against whom the *Daily Mail* was running a campaign, and on one or two other occasions speeches actually shown were badly mutilated'.[32]

Baldwin's visual prominence was an extension of his radio image, and film's impact was magnified further with the advent of 'talkies'. Sir Henry Clavering was a key figure: 'When he took over the Films Department it was being run on very amateurish lines because we were lacking in expert and technical advice.' Gower described him as 'invaluable' and 'one of the reasons why we, as a party, are so far ahead of the other parties in the development of film propaganda which is likely to become increasingly important as time goes on'.[33] Newsreels were designed to be made and distributed as quickly as possible and seen by as many people as possible, and were popular in the industrial areas of Scotland, Lancashire, the north of England, south Wales, Yorkshire and the Midlands. Cinema seats were cheap – 43 per cent cost 6d (2.5p) or less – and the most avid cinema goers were the working class, especially the young and women. Newsreel output was high: 520 were produced in 1930 alone and their content was modelled on the popular press, political speeches were allocated at most four to five minutes.[34] Given film's conservative presentation of British society it is not surprising that party strategists saw film as a means of reaching 'the unconverted working classes, a section of the populace which no traditional methods of publicity appeared effectively to reach'.[35] Clavering and Ball devoted enormous effort to promoting a positive image of the Conservatives and the National Government on film.

The party's own daylight cinema vans were first deployed in 1925. A cinema van tour in April–November 1926 lasted 31 weeks and cost £40 per week, which made it very cost effective compared to conventional propaganda techniques. In a village of 600 adults, 400 would attend with a special 4 pm showing for children facilitated by teachers allowing their charges to leave early. Little advertising was needed because the van itself proved a great crowd-puller: 'no two or three speakers in a village would ever draw the same crowds nor make the same impression as a film display and a speech'. Showings became news items in the local press, generating further publicity.[36] By 1935 the party had ten touring cinema vans (Labour had two), which 'attract large crowds of people, a high proportion of whom never attend ordinary political meetings, and if more vans were available it would be possible to reach a higher percentage of the apathetic voters, upon whose votes the result of elections so largely depends'.[37]

Clavering's links with the newsreel companies helped secure exposure for Baldwin between elections. As a result, 'No previous party leader and prime minister had been photographed, heard and "seen live" as much as he was, nor were any of his contemporaries able to present themselves so attractively.'[38] Baldwin paid close attention to technique and appearance; the transmission of his message was greatly helped again by the common ethos of the newsreels and the party which, in turn, corresponded with Baldwin's style and political objectives.[39] Newsreels compared Britain's stability with civil strife abroad, an image reinforced by Baldwin's speeches extolling England and the common-sense virtues of its people.[40]

The Conservatives lost the 1929 election despite running a sophisticated and innovative campaign and the National Government's victories in 1931 and 1935 were of such a magnitude that Baldwin's media appearances could have only marginal effect. This, however, is not the point. Faced by a new and complex electorate the party took an old message and recast it using the new technologies of mass communication. This deeply impressed contemporaries and has been identified as an important factor in the Conservative dominance of inter-war politics.

MARKETING THE *INDUSTRIAL CHARTER*

In the aftermath of defeat, the Conservative Party concluded it needed a statement of aims to distance itself from the image that had cost it the 1945 general election.[41] The *Industrial Charter* is portrayed as one of the pivotal statements of post-war Conservatism, unequivocal proof that the Conservative Party of the 1920s and 1930s – the party of mass unemployment – had changed irrevocably.[42] On the day after the *Charter*'s publication the Advisory Committee on Policy and Political Education (ACPPE) noted that it had attracted considerable media attention. Sales had been good and it attracted criticism from both Beaverbrook's *Daily Express* and Labour's *Daily Herald*, which suggested it was on the right lines.[43] However, despite the importance invested in the *Charter* it had remarkably little impact.

The pioneering opinion research organisation Mass-Observation (MO) was commissioned to 'discover the effect on the general population' of the *Industrial Charter*. The survey used a qualitative research methodology and an early version of 'focus groups', but MO warned: 'the basic difficulty in a survey of this kind is to discover a reasonable degree of interest in any group of the population. A very large number of people know little about party politics and care little.'[44] MO found almost universal ignorance of Conservative policy; those who did express a view did so in general principles (for example, the Conservative Party opposed nationalisation). These general perceptions supported a party image that MO argued was fairly accurate and distinguished the Conservatives from Labour, but MO concluded the *Charter* did not have any serious impact because the idea of a Conservative industrial policy was incomprehensible to public opinion.[45]

Mass-Observation found 20 per cent of those questioned claimed to have heard of the *Charter*, whereas 30 per cent had heard of *Keep Left*, the manifesto of a dissident Labour group; men were three times more likely than women to have heard of the *Charter*. Recognition was exaggerated because a smaller number actually recognised the pamphlet when they saw it and only 25 per cent of those who said they had heard of it could give any detail on its content. When MO repeated this survey a few weeks later, 90 per cent stated they had never seen it before. Of those who had seen it only 5 per cent claimed to have read it (the shortened version); 4 per cent claimed to have heard of the *Charter* 'but there are thus still four people out of every five to whom the *Industrial Charter* means nothing at all'.[46] Knowledge, if this can be so described, was derived from three sources: the press, radio and other people; place of work (apart from bookstalls) was the most likely place for an individual to have seen the *Charter*. MO compared its impact with two other pamphlets and found a common pattern of political apathy and ignorance.[47]

Respondents were asked to guess who had produced the pamphlet (the Conservative identification was blacked out): 75 per cent refused; a majority of Conservatives believed it was a government publication; a majority of Labour supporters thought it was a Conservative Party pamphlet. Some respondents were asked to read the 'Workers' Charter' (part of the *Industrial Charter*) and were then asked who they thought had written it: 25 per cent (50 per cent of women) refused but of those who did there was a general conviction of a left-wing origin, equally Labour or communist. Labour, Conservative and non-voters thought it communist-inspired and the largest group of middle-class voters, who were most likely to have read it and guess correctly its origins, interpreted the *Charter* as communist. MO concluded: 'there is little evidence of an increased political consciousness' even after reading the *Charter*.[48]

Labour voters were more favourably disposed to the *Charter* and 'four times as many Labour voters approved of it as Conservative voters'.[49] Of those who read it, the general response was approval countered by a conviction that it was impracticable and would never be implemented, an attitude common in all classes.[50] The most popular theme was equality of opportunity but, because the pamphlet was not clearly attributed to any political party and because no party would oppose equality of opportunity, this approval was party neutral.[51] Ironically, the proposal to provide everyone with a contract of employment (regarded by the *Charter's* authors as a significant and popular reform) was disliked widely, but was misinterpreted as making it easier to dismiss employees. Of the tiny minority who had read it, 75 per cent claimed to understand it: 'It does not of course follow that because people say they understand a pamphlet they in fact do [but] it seems clear that the [*Charter*] raised no major difficulty of understanding' when it was read. The problem was persuading people to read it.[52]

In early January 1948 Derek Heathcoat-Amory (one of the *Charter*'s authors) concluded it 'has been accepted by a satisfactorily large proportion of the party. It has been well received by the press … It has helped to confirm and consolidate a shift in the party's centre of gravity in the right direction.' However, he conceded, 'It has not "got over" to any great extent to the working man [sic] or made much impression on him. The cheap edition was, I should say, unsuccessful. Michael Fraser, deputy director of the Conservative Research Department (CRD), agreed it had failed to penetrate the mass consciousness because of a lack of Conservative credibility.[53] Fraser felt that the report made 'the reader despair of democracy' and he wondered (jokingly) if MO was a subversive organisation out to undermine democracy. Fraser believed MO's methods and its use of the popular version made the results unreliable as a guide to opinion and strategy. The poor results achieved with the version designed for the mass market suggest even worse results would have been produced by using the full version. Fraser noted that apathy, ignorance and cynicism were not new and their effects were often exaggerated because voters 'have up to date usually succeeded in combining a remarkable lack of political knowledge with a surprisingly sound instinct on really major issues'.[54]

Fraser agreed mass ignorance was remarkable given the *Charter*'s coverage, but the secret of effective propaganda was repetition and the initial launch had not been followed up. Confusion over authorship was understandable because MO had disguised the *Charter*'s origin; given that it was designed to demonstrate that the Conservative Party had radically changed, MO was indeed confirming a change of image. Fraser concluded: 'Although at first sight its results are frightening the final impression left by this report is fairly encouraging.'[55] R. A. Butler regretted the failure to capitalise on the *Charter*; he subsequently noted 'the growing opposition to documents on the *Charter* lines and the general concern about the necessity for producing material as a basis for an election programme'.[56] A major justification for the *Charter* was that it would give Conservatives a weapon to fight Labour, but by the end of 1947 'the Conservative Party was again on the defensive throughout the country'.[57] When constituencies sought advice about using the *Charter*, the director of Information Services replied:

It will not be possible in the present circumstances to answer your queries in a way that would commit the party to action along the lines of a specific programme. Until we are in power, we cannot make any definite pledges about how soon we can implement the policy recommendation of the *Industrial Charter*; so much depends upon the type of mess with which we are confronted.[58]

Poor follow-up of the launch was a factor but more important was the *Charter*'s complexity which left mass opinion unmoved: 'it is difficult not to come to the conclusion that to most people, Conservatives included, a Conservative Industrial Policy *is not yet in any way a living idea*'.[59] More seriously, the *Charter* could not impact on public opinion because it conflicted with the mass perception of the Conservatives, so the extent of coverage was irrelevant. The authors of the popular version recognised this: 'I have tried to avoid the old clichés and slogans … and have aimed at the language of the cinema … The difficulty is that it is literally impossible to be both brief and intelligible to Demos.'[60] Ironically, the *Charter*'s left image could actually harm the Conservatives who already had a clear image: 'There seems very little doubt in most people's minds that the Conservatives stand for free enterprise, against government control and nationalisation.'[61] This image, not the *Charter*'s, was taken up by Conservative propagandists.

The *Charter* was 'big-bang' propaganda. A major document launched in a blaze of publicity, so obviously challenging 'traditional' Conservatism would, it was hoped, shatter the party's current image and implant a new image in the electorate's mind. Unfortunately, its central message was not picked up by the electorate. The *Charter* was intended as an instrument of mass persuasion, but party strategists were unclear about their audience. Was it opinion formers who would then project the image of a remade Conservatism? Or party activists who needed a morale boost and something to fight Labour? Was it the electorate? Was it all three? Before the war, party propagandists had 'definitely decided against using the ordinary political leaflet' but to target specific groups.[62] The *Charter* was complex and not targeted; it lacked a simple, easily assimilated message; it was a lesson in how not to communicate with the electorate.

OPINION RESEARCH

In 1937 the British Institute of Public Opinion (BIPO) began operating. However, opinion research was ignored by the Conservative Party until its interest was stimulated by the 1945 defeat.[63]

Conservative interest increased further when discontent with the Labour government failed to translate into Conservative support and the 1950 and 1951 general elections increased Conservative puzzlement. Macmillan noted voters 'grouse and tell the Gallup Poll man that they will never vote socialist again – but when the election comes, they vote the party ticket'.[64]

In 1948 CCO approached the Colman, Prentis and Varley (CPV) advertising agency for advice on a poster campaign and CPV's research department suggested market research assess the posters' effects. Mark Abrams, a founding father of British polling, claims the party 'was interested only at a dilettante level, and remained uninterested, until 1951'.[65] In fact, CCO created the Public Opinion Research Department (PORD) in 1947 under Brigadier Dudley Clarke. Despite merging with the publicity department in 1952, PORD made several important contributions to party strategy. PORD, for example, focused attention on the floating voter. The narrow gap between Labour and Conservative meant that the ex-Labour and floating voter held the key to victory.[66] These had decided the 1948 US presidential election and 'If we are to avoid that happening here, most of our methods of approach to the elec-torate will surely have to be shaped from now onwards to fit the particular condition of this all-important group.' Polls were the only way of penetrating 'this all-important group' and formulating an appeal.[67] During the election Churchill expressed concern about his electoral attractiveness and the negative image of the Conservatives as the party of the rich and of mass unemployment. Others were more optimistic: 'If, before the next election, none of these fears [unemployment, welfare cuts etc.] have proved reason-able, we may be able to force the Opposition to fight on socialism. Then we can win.'[68] The structure of opinion as revealed in polls and election results explored both and the results helped pull the party to the centre-ground after 1951.

The claim that the Conservative Party was not seriously inter-ested in polling between 1951 and 1955 is incorrect, but polling seemed unable to grasp the complexity of post-war electoral politics.[69] Gallup's finding that 'there seems to have been little long-term trend' towards the Conservatives among voters was of great concern.[70] The CRD ascribed the 1955 Conservative victory to Labour abstentions produced by prosperity, its left–right divisions, and lack of an inspirational appeal rather than a positive endorse-ment of Conservatism. Most importantly, polls did identify a critical change in the party's image: 'Successful post-war Conservative administrations, plus the growing distance of time, rendered the pre-war myths about the Conservatives' irrelevant to the mass of voters.[71]

Oliver Poole, the party chairman, was instrumental in promoting the party's use of opinion research. His 'greatest achievement' was to focus on 'younger voters between twenty-five and forty, many of them manual workers earning between £15 and £25 a week'. When asked to define their status:

> a good number would describe themselves as middle class. Married, with not more than two children, buying their own house ... with a TV set in the living-room and a washing-machine in the modern kitchen, to such people the appeal of a party proclaiming itself to be a working-class party and calling all the time for working-class solidarity was not strong.[72]

Poole's conviction was confirmed by his observation of these voters shopping in Watford on Saturday mornings. In the spring of 1957 he commissioned CPV to begin preparatory work on the next general election campaign and *'on their own initiative and without any noticeable encouragement from their client'* CPV surveyed the campaign's effect.[73] Poole used National Opinion Polls Ltd (NOP) owned by the *Daily Mail* but Gallup remained the main source of poll data. Nevertheless, Abrams argues 'in the early part of the 1957 to 1959 period, Conservative headquarters' attitude towards polling was distant and uninterested' and he dates the party's shift in attitude with the publication of *Marginal Seat* in 1958. R. A. Butler's preface (Butler was CRD chairman) acknowledged the importance of behavioural research to Conservative political strategy and that this flowed from the Rochdale (12 February 1958) and Torrington (27 March 1958) by-elections. In Rochdale there were a large number of Conservative defections to the Liberals, which helped Labour win; in Torrington the Conservative candidate was defeated by a Liberal. From this point Conservative 'interest in public opinion became almost continuous'.[74]

In the aftermath of Rochdale, NOP was asked to identify precisely which Conservative voters had defected to the Liberals, and why they had done so.[75] The survey was important not because it uncovered new factors at work in the electorate but because it attached values to the factors which had undermined Conservative support. Of particular importance was its confirmation of a substantial loss of support among the lower middle/skilled working class, who provided 45 per cent of Conservative defectors. The main reason for defection was not the attractiveness of Liberal policies (cited by only 8 per cent of defectors) but general dissatisfaction with government (36 per cent) and the Conservative candidate (24 per cent).[76] Rochdale, it was feared, heralded a shift in established patterns of electoral behaviour because 'From 1951 to mid-1957 it was possible to say whatever might happen in safe seats, by-elections in marginal seats would be fairly close to the Gallup Poll prediction. This no longer holds.'[77] Close attention was to be paid to the vagaries of public opinion: 'The day when policy could, however, be framed with complete disregard for public opinion are long past and we [the Conservative Party] have to take account of a correct measure of public opinion rather than a biased one. Moreover, though policy should perhaps disregard opinion propaganda cannot.'[78]

By the later 1950s the Conservatives had considerable experience with opinion research and, outside Conservative ranks, there was a belief that their electoral success was not unconnected to opinion research.[79] The Conservative Party had, however, made no assessment of the utility of polling or what contribution, if any, it had made to strategy. Polls were influencing important decisions so the party had to be assured of their reliability.[80] The CRD therefore established the Psephology Group in March 1960. Before meeting representatives of polling organisations, James Douglas prepared a briefing paper to guide the group's work. Douglas argued BIPO/Gallup were the most accurate and most experienced, but since 1945 elections had been decided by relatively small shifts of opinion.[81] The group's second meeting discussed the political significance of the errors made by polls in the various elections, so it began its enquiry by expressing scepticism about the utility of polling.

This scepticism underpinned the Psephology Group's meeting with NOP. NOP expected a sampling error of ±2 per cent but the error would be correspondingly greater for sub-groups. Eliminating sampling error required very large and complex samples, which were costly and time consuming; to be of use poll data had to be gathered and used quickly and cost was a factor even for the Conservative Party. A ±0.5 per cent sampling error required a sample of 10,000 compared to the usual sample of 1,500–2,000. Large and complex samples were unnecessary because random samples were subjected to reliability tests and NOP doubted the value of panel surveys designed to explore deeply held values but recognised their attraction to a party.[82] The group was particularly interested in Gallup's evidence because of its experience and overestimation of Conservative support in 1950, 1951 and 1955, and an underestimate in 1959. These variations were blamed on Gallup's sample, which contained too many old people (more inclined to vote Conservative), on middle-class female pollsters' reluctance to interview working-class men (Labour's strongest supporters) and on a failure to appreciate the importance of differential turnout between Labour and Conservative supporters which benefited the Conservatives.[83]

David Butler, the Nuffield College psephologist, advised that on questions of gathering data pollsters were undoubtedly expert, but on interpreting the data and making political judgements 'there was no reason to believe that pollsters were any more reliable than academics, political journalists or the staffs of political parties'. The refining of methodology, sample changes, improved questionnaire design, limited comparison between surveys but trends over time were more valuable than 'snapshot' individual polls. Butler argued polls could not be used as forecasts or as a substitute for political judgement, but could provide useful information on, for example, which social groups voted for which party and which issues concerned the electorate. Polls had an important but limited contribution to make to the formulation of a party's electoral strategy.[84]

The group acknowledged that five general elections was too small a sample on which to come to any definitive conclusion about accuracy.[85] 'To be able to estimate the proportion of the population that will vote for a party to within 2 per cent seems very good', argued the report, but 'In relation to the sort of swings of public opinion that have determined the fate of governments at recent elections it is less impressive.'[86] Between elections respondents answered in the knowledge that no election was being held, which led to marked fluctuations in opinion; support was affected by the general election campaign which tended to polarise opinion. The report concluded: 'Polls provide a valuable but rough guide to election results.'[87] These weaknesses did not reduce the polls' value because of 'the trends they appear to show and of the extent to which these trends are confirmed by other reliable polls'.[88] NOP's entry into general election polling in 1959 was significant because if 'a movement in public opinion is picked up by several polls at the same time or appears in several consecutive polls of the same organisation then one can have considerably greater confidence in the findings even if they are based on quite small percentage changes that would be within the allowable margin of error on a single poll'.[89]

It was already known that non-voters were not distributed equally throughout the electorate or in proportion to party strength. In 1959 non-voters were twice as likely to be Labour as

Conservative so Labour abstainers were an important segment of the electorate which 'if ever it was to be activated [would] sweep us far into opposition. They thus represent a danger, but they also represent an opportunity. People do not normally change over immediately from being socialist to being Conservative. They first get disgruntled with the Labour Party and not bother to vote or vote Liberal, and then only gradually change later their political allegiance. The non-voting socialist is thus a potential recruit for the Conservative Party.'[90] Despite their importance, the Conservatives had inadequate information on them so it was difficult to formulate an effective response. Polling could elicit this information.

Polling could also illuminate the impact of the campaign. In the 1950, 1955 and 1959 campaigns Conservative support rallied: 'It would seem that during the early stages of [the] election campaign, the electorate is conscious of its grumbles against the government, but when, finally, it is forced to make up its mind, it cannot quite bring itself to the decision of changing the government.'[91] Campaigns could influence behaviour but more important was a party's image of competence which influenced both the decision to vote and for which party to vote. Two-thirds of voters supported the same party all their lives so the behaviour of non-voters was all-important: 'Elections are won by people who bother to turn out to vote.'[92]

Weakening class identification, the changing blue/white collar occupational balance, the growth of 'middle class' consumption patterns and home ownership were weakening Labour partisanship. Between 1951 and 1959 the Conservative Party had made gains in the 21–30 age group because 'when people acquire the responsibilities of marriage and starting a family they are most likely to turn to the Conservative Party and the values for which it stands'.[93] They were drawn to the Conservatives for *instrumental*, not ideological, reasons, because 'They think the Conservative Party is more likely to be effective in working for world peace and making the country prosperous. They see the Labour Party as predominantly standing for the working class and out to help the underdog ... they see the Conservative Party as the more competent.' This group identified themselves as middle-class and were optimistic about their future, however, 'this age group even more than its elders wants to see more money spent on hospitals, houses, roads and ... schools ... They are prepared to see higher taxation to pay for these things ... This is perhaps another indication that what attracts them to the Conservative Party is the "competence" image rather than the traditional policy distinctions.'[94] Underlying this was growing affluence. Crude embourgeoisement theories – 'when a working man [sic] has a television set, a refrigerator or a car he is more likely to vote Conservative'[95] – were rejected but affluence had eroded the class basis of politics. A solid residuum of class loyalty remained, suggesting a much more complex electorate than that indicated by embourgeoisement. The conclusion drawn was: 'We must keep bright our "image" – competence, opportunity, home ownership, etc.'[96]

Deferential working-class Conservative voters would decline in favour of instrumental voters. Though less securely tied to Labour, their background and attitudes inclined them to Labour so, although many currently voted Conservative, they could drift away. The party was winning over about one-third of the working-class electorate and 'The Conservatives cannot rule unless they succeed in obtaining considerable support within this group.'[97] The working class voted Conservative because it regarded Conservative governments as competent economic managers. Society was changing and becoming wealthier and the Conservatives had benefited, but no causal link between social change and electoral behaviour was identified and Britain was a long way from being a middle-class society.[98] Acquiring consumer goods did not directly affect voting, the exception being home ownership. Of working-class adults who did not vote Labour, one-third were owners or were in the process of buying their house and, the report concluded, 'It would seem that so far as a property-owning democracy is concerned "l'appetit vient en mangeant" [The appetite increases through eating].'[99]

The Psephology Group believed turnout was not 'solely or even perhaps predominantly determined by organisation [but] by the pulling power of the policies advocated both positively by giving one's supporters something to vote for and negatively by frightening voters on the other side'.[100] Opinion research indicated the most damaging losses came not from 'core' voters but from 'movements in the centre of the political spectrum [which] prove decisive'. In Rochdale 'it was the loss of the lower middle-class and upper-working-class votes … that proved decisive' and it was their retention in 1959 which gave the Conservatives their third consecutive victory. The report continued: 'A movement in the centre of this sort essentially affects people who are not very active politically and is characterised by a general disgruntlement with politics as a whole.'[101] The implications for strategy were clear: 'The critical class lies, so to speak, at the juncture of the lower middle class and working class.' Though difficult to isolate, winning this group's support was the key to electoral victory.[102]

Events proved the Psephology Group's scepticism of the consequences of social change to be well founded as well as exposing the limits of opinion research. 'What has happened since 1960 is that the two vulnerable groups, the young and the "new middle class", have been estranged.' Many working-class Labour voters had been won in the 1950s 'because for them Conservative freedom really seemed to work' and because Labour was perceived as a divided party. Discontent among the affluent working class after 1961 accounted for 70–80 per cent of defections in Conservative by-election defeats.[103] Working-class instrumental voters 'are not the sort of people for whom socialism is a bogey. For most of them a Labour government would be a perfectly normal choice approved by most of their fellows. In voting Conservative in 1955 and 1959 they were probably conscious of being rather daring, emancipated and smart. They no longer think it smart.' Many were now accustomed to prosperity under a Conservative government so 'their political movements have been influenced by nothing much more deep-seated than a change of mood, fashion tinged with self-interest and a fairly shrewd, though superficial assessment of their rulers'.[104]

Polling evidence showed that 'what has been achieved still seems good but it is no longer seen as in danger and it is no longer sufficient'. What the Conservatives had done was discounted; 'Above all, the present [government's] image of ineffectualness and indecisiveness needs to be attacked.'[105] The review admitted that despite opinion research the Conservative Party still did not fully understand these changes or how to create commitment among these voters. The party had won over large numbers of non-traditional voters in the 1950s but these were now drifting away from the Conservative Party and would give Harold Wilson and Labour victory in 1964 and 1966.

CONCLUSION

Baldwin grasped intuitively effective political communication: 'If a thing had got to be believed you want to repeat it so that ultimately the public, by reiteration, got hold of the idea that you were putting across.'[106] Mass electorates do not receive complex messages and frequently misinterpret what they do receive. Propaganda must have simple, generalised, easily assimilated images rather than detailed policy, but until opinion research came along parties had no means of estimating their propaganda's effectiveness other than electoral victory.

Strategists were pulled in two directions: maintaining party principles and doctrine while accommodating them to the needs of a mass audience. This required reducing the 'vertical distance' between elite and mass. Baldwin bridged this gap; the *Charter* did not; opinion research offered a means of 'collapsing the cultural distance' between elites and the mass.[107] This confirms Converse's conclusion that masses were capable of first-level knowledge (linking two factors without displaying any real understanding, for example 'Labour favours nationalisation'), but not second-level knowledge (complex causal chains, for example 'a Conservative industrial policy') which require 'an act of creative synthesis characteristic of only a minuscule proportion of any population'.[108] Compared to the inter-war period, electoral politics after the Second World War were complex and difficult to fathom, especially when social change accelerated with affluence. In this unstable environment polling offered a 'scientific' method of understanding the electorate and providing a means whereby the party's appeal could be honed and targeted.

Butler's comment in *Marginal Seat* that its conclusions about electoral apathy would come as no surprise to anyone engaged in politics; and his advice concerning the indispensability of political nous and judgement was sometimes overshadowed by exciting new techniques. Political communication remained an inexact science. Despite new techniques the electorate repeatedly confounded politicians and their strategists. Baldwin's loss of the 1929 election, the electorate's refusal to be wooed by the *Industrial Charter*, and electoral volatility in the late 1950s and early 1960s demonstrate there is no substitute for an image of governing competence.

NOTES

1.   Peter Lilley, speech at 'Listening to Britain' launch, 14 July 1998.
2.   R. Cockett, 'The Party, Publicity, and the Media', in A. Seldon and S. Ball (eds), *Conservative Century: The Conservative Party since 1900* (Oxford, 1994), 547–77.
3.   Conservative and Unionist Party, *The Industrial Charter* (London, May 1947).
4.   K. Middlemas and J. Barnes, *Baldwin* (London, 1969), 502–3.
5.   Davidson to Hoare, 28 December 1923, House of Lords Record Office (HLRO), Davidson MSS; see also S. Nicholas, 'The Construction of a National Identity: Stanley Baldwin, Englishness and the Mass Media in Inter-war Britain', in M. Francis and I. Zweiniger-Bargielowska (eds), *The Conservatives and British Society 1880–1990* (Cardiff, 1996), 128. Davidson saw 'political warfare' as his main task: R. Rhodes James

(ed.), *Memoirs of a Conservative: J. C. C. Davidson's Memoirs and Papers 1910–1937* (London, 1969), 177.

6. Davidson to Baldwin, 14 January 1928, Davidson MSS; see also D. Jarvis, 'British Conservatism and Class Politics in the 1920s', *English Historical Review*, 111 (1996), 59–84.

7. Londonderry to Bonar Law, 1 December 1921, HLRO, Bonar Law MSS, 107/1/82.

8. 'Democracy and Its Task' (4 March 1927), in S. Baldwin, *Our Inheritance. Speeches and Addresses by the Rt Hon. Stanley Baldwin MP* (London, 1928), 29.

9. Baldwin to Davidson, 30 July 1924, in James (ed.), *Memoirs of a Conservative*, 196.

10. Robertson Scott memorandum, 28 January 1938, Cambridge University Library (CUL), Add. 8770.

11. P. Williamson, *Stanley Baldwin: Conservative Leadership and National Values* (Cambridge, 1999), 78–83.

12. Ball to Baldwin, 6 December 1935, CUL, Baldwin MSS, 48/258. Sir Joseph Ball, an ex-MI5 officer, was appointed director of publicity in 1927 and head of the Research Department in 1929; he was in charge of the party's propaganda and intelligence effort: Cockett, 'The Party, Publicity and the Media', 549ff.

13. Robertson Scott memorandum, 28 January 1938.

14. T. Stannage, *Baldwin Thwarts the Opposition: The British General Election of 1935* (Beckenham, 1980), 177.

15. D. Cannadine, 'Politics, Propaganda and Art: The Case of Two Worcestershire Lads', *Midland History*, 4 (1977), 98; Williamson, *Stanley Baldwin*, 87.

16. Gower to Baldwin, 2 November 1935, Baldwin MSS, 203/40. A career civil servant in the No.10 Private Office, Sir Patrick Gower served Law, Macdonald and Baldwin until Davidson persuaded him to join Central Office in 1928. He became Baldwin's media adviser and in 1929 the party's chief publicity officer.

17. Middlemas and Barnes, *Baldwin*, 479–80; Nicholas, 'The Construction of a National Identity', 141.

18. C. Stuart (ed.), *The Reith Diaries* (London, 1975), entries for 15, 16 and 17 October 1924, 90; A. Briggs, *The History of Broadcasting in the United Kingdom, Vol. 1: The Birth of Broadcasting* (Oxford, 1961), 268.

19. Robertson Scott memorandum, 28 January 1938.

20. R. McKibbin, *Classes and Cultures: England 1918–1951* (Oxford, 1998), 457; Stannage, *Baldwin Thwarts the Opposition*, 178.

21. K. Middlemas (ed.), *Thomas Jones: Whitehall Diary, Vol. 2: 1926–1930* (Oxford, 1969), entries for 18 and 22 April, 182; Baldwin to Reith, 13 April 1929, *Reith Diaries*, 102; A. Briggs, *The History of Broadcasting in the United Kingdom, Vol. 2: The Golden Age of Wireless* (Oxford, 1965), 135.

22. Reith to Baldwin, 14 April 1929. *Reith Diaries*, 102.

23. Williamson, *Baldwin*, 85; Middlemas and Barnes, *Baldwin*, 502.

24. James (ed.), *Memoirs of a Conservative*, 171.

25. Lloyd to Baldwin, 8 November 1935, Baldwin MSS, 203/58.

26. Robertson Scott memorandum, 28 January 1938. Reith described a Baldwin speech as 'an excellent twenty minutes talk, which will, I expect win the election for him': *Reith Diaries*, 16–17 October 1924, 90.

27. Briggs, *History of Broadcasting, Vol. 2*, 139, 141.

28. Stannage, *Baldwin Thwarts the Opposition*, 183.

29. Lloyd to Baldwin, 8 November 1935, Baldwin MSS, 203/57–8.

30. The BBC did not undertake audience research until 1937.

31. Ball to Baldwin, 6 December 1935, 48/231.

32. Ibid., 48/234.

33. Gower to Baldwin, 5 April 1935. Baldwin MSS, 170/84. Gower was responding to charges brought by a Colonel Lane ('an anti-Semitic lunatic') who accused Clavering *inter alia* of 'destroying the Conservative Party'. Clavering was one of the founders of the Cinematograph Renters Association and a key figure in the Cinematograph Exhibitors Association, and was made honorary organising director of CUFA in 1930: Cockett, 'The Party, Publicity and the Media', 559.

34. N. Pronay, 'British Newsreels in the 1930s: 1. Audience and Producers', *History*, 56 (1971), 411–18.

35. T. J. Hollins, 'The Conservative Party and Film Propaganda between the Wars', *English Historical Review*, 96 (1981), 363.
36. W. Courtenay, 'Report of Tour of Daylight Cinema Van, April–November 1926', 2, in Pembroke Wickes to Baldwin, 14 January 1927, Baldwin MSS, 48/75.
37. Ball to Baldwin, 6 December 1935, 48/238.
38. Williamson, *Baldwin*, 86.
39. N. Pronay, 'British Newsreels in the 1930s. 2. Their Policies and Impact', *History*, 57 (1972), 67.
40. T. Aldgate, 'The Newsreels, Public Order and the Projection of Britain', in J. Curran, A. Smith and P. Wingate (eds), *Impacts and Influences: Essays on Media Power in the Twentieth Century* (London, 1987), 150; T. Aldgate, 'Ideological Consensus in British Feature Films 1935–47', in K. R. M. Short (ed.), *Feature Films as History* (Beckenham, 1981), 100.
41. National Union (NU) Central Council minutes, 28 November 1945, and NU Executive Committee, 14 November 1946, Conservative Party Archives (CPA), Bodleian Library.
42. B. J. Evans and A. J. Taylor, *'From Salisbury to Major: Continuity and Change in Conservative Politics* (Manchester, 1996), 81–5.
43. Advisory Committee on Policy and Political Education (ACPPE), 13 May 1947, CPA.
44. 'A Report on the *Industrial Charter'*, September 1947, University of Sussex, Mass-Observation (MO) Archive, File Report 2516, 1.
45. Ibid., 11
46. Ibid., 24, emphasis added.
47. Ibid., 29.
48. Ibid., 22.
49. Ibid., 28–9.
50. Ibid., 28.
51. Ibid., 30.
52. Ibid., 30.
53. D. Heathcoat-Amory, 'The *Industrial Charter*: An Assessment', January 1948, 1; Memorandum, Michael Fraser to D. Clarke, 8 January 1948, CPA, CRD 2/7/1.
54. Michael Fraser, 'Comments on the MO Report on the *Industrial Charter'*, 12 January 1948, para 5a, CPA, CRD 2/7/1.
55. Ibid., para 11d.
56. ACCPE, 6 July, 27 October 1948, CPA, Tactical Staff Committee files, temporary classification CCO/600.
57. Tactical Staff Committee, 10 December 1947, CPA, CCO 600.
58. E. D. O'Brien to R. O. Wallington, 4 March 1948, CPA, CRD 2/7/1.
59. 'A Report on the *Industrial Charter'*, MO, File Report 2516, 23, emphasis added.
60. Stelling to Clarke (director of publicity), 11 November 1947, CPA, CRD 2/7/1. The *Daily Mirror* criticised the patronising language of the popular version.
61. 'A Report on the *Industrial Charter'*, MO, File Report 2516, 13.
62. Ball to Baldwin, 6 December 1935, 48/259.
63. R. Sibley, 'The Swing to Labour during the Second World War: When and Why?', *Labour History Review*, 55, 1 (1990), 23–4; Lord Moran, *Winston Churchill: The Struggle for Survival 1940–1965* (London, 1966), 335. BIPO was the British end of the Gallup organisation.
64. Harold Macmillan's diary, 21 October, 1951, in H. Macmillan, *Tides of Fortune 1945–1955* (London, 1966), 335.
65. M. Abrams, 'Public Opinion Polls and Political Parties', *Public Opinion Quarterly*, 27 (1963), 11.
66. Clarke to chief publicity officer, 22 November 1949, CPA, CRD 2/21/1.
67. 'The Approach to the Ex-socialist Floating Voter', 30 December 1949, CPA, CRD 2/21/1.
68. M. Gilbert, *Winston S. Churchill, Vol. 8: 'Never Despair' 1945–1965* (London, 1988), 638; Macmillan, *Tides of Fortune*, 355.
69. Abrams, 'Public Opinion Polls and Political Parties', 11.
70. Gallup Polls, 14 June 1954, 2 December 1955, CPA, CRD 2/21/5.
71. 'The General Election of 1955', general director's report to Eden, 22 June 1955, 1; Stebbings to Fraser, 'General Election Campaign 1955', 9 June 1955, 1, CPA, CRD 2/28/54.

72. D. Hennessy, 'The Communication of Conservative Policy 1957–59', *Political Quarterly* 32 (1961), 249.
73. Abrams, 'Public Opinion Polls and Political Parties', 11–12, emphasis added
74. A. Milne and R. MacKenzie, *Marginal Seat* (London, 1958), vii, for Butler's admission.
75. 'Abstract of National Opinion Polls Ltd Report: Rochdale By-election', 27 February 1958, CPA, CRD 2/21/5.
76. 'Draft Report on Rochdale', n.d., CPA, CRD 2/21/5.
77. 'Gallup Polls and By-elections', 31 March 1958, CPA, CRD 2/21/5.
78. 'Public Opinion', 21 February 1958, 4, CPA, CRD 2/21/5.
79. A. Crosland, *Can Labour Win?* (Fabian Society Tract, 324, May 1960), 24, n.1.
80. 'Psephology Group Chairman's Notes', 24 March 1960, Psephology Group, 60/1, minutes of 1st meeting, 28 March 1960, CPA, CRD 2/21/6. The group consulted Dr Durant (Gallup), Mr Shields (NOP), Dr M. Abrams (director of research, London Press Exchange), David Butler (Nuffield College) and a friendly political correspondent.
81. James Douglas, 'Comments on Dr M. Abrams, Why Labour Has Lost Elections', Psephology Group, 60/2, CPA, CRD 2/21/6.
82. Psephology Group, 60/3, minutes of 2nd meeting, 11 April 1960, CPA, CRD 2/21/6.
83. Psephology Group, 60/5, minutes of 3rd meeting, 25 April 1960, CPA, CRD 2/21/6.
84. Psephology Group, 60/9, minutes of 4th meeting, 9 May 1960, CPA, CRD 2/21/6.
85. 'First Report of the Psephology Group to the Chairman of the Conservative Party Organisation', 15 October 1960, paras 6–7, CPA, CRD 2/21/6.
86. Ibid., para 8.
87. Ibid., para 10.
88. Ibid., para 12.
89. Ibid., para 18.
90. Ibid., para 22.
91. Ibid., para 26.
92. Ibid., para 28.
93. Ibid., paras 47 and 51.
94. Ibid., paras 52–3.
95. Ibid., para 62.
96. Dear to Fraser, 'Psephology Report: Political Lessons which Emerge', September 1960, 1, CPA, CRD 2/21/6.
97. 'The General Election of 1959', 5, CPA, CCO 4/8/104.
98. 'First Report of the Psephology Group', paras 58–9, CPA, CRD 2/21/6.
99. Ibid., para 63.
100. Ibid., para 30.
101. Ibid., para 31.
102. Ibid., para 60.
103. Psephology Group, 63/19, 'Psephology Report Reviewed in the Light of Current (March 1963) Conditions', 10 April 1963, paras 6–9, CPA, CRD 2/21/6.
104. Ibid., paras 10–11.
105. Ibid., para 16.
106. James (ed.), *Memoirs of a Conservative*, 171.
107. D. L. Le Mahieu, *A Culture of Democracy: Mass Communication and the Cultivated Mind in Britain Between the Wars* (Oxford, 1988), 104.
108. E. Converse, 'The Nature of Belief Systems in Mass Publics', in N. R. Luttberg (ed.), *Public Opinion and Public Policy* (Homewood, IL, 1974 rev. edn), 305–8.

6

Conservative Women and Voluntary Social Service, 1938–51[1]

JAMES HINTON

Culturalist challenges to the working assumptions of the 'new social history' have been fruitful not only in reinvigorating work in political history, but also in throwing new light on the origins of social identities more generally.[2] David Cannadine's recent synthesis, *Class in Britain*, for example, works on the assumption that party politics 'are as much about the attempt to create, manage and manipulate social identities as they are the direct expression of them'.[3] In exploring Conservative electoral mobilisation, a number of writers have shown how a focus on the efforts of politicians to shape their own constituencies of support can illuminate the formation of both working-class and middle-class identities.[4] Less helpful, however, is Canadine's stress on the discourse of partisan politics as the *main* source of class identities, and his apparent dismissal of collective identities formed in more every-day experience as 'unfathomable'.[5] There is a danger that, in seeking to rehabilitate the creative agency of politics, historians find themselves marginalising other social processes. The evolution of class identities cannot be reconstructed out of the discourses of national political life alone.[6] Just as it is a mistake to write the history of political parties as though they simply reflected the needs and interests of their various constituencies of support, so it would be unhelpful to neglect the fact that each of these constituencies was engaged in an everyday politics of its own.[7] In the case of the publicly active middle-class women discussed here, this everyday politics revolved around the exercise of local social leadership through a range of associations of which the Conservative Party was not necessarily the most important. Viewing these women's partisan activities from the vantage point of their broader associational lives suggests a need for some revision of established accounts of both the evolution of Conservative politics and the middle-class identities in which those politics were embedded.

This chapter examines relationships between Conservative politics and the associational life of middle- and upper-class women in English provincial towns during the 1930s and 1940s. Particular attention is paid to the process by which the Women's Voluntary Service (WVS), set up in June 1938 to recruit women to assist local authorities with air-raid precautions and evacuation, colonised this associational world, appointing as its local organisers 'women of standing who are already acknowledged leaders of the borough'.[8] After war broke out the WVS rapidly expanded its brief, becoming a maid-of-all-work filling gaps as its branches materialised at the behest of both local authorities and Whitehall departments. By 1943 membership had risen to nearly 1 million and it remained at that level for the remainder of the war.[9] While the WVS was, from the outset, anxious to involve working-class women – and it succeeded in doing so to a degree unusual in the world of voluntary work[10] – it was nevertheless led from the top of the social hierarchy. At all levels its leading personnel were overwhelmingly drawn from the upper layers of English society, among them a large number Tory activists. When electoral activity went into suspension during the war, the WVS provided an outlet for many women previously active in Conservative politics, including the two people who were to have prime responsibility for reconstructing the party's women's organisation after the war – Marjorie Maxse and Evelyn Emmet.[11] With the return of peace, electoral politics and a Labour government in 1945, Conservative WVS members faced a dilemma over the correct balance to strike between voluntary work and partisanship; a dilemma intensified by the fact that Lady Reading, who had controlled the WVS from the outset, was not a Conservative and sought to ensure the future of her organisation by identifying its goals closely with those of the Attlee administration. The WVS, therefore, provides a valuable site for exploring the interplay between Conservative politics and non-partisan public activity in the making of mid-twentieth-century female middle-class identity.

'THE WOMEN'S SPHERE'

Until recently historians of twentieth-century urban society have been more interested in the rise of labour than in the continuities of middle-class power.[12] The dominant narrative in the existing literature revolves around the withdrawal of the bourgeoisie from civic leadership since the later nineteenth century. Not wishing to live in the muck that generated their brass, businessmen moved away to the countryside or the suburbs. The emergence of organised labour, the growth of a more self-assertive petty bourgeoisie increasingly influential in local government, the democratising effects of the modern party system and the growing importance of town hall bureaucrats – all served to force traditional civic leaders into uncomfortable negotiation with rival centres of authority in the towns, inhibiting the free exercise of their patronage and power.[13] During the inter-war years Labour gained control of nearly one-quarter of country boroughs,[14] and the separation between non-Labour local politicians, mostly drawn from the butchers and builders of the local petty bourgeoisie, and the controllers of industry continued apace as family firms were gobbled up by national combines.[15] Withdrawal from local politics did not, however, necessarily imply withdrawal from social leadership, as Clements demonstrates in his study of post-war Bristol, where an established urban upper class continued to dominate associational life long after it had abandoned local politics to Labour and the Tory shopocracy.[16] Bristol may have been exceptional in the degree to which the local economic elite retained its civic commitment: this had certainly been J. B. Priestley's impression in the mid-1930s.[17] However, more recent studies of some lesser cities, notably Norwich and Leicester, indicate the continued social leadership exercised by civic-minded businessmen well after they had ceased to be actively involved in local politics.[18]

Since the later nineteenth century women had become increasingly prominent in philanthropic activity, and it may well be that the tendency of men to withdraw from public life was compensated to some degree by the efforts of their wives, daughters and unmarried sisters: a feminisation of paternalism.[19] Reflecting on evidence of inter-war social activism by the womenfolk of the Norwich business elite, Barry Doyle has recently remarked that the 'input from the wives, daughters and sisters of the "public men" has been greatly underestimated in accounts of the functioning of urban middle-class power in the period after 1900'.[20] Participation in women-only organisations, or in distinct women's sections of mixed organisations, played a significant role in the lives of hundreds of thousands of middle-class women. This vigorous female public sphere provided women – most of them non-earning housewives, but also spinsters of independent means and career women – with opportunities to meet and socialise outside the home; to educate and amuse themselves; to undertake good works; to pursue campaigns around a wide and varied agenda of 'women's issues', and, in all this, to establish their places within the complex pecking-orders that characterised middle-class status; to assert a distinctive feminine presence in local civic life; and to exercise leadership over women less privileged than themselves. Although it has been argued that the rise of state welfare in the twentieth century tended to deprive middle-class women of the kinds of authority that they had grown used to exercising in the philanthropic world,[21] it is easy to exaggerate the degree to which public provision sidelined the voluntary sector. The inter-war years have been seen as the heyday of local social services.[22] While local elective office remained overwhelmingly masculine – in 1937 only about 5 per cent of provincial local councillors were women and over one-third of city and borough councils had no women members at all[23] – much of the welfare legislation involved local authorities in extending their partnerships with voluntary organisations; significant numbers of women were co-opted on to council committees in recognition of their prominence as voluntary social workers.[24] Regretting the fact that there were only two women councillors in Blackpool by 1939, the mayor suggested (with doubtful logic) that this must reflect a feminine disinclination for politics, since 'most of the charitable causes in this town are run by women and they raise the bulk of the money'.[25]

While such women were often Conservatives, their local prominence normally reflected activity in a range of women's organisations, most of them non-partisan. The largest women's organisation was probably the Mothers' Union, an offshoot of the Anglican church claiming half a million members in 1950.[26] Many other male organisations had thriving women's auxiliaries – the Inner Wheel for the wives of Rotary Club businessmen, and the women's sections of the British Legion, for example.[27] Auxiliary medical organisations included Nursing Associations, whose main business was raising charitable funds to pay the salary of the district nurse, St John's Ambulance and the more fashionable Red Cross. The proliferation of women's organisations after the First World War was informed by the recent struggle for the vote; a common objective was education for citizenship and the promotion of active participation in political life. The Women's Institute (WI), the most successful of these bodies, had over 330,000 members by 1940, but it only touched the fringes of the towns.[28] Its urban equivalent, the Townswomen's Guilds, had been founded in 1929. Membership of the Townswomen's Guilds in 1939 was 54,000; it held up well during the war and went on to double during the Attlee years, reaching a total of 114,000 by 1949. The Townswomen's Guilds were composed mainly of housewives; career women joined the Business and Professional Women, who claimed 14,500 members in 240 clubs by 1951. Started in 1938, these clubs were designed to cater for the same groups of women as the older Soroptimists, whose membership was restricted by adherence to the Rotarian principle of allowing only one representative of each of an elaborately drawn schedule of occupations to join any local club.[29] Other organisations providing local social, educational and campaigning platforms for educated middle-class women included the National Council of Women and the Electrical Association for Women.[30] Membership of these organisations frequently overlapped.[31] In Nottingham, for example, an active woman might find herself lunching at the Mikado Cafe several times a month under the auspices of a number of different organisations.[32] In Halifax, where the local newspaper carried reports of the activities of all the local women's organisations in weekly column entitled 'The Women's Sphere', the close association among their leading personnel is clear from their frequent attendance at each other's annual dinners.[33] The organised life of middle-class women revolved around luncheon clubs, whist drives, garden fetes, tours of local factories or coach outings to stately homes, tea-time cafe meetings with improving talks, evening meetings of branch or committee, bring-and-buy sales, flag days for the local hospital fund, the administration of charitable funds, hands-on personal service in the maternity and child welfare clinic, and the provision of leadership and moral guidance to young women in girls clubs or the girl guides.

This was an overwhelmingly middle-class world. In their anxiety to free women's organisations from the condescension of posterity some recent historians have tended to underestimate the salience of class in the female public sphere.[34] The Mothers' Union provided tea and gossip to women of all classes, but its inner life probably had more to do with reinforcing deference than dissolving class identities.[35] Similarly, the British Legion provided an arena within which ex-army wives could continue to officer the rank and file.[36] Most Townswomen were middle class, and where the membership of individual guilds was mixed the middle-class women occupied the leading positions.[37] Large numbers of working-class women, refusing to accept middle-class leadership, organised themselves separately through the Women's Co-operative Guild (87,000 members by 1939) and Labour Party women's sections (178,000 members by 1938).[38] While leaders of middle-class associational life frequently expressed eagerness to forge links with these organisations, working women regarded such overtures with suspicion or downright hostility. Generations of working-class women had been subject to often arrogant interference by female philanthropists, and the new organisations were reluctant to associate with the middle-class women whose claims to social leadership they existed to contest.[39]

The Conservative Party at local level was intimately linked with middle-class associational life, as Bates has demonstrated in his study of the West Midlands Conservative Party between the wars.[40] Conservative women's branches subsisted on a staple diet of social activities and fund-raising spiced by the occasional more-or-less political talk. Apart from the occasional ball or garden fete the majority of funds were raised by that most popular of middle-class leisure pursuits: the whist drive. The formulaic minute entered by the secretary of the Stanley ward women's branch in Blackpool for each annual general meeting from 1938 to 1940 read, with slight variations: 'A light supper and whist drive followed, and this ended a very pleasant evening.'[41] In Portsmouth the secretary of a women's branch measured the party's wartime decline by the number of tables she could expect to fill at a whist drive.[42] A 1937 headline in the *Surrey Weekly Press* succinctly described the Tory women of Guildford: 'Conservatives at Whist'.[43] The money raised on such occasions was regularly given to local charities as well as to party funds, and branches were careful to avoid encroaching on the fund-raising activities of local charities or clashes between party meetings and those of non-partisan organisations in which their members were involved.[44] The 1938/39 annual disbursement of funds by Stanley ward included the following items: Victoria Hospital (3 guineas); Social Service (2 guineas); Chief Constable Fund (1 guinea); Sick Poor (1 guinea); Blackpool Women's Unionist Association (2 guineas).[45] Whether this was the normal order of priorities in women's branches the present research does not reveal.

MOBILISING FOR WAR

Involved as they already were in local philanthropic endeavour, it was quite natural for Conservative women to take an active part in the mobilisation of the WVS.[46] Data exists on the first 500 local organisers appointed by the WVS between the summer of 1938 and March 1939.[47] About 10 per cent held office in the Conservative Party, and as many again – local councillors not identified politically – were probably also Conservatives. (By contrast only seven Labour activists were identified.) The same data reveal something of the overlap between Conservative politics and non-partisan associational life. At least one-third of the 51 local WVS leaders identified as Conservatives also held office in other organisations. Six of them ran the local Personal Service League (established in 1932 to raise funds from the upper classes to distribute clothes, boots and blankets to the unemployed),[48] and the remainder were spread evenly between the WI, Red Cross/St Johns, British Legion, Nursing Associations, Girl Guides and a variety of hospital charities. The WVS was a natural home for women like the Glamorganshire Conservative leader who, despite her political affiliation, 'works a great deal with all sections and [in 1938] undertook to help organise Cardiff Rural District [for the WVS] because she had so many links with the working women in outlying districts'.[49] Conservative women played a central role in establishing the WVS not only in Tory strongholds like Blackpool or Tunbridge Wells, but also in many more mixed localities (Southampton, Guildford, Scunthorpe) and in towns where Labour dominated the local council (Ipswich, Sheffield).[50] The WVS provided Conservative activists with a means of strengthening their claims to social leadership in an arena stretching far beyond the contours of political partisanship.

The relationship between voluntary work and political activism could, however, be an ambivalent one – the 'women's sphere' constituted, at one and the same time, the milieu in which Tory women recruited, and a rival set of interests threatening to draw activists away from party work.[51] In the autumn of 1938, for example, the WVS administrator in Lancashire blamed the post-Munich 'apathy' of her members partly on 'the vigour with which Lancastrians fight the municipal elections': political activity could sap the energies needed for voluntary work, and vice versa.[52] The wartime cessation of electoral politics eased such tensions, and engagement with war-related activities may have helped Conservative women's branches to hold themselves together for the duration. Conservatives in the south-east launched a fund for prisoners of war with the explicit object of encouraging dormant branches to revive 'by giving them some definite object for which to work'.[53] Although Conservatives took the wartime political truce seriously, the abandonment of political propaganda was not intended to lead to the dissolution of party activity altogether. With men disappearing into the forces, the survival of the party on the ground depended largely on the women, and sustaining a healthy Conservative Party machine was vital, they believed, not only for the future but also for the health of the home front in wartime.[54] For the women of Blackpool's Stanley ward, the outbreak of war 'curtailed activities for a short period ... [but] after the first big shock, we soon got down to rearranging our lives according to the changed circumstances'. The 'rearrangement' was not extensive: 'It was decided to carry on with the whist drives as usual, the proceeds to buy wool for knitting comforts, such as socks, scarves, gloves, and mittens for HM Forces.'[55] The chairman of one ward branch in Southampton urged a similar continuity, maintaining the whist drives in order 'to help members forget their troubles ... in the difficult times we were passing through'. Alongside knitting and occasional talks on home-front activities this proved sufficient to keep the branch active: political talks, however, were suspended indefinitely.[56] The same pattern of whist drives, donations to war charities and knitting for the troops is apparent wherever information on the activities of wartime women's branches survives – Redhill, West Bridgeford, Sheffield and throughout the North West Area.[57] While war work was perceived by party organisers as a means of holding the political organisation together, some local activists allowed it to supplant politics altogether. In March 1940, for example, the secretary of the Stanley ward branch closed the minute book with the following entry: 'All political work was suspended and the officials and committee decided to carry on under the name of the Ladies Benevolent Fund.' When, in October, she received a circular from the Blackpool Conservative Association urging members not to allow the wartime suspension of political propaganda to lead to the dissolution of Conservative organisation, she made no attempt to revive branch meetings. Rather, with a thrifty eye on the wartime paper shortage, she turned the glossy paper over and used the back to draft an appeal for furniture, sheets and blankets for WVS volunteers staffing her local first aid post.[58]

The enthusiasm with which Tory women threw themselves into war work was sometimes an embarrassment to the WVS. In 1938, anticipating complications with Labour, Lady Reading had tried to keep the Conservative Party at arm's length.[59] Conservatives were not always very sensitive to the need for the WVS to present a non-partisan face. In the west Midlands, at the outbreak of war, the Tory agent had tried unsuccessfully to persuade the WVS to devolve certain tasks exclusively to Conservative Party branches as a means of keeping them together and active.[60] In working-class Scunthorpe all three of the original WVS leaders were Tory activists and they resisted pressure to invite non-Tory women into the leadership on the grounds 'they had always worked together and would find an outsider difficult'. They also produced a letter from the mayor – a wealthy landed aristocrat and former Tory MP – saying that so far as he was concerned their politics were irrelevant![61] Once war broke out such claims became easier to sustain. So long as the political truce continued, it was argued, there need be no contradiction between the non-partisan stance of the WVS and the leading roles adopted by Tory women. When, in 1944, questions were raised about the position of the deputy leader in Darlington, who had doubled as agent for the local Conservative Party throughout the war, the WVS ruled that there was no incompatibility between the two roles since the agent's work was essentially non-partisan, limited to organising social events and undertaking individual case-work on behalf of the Tory MP.[62] The Sunderland organiser who ran the WVS from the local Tory party offices throughout the war, successfully resisting all attempts to move her to less obviously partisan premises, was only taking the same doctrine to its logical conclusion.[63] It was difficult for some Conservatives to perceive any distinction between partisanship and patriotism.

NATION BEFORE POLITICS?

The post-war return of party politics was problematic for Conservative members of the WVS. Leading Conservatives who had put partisan activity to one side during the war, now wished to return to the political fray. Marjorie Maxse departed at the end of 1944 to take responsibility for rebuilding the Conservative women's associations, and other leading Tories found it increasingly difficult to juggle WVS responsibilities with the reviving demands of political commitment.[64] Many of the activists withdrew when electoral politics returned. Some of them argued that the WVS, with its novel mixture of voluntary service and accountability to the government of the day, could not – and indeed should not – survive the special political circumstances of the electoral truce. Evelyn Emmet, the Conservative WVS leader in east Sussex, warned of the 'dangerous implications' of maintaining such close links between voluntary work and the state once partisan politics returned.[65] Lady Davidson, a centre organiser in rural Sussex and, like Emmet, a leading Conservative, decided in June 1945 to join the other centre organisers in the district in resigning *en bloc*: 'so many of us feel that we must now be free to go forward to the many jobs waiting to be done'. The WVS, she implied, had no monopoly on patriotism and whatever activity they chose – Davidson listed citizen's advice bureaux, community centres, WI, clinics, Mothers' Union, youth work, moral welfare and housing – they would be 'the same women, imbued with the same spirit of wishing to take part in the great battle against evil, fighting for God, King and Country'.[66] Ruth Balfour, before resigning the leadership of the WVS in Scotland, had pressed for the organisation to be wound up on the grounds that peacetime welfare work would be better undertaken through established voluntary organisations: 'The aim should be for diversity not uniformity and for freedom of voluntary societies from government control.'[67] In east Sussex the regional administrator, worn out by 'the great strain of swimming against the tide', reported in June 1945 that, in the absence of any demand for WVS services from the local authorities in the region, it 'would be extremely difficult if not impossible to try and harness goodwill which will have gone back to the Guides, WI, British Legion, and other organisations from whom we took many of our best members in the early years of the war'.[68] A few Tory women went further, reacting to the 1945 election by withdrawing from *any* voluntary work, on the improbable theory that the resulting social misery would bring the government to its knees.[69] But most WVS members either retired into inactivity, or chose to transfer their efforts to the established organisations. Some of the rapid post-war growth of the WI and the Townswomen's Guilds can probably be explained by re-engagement of members who had spent the war years in the WVS. In many areas, by 1947, the WVS had virtually ceased to exist and, as late as February 1951 after several years of strenuous rebuilding, the membership claimed was no more than 200,000, one-fifth of wartime levels.[70]

Lady Reading, the autocratic leader of the WVS since its foundation, had no time for partisan politics, and her conduct of the organisation during the Attlee years did nothing to make life easier for its Conservative members. During the war she had developed a clear idea of how voluntary social service needed to be modernised. Contemptuous of the local autonomy and internal democratic procedures prized by most of the established women's organisations, Reading saw the WVS as pioneering a new kind of relationship between the state and voluntary work, one in which traditions of middle-class philanthropy could be brought into line with the more egalitarian and, above all, the more planned society that appeared to be emerging.[71] Delivering patriotic co-operation with Labour's austerity programme was central to her strategy for establishing the long-term future of the WVS as a recognised arm of the national and local state. In sharp contrast to the anti-austerity rhetoric mobilised in Conservative Party propaganda directed at women, Reading repeatedly linked the capacity of her members to bear the frustrations of the post-war world with forti-tude and good humour with their role in preserving, not only their individual 'characters', but the 'national character' itself.[72] Accepting responsibility for austerity in their own lives was both a patriotic duty and a necessary condition of sustaining their claim to leadership in the community at large.

As austerity tightened in 1946 Lady Reading urged members to 'look at the situation in an unbiased and humanitarian way, we must be clearing our minds of the difference between party politics and national dilemmas which are the natural aftermath of war'.[73] When, in the summer of 1946, the WVS instructed members to explain details of the bread-rationing scheme, signifi-cant numbers refused to take part, and an irate Conservative Central Office subsequently extracted guarantees that more care would be taken in future to prevent 'party political propaganda' from creeping into literature distributed by the WVS.[74] At the height of the 1947 fuel crisis Reading rallied her regional adminis-trators to combat 'the apathy and disintegration which was every-where apparent', stressing that 'the next few months were going to be very difficult and the influence of people thinking on broad lines would be needed'.[75] In May 1948 she praised centre organis-ers for the way they 'had subjugated political feelings and had understood the necessity of looking at broad issues and avoiding political bias'.[76] Sixteen months later, with the devaluation of the pound triggering a rising volume of criticism of the Labour government, she again appealed to her members to resist the temptation to make political capital out of the crisis, urging them to preach the national necessity of austerity and to practise it in their own domestic lives.[77]

Lady Reading's enthusiasm for austerity certainly alienated many Conservative women. Following the 1946 row over bread rationing local organisers in rural Nottinghamshire demanded the formal closure of the WVS, citing – alongside a desire to spend more time looking after their families and to give any time they could spare to established organisations – 'a strong feeling against working for the present government'.[78] A year later, the organiser of the by then inactive Blackpool WVS offered her resignation on the grounds that being 'actively interested in politics as a Conservative, and as the WVS works directly with a socialist government' she was not the person to get things moving again.[79] By 1949 members of the South East Area Conservative Women's Advisory Committee were condemning the WVS as 'government stooges' being used 'to cover up the deficiencies of the socialist administration'.[80] But not all Conservatives felt like this. Lady Hillingdon, who had represented the party on the WVS Advisory Committee from the outset and had replaced Maxse as WVS vice-president in 1944, was at one with Lady Reading in 1949 in urging members to 'put the nation before politics … our effort is for the nation and our national conscience must come in front of our political conscience'.[81] Such appeals testify to the fact that most local WVS leaders were political opponents of the Labour government. Those Conservative women who worked to revive the WVS in the later 1940s did so presumably in the belief that maintaining the commitment of people like themselves to the everyday exercise of social leadership was at least as important to the defence of the existing social order as indulging in the strident rhetoric of anti-socialist resistance. And such attitudes were not confined to the Conservative women who remained with the WVS. Others continued to combine political activism with work in established voluntary organisations whose independence from state control made them less likely than the WVS to appear as handmaidens of socialism. To the extent that Tory activists constructed their sense of pubic duty around these broader considerations, then they had a chance of remaining 'natural' rulers rather than mere political opponents of the Labour government. These ongoing tensions between political activism and voluntary social work mean that it is impossible to grasp the mentalities of party activists by studying their political activism in isolation from the larger textures of their public lives.

Existing accounts of post-war Conservatism largely ignore the wider context of the female associational world. They focus instead on a figure made famous by the sophisticated propaganda of

Conservative Central Office in the late 1940s: the frustrated housewife–consumer, and, in particular, the middle-class housewife who
felt herself the victim of socialist incompetence and class envy.
When the left-wing Labour champions of the coalminers –
Shinwell and Bevan – appeared to say, between them, that they
'didn't care a tinker's cuss' for the comfort of the middle classes
whom they regarded as 'lower than vermin', Tory propagandists
had little difficulty fashioning a narrative of middle-class victim-
hood at the hands of the socialist state.[82] As deepening austerity
gave momentum to the anti-socialist cause, some Tory leaders
urged activists:

> to resume full political activities even at the cost of giving up
> … other work which they had taken up while political activi-
> ties lapsed [during the war]. Our thoughts must turn to the
> bitter fight in which we are now engaged, and in which we
> must continue until the shackles of socialism are broken and
> our liberties restored. It is our task to weld the political influ-
> ence of women into a formidable weapon in the ordnance of
> the right.[83]

Such anti-socialist partisanship, however, never blinded Tory
women to what Maxse described as 'the value of contacts with
outside organisations and their work'.[84] In October 1946, for
example, a speaker from Central Office urged members of the
South East Women's Advisory Committee to expand their activity
in Women's Institutes, Townswomen's Guilds, the National
Council of Women and other educational and charitable bodies in
order to improve their contact with people with a non-partisan
interest in public affairs.[85] Participation in voluntary social work,
another speaker told the Eastern Women's Advisory Committee in
1950, was crucial to establishing the credentials necessary to stand
successfully for local government office.[86] Reacting against a 1948
Labour Party initiative to encourage its own female members to
challenge the traditional Tory monopoly on voluntary work, the
Central Women's Advisory Committee asked regional groups to
'find out what community work is being done by Conservative
women'.[87] These women knew in their bones that sustaining the
right to rule had more to do with taking responsibility and delivering public service than it did with the quintessentially subaltern
characteristics projected by the merely anti-socialist British
Housewives League: grumbling and moaning.[88]

Attention to the attitudes and activity of middle-class women,
active as social leaders in the public sphere, suggests a need to

revise a currently established view of middle-class identity in late 1940s Britain which puts the emphasis on anti-socialism and the revolt against austerity. The study of election propaganda can reveal much about partisan electoral strategies, but we should beware of reading from it the psychology or social identity of any real people, and particularly not of the activists who deployed such propaganda.[89] The WVS material suggests the continuing importance of non-partisan social leadership to the identity of the kind of women who supplied the Tory party with many of its activists. Faced with the apparent logic of emergent socialism some upper-class women, like Lady Reading herself, came to believe that the best way to defend their leadership was to put partisan politics to one side and to concentrate on implanting themselves firmly in the apparatus of controls and the welfare state. Others saw outright partisan opposition to socialism and all its works as their only resort. Between these two responses, however, lay a broad group of Conservative women for whom it was important to find some way of balancing the exercise of everyday social leadership with the need for partisan opposition to the Labour government. A speaker at a meeting of Tory women activists in June 1949 addressed this dilemma clearly:

> Twenty years back when they were busy holding garden fetes, socialists and communists were on the soap-boxes with lies and half-truths. The material, the British people, is still all right, but the stitches put in it by repetition must be unpicked. She urged the meeting not to be put off by the number of other organisations in which they had to take an interest. Worthy as some of these may be, it must be a case of 'as well as' and not 'instead of' politics.[90]

The complete Tory woman juggled social leadership with anti-socialist propaganda – or, as Marjorie Maxse preferred to call it, with the advocacy of 'Conservative truth'.[91]

CLASS AND PARTY

Lewis and Maude, writing in the late 1940s, noted the paradox that, while middle-class people were for ever bemoaning their powerlessness, they could not bring themselves to believe that they were not in fact indispensable to national survival: an attitude they describe as 'an amalgam of dread and confidence'.[92] What is striking about the public women whose activities have been examined here is not the dread but the confidence: their capacity for constructive engagement with the social upheavals of the era. While Tory electioneering rhetoric might characterise the decade as one of middle-class decline, women active in the public sphere (including large numbers of Conservative women) had in fact been busily asserting their indispensability in many areas of social life – civil defence and evacuation, the patriotic management of austerity both during and after the war, the multiple strands of 1940s welfare reform. For partisan reasons many of these women in the later 1940s were prepared to deploy the rhetoric of anti-socialism, but it is doubtful how far they embraced the identity offered by that rhetoric. A Tory woman who at election time saw herself as fighting to free the middle classes from socialist tyranny might at other times see herself, not as a victim, but as a respons-ible social leader whose indispensability to the life of the com-munity would guarantee the influence of her class no matter who held office at Westminster or the town hall.

This chapter points towards an interpretation of twentieth-century class relations in which middle-class identity was shaped less by occasional anti-socialist panics than by a continuing confi-dence that middle-class England remained in control of the forces of progress. The everyday politics of class cannot be reduced simply to the history of party politics, and there is little merit in substituting political for social determinism in the way we imagine the relationship between class and party. Class had a life beyond politics, a life that is far from 'unfathomable'. Exploration of the rich archival records of Britain's voluntary organisations can provide important correctives to over-politicised accounts of class identity produced by privileging the noisy posturing of the partisan battle for votes. Precisely because non-partisan public activity was so central to the lives of many Conservative women, the traditions of local social leadership into which the Conservative Party had long been able to tap may have been much less disturbed by the political upheavals of the mid-twentieth century than concentration on either formal party organisation or the electoral record would suggest.

NOTES

1.   This chapter has benefited from discussion at the 'Mass Conservatism' conference at Manchester in 1998. I am particularly grateful to the Women's Royal Voluntary Service (WRVS) for permission to use its archives and to the Modern Records Centre at Warwick University for housing them while I worked on them. I thank also the keepers of the following national archives: Conservative Party Archive (CPA), Nuffield College

Social Reconstruction Survey (NCSRS), Mass-Observation (MO), Public Records Office (PRO) and the local records offices in Preston, Halifax, Sheffield, Nottingham, Coventry, Guildford and Southampton. The research on which this chapter is based will be fully reported in my forthcoming book, *Continuities of Class: Women, Social Leadership and the Second World War* (Oxford, 2002).

2. James Thompson, 'After the Fall: Classes and Political Language in Britain 1780–1900', *Historical Journal*, 39, 3 (1996); Marc W. Steinberg, 'Culturally Speaking: Finding a Commons between Post-structuralism and the Thompsonian Perspective', *Social History*, 21, 2 (1996); D. Wahrman, 'The New Political History: A Review Essay', *Social History*, 21, 3 (1996).

3. D. Cannadine, *Class in Britain* (London, 1998), 107.

4. J. Lawrence and M. Taylor (eds), *Party, State and Society: Electoral Behaviour in Britain since 1820* (Aldershot, 1997); R. McKibbin, 'Class and Conventional Wisdom: The Conservative Party and the Public in Inter-war Britain', in R. McKibbin, *Ideologies of Class* (Oxford, 1990); D. Jarvis, 'British Conservatism and Class Politics in the 1920s', *English Historical Review*, 111, 440 (1996), 59–84.

5. Canadine, *Class in Britain*, 168–9, 188.

6. A point well made by Duncan Tanner, 'Labour 1910–31', in Lawrence and Taylor, *Party, State and Society*, 123.

7. For a theorisation of this relationship between 'formal' party politics and the 'practical' everyday politics of class in a working-class context see M. Savage, *The Dynamics of Working-class Politics: The Labour Movement in Preston 1880–1940* (Cambridge, 1987); M. Savage, 'Urban History and Social Class: Two Paradigms', *Urban History*, 20, 1 (1993). Perhaps because of the dominance of the linguistic turn and increasing scepticism about the existence of 'class' as anything other than a projection of political life, Mike Savage's subtle handling of the relationship between class and party has not been followed up as fully as it might have been.

8. Huxley to Mayoress, 9 October 1939, in WRVS, R6/4 Southampton.

9. J. Hinton, 'Voluntarism and the Welfare/Warfare State: Women's Voluntary Services in the 1940s', *Twentieth Century British History*, 9 (1998), 274–305.

10. R. C. Chambers, 'A Study of Three Voluntary Organisations', in D. V. Glass (ed.), *Social Mobility in Britain* (London, 1954), 392–3.

11. I. Zweiniger-Bargielowska, 'Explaining the Gender Gap: The Conservative Party and the Women's Vote 1945–1964', in M. Francis and I. Zweiniger-Bargielowska (eds), *The Conservatives and British Society 1880–1990* (Cardiff, 1996), 207–8. Dame (1952) Marjorie Maxse (1891–1977), chief organisation officer, Conservative Central Office, 1921–39; vice-chairman, WVS, 1940–44; vice-chairman, Conservative Party organisation, 1944–51. Baroness (1955) Evelyn Emmet of Amberley (1899–1980), member of London County Council, 1925–34; Sussex county organiser WVS, 1938–45; chairman, Conservative Women's National Advisory Committee, 1951–54; MP for East Grinstead, 1955–64.

12. On the under-researched nature of this subject see W. D. Rubinstein, 'Britain's Elites in the Inter-war period 1918–39', in A. Kidd and D. Nicholls (eds), *The Making of the British Middle Class? Studies of Regional and Cultural Diversity since the Eighteenth Century* (Stroud, 1998), 186, 199.

13. John Garrard, 'Urban Elites 1850–1914: The Rule and Decline of a New Squirearchy?', *Albion*, 27 (1995), 583–621.

14. Report of National Executive Committee to Labour Party Annual Conference, 1939, 91.

15. L. Hannah, *The Rise of the Corporate Economy* (London, 1976); M. J. Daunton, 'Payment and Participation: Welfare and State-formation in Britain 1900–1951', *Past and Present*, 150 (1996), 201–2; F. Carr, 'Municipal Socialism; Labour's Rise to Power', in B. Lancaster and T. Mason (eds), *Life and Labour in the Twentieth-century City: The Experience of Coventry* (Coventry, 1986); M. Savage and A. Miles, *The Remaking of the British Working Class 1840–1940* (London, 1994), 63–4.

16. R. V. Clements, *Local Notables and the City Council* (London, 1969).

17. J. B. Priestley, *English Journey* (first published 1934, Penguin edn, 1987), 29–40; R. Trainor, 'Neither Metropolitan nor Provincial: The Inter-war Middle Class', in Kidd and Nicholls (eds), *The Making of the British Middle Class?*, 210.

18. B. M. Doyle, 'The Structure of Elite Power in the Early Twentieth-century City: Norwich 1900–35', *Urban History*, 24 (1997), 181; Peter Jones *et al.*, 'Politics', in D. Nash and

D. Reader (eds), *Leicester in the Twentieth Century* (Leicester, 1993), 92–4.

19. Garrard, 'Urban Elites', 609; F. K. Prochaska, *Women and Philanthropy in Nineteenth-century England* (Oxford, 1980).
20. Doyle, 'Structure of Elite Power', 192.
21. Jane Lewis, 'Gender, the Family and Women's Agency in the Building of "Welfare States": The British Case', *Social History*, 19, 1 (1994).
22. Matthew Thomson, *The Problem of Mental Deficiency: Eugenics, Democracy and Social Policy in Britain c. 1870–1959* (Oxford, 1998), 219. For details of local co-operation between statutory and voluntary agencies in the 1930s see Political and Economic Planning (a pressure group and research body), *Report on the British Social Services* (1937), 105–6, 156–67, 172–5.
23. M. Pugh, *Women and the Women's Movement in Britain 1914–1959* (Basingstoke, 1992), 57–8; in London the proportion of women was three times greater.
24. Thomson, *Problem of Mental Deficiency*, 229–30.
25. Undated press cutting in Preston Women's Citizens' Association, Lancashire Record Office, DDX 1749, Box 5.
26. Caitriona Beaumont, 'Women and Citizenship: A Study of Non-feminist Women's Societies and the Women's Movement in England 1928–1950' (PhD thesis, University of Warwick, 1996), 17; F. Prochaska, 'A Mothers' Country: Mothers' Meetings and Family Welfare in Britain 1850–1950', *History*, 74 (1989).
27. Dr Roper Power, 'The Voluntary Social Services in Hertfordshire' (n.d., 1942), 12, Nuffield College Social Reconstruction Survey (NCSRS), E2/7; James McIntyre, 'Report on Voluntary Service in Devon', (n.d., 1942), 33, NCSRS, E2/5.
28. Beaumont, 'Women and Citizenship', 264.
29. Dorothy Hall, *Making Things Happen* (National Federation of Business and Professional Women's Clubs of Great Britain, 1963), 4–5, 265; Miss Gordon Holmes, *In Love with Life. A Pioneer Career Woman's Story* (London, 1944), 177.
30. S. Worden, 'Powerful Women: Electricity in the Home 1919–1940', in J. Attfield and Kirkham, *A View from the Interior: Feminism, Women and Design* (London, 1989); Electoral Association for Women (EAW), minutes of Nottingham Branch, *passim*, Nottingham Archives, DD. 1357/1/4/1; National Council for Women (NCW), minutes of Coventry branch, *passim*, Coventry Record Office, PA/1269; minutes of Halifax NCW, *passim*, Calderdale Archives, NCW/1; Pugh, *Women and the Women's Movement*, 69; Beaumont, 'Women and Citizenship', 264–5.
31. Examples of such overlapping are legion in the minutes examined. When the national conference of the EAW was held in Nottingham in 1941, the local branch sought help in providing accommodation for delegates from the Soroptimists, the Inner Wheel, the Business and Professional Women's Club, the City Business Club, and the NCW: EAW, Nottingham Branch, Nottingham Archives, DD. 1357/1/4/1.
32. The Soroptimists, the NCW and the Women's Conservative Association all met at the Mikado.
33. *Halifax Courier*, *passim*
34. For example, M. Andrews, *The Acceptable Face of Feminism: The Women's Institutes as a Social Movement* (London, 1998), which stresses female solidarity to the virtual exclusion of the operations of class within the WI.
35. McIntyre, 'Report on Voluntary Service in Devon', 55; P. Hollis (ed.), *Women in Public: Documents of the Victorian Women's Movement 1850–1900* (London, 1979), 276–7.
36. Power, 'Voluntary Social Services in Hertfordshire', 12; McIntyre, 'Report on Voluntary Service in Devon', 33.
37. Power, 'Voluntary Social Services in Hertfordshire', 17; T. Bottomore, 'Social Stratification in Voluntary Organisations,' in Glass, *Social Mobility*, 363–4. In the Durham mining town of Birtley, the guild was run by the colliery managers' wives: M. Stott, *Organisation Woman: The Story of the National Union of Townswomen's Guilds* (London, 1978), 32–3.
38. Jean Gaffin and David Thoms, *Caring and Sharing: The Centenary History of the Co-operative Women's Guild* (Manchester, 1983), 268; Pamela M. Graves, *Labour Women: Women in British Working-class Politics 1918–1939* (Cambridge, 1994), 212–13.
39. Ibid., 125; Gillian Scott, *Feminism and the Politics of Working Women: The Women's Co-operative Guild from the 1880s to the Second World War* (London, 1998); Ann Summers, 'A

Home from Home: Women's Philanthropic Work in the Nineteenth Century,' in S. Burman (ed.), *Fit Work for Women* (London, 1979); Ellen Ross, *Love and Toil: Motherhood in Outcast London 1870–1918* (London, 1993); E. Ross, 'Good and Bad Mothers: Lady Philanthropists and London Housewives before the First World War', in K. D. McCarthy (ed.), *Lady Bountiful Revisited: Women, Philanthropy and Power* (New Brunswick, 1990); S. Pederson, 'Gender, Welfare and Citizenship in Britain during the Great War,' *American Historical Review*, 94 (1990), 992–3; Jane Lewis, 'The Working-class Wife and Mother and State Intervention', in J. Lewis (ed.), *Labour and Love: Women's Experience of Home and Family 1850–1940* (Oxford, 1986).

40. J. W. B. Bates, 'The Conservative Party in the Constituencies 1918–1939' (DPhil thesis, University of Oxford, 1994), ch. 7.

41. Stanley ward No 1, Women Unionists, minutes, *passim*, Lancashire Record Office, LC/5/12/1.

42. Interview with secretary of Portsmouth Women's Conservative Association (n.d., 1941), in Mass-Observation Archive (MO), University of Sussex Library, TC 17/D.

43. *Surrey Weekly Press*, 19 November 1937.

44. See, for example, the minutes of the Shirley ward Women's Conservative Association, Southampton Record Office; Bates, 'Conservative Party in the Constituencies', 224–5.

45. Stanley ward No. 1, Women Unionists, minutes, 23 February 1939, Lancashire Record Office, PLC/5/12/1.

46. North West Area, Women's Advisory Committee (WAC), General Purposes Committee, minutes, 23 May, 22 June 1939, Conservative Party Archive (CPA), ARE 3/11/3; women who resigned office to take on WVS work were encouraged to keep in contact, Unionist Women Organisers, *Wartime Newsheet*, No. 1, January 1940, CPA, CCO 170/2/3/2.

47. Details of the social status and associational affiliations of the 556 WVS leaders appointed during the first seven months of the WVS's existence (July 1938–February 1939) were recorded in the Executive minute books. About 50 of these were head-office appointments.

48. Personal Service League, leaflet, November 1938, in MO, TC Women, Box 4, File G; *Hull Daily Mail*, 26 November 1933; *Newcastle Sunday Sun*, 25 June 1936; *Western Daily Mail*, 15 October 1936.

49. E. Wade, Report on visit to Barry, 2 December 1938, WRVS R8/8 Glamorganshire.

50. For details see J. Hinton, *Continuities of Class: Women, Social Leadership and the Second World War* (Oxford, 2002).

51. Bates, 'Conservative Party in the Constituencies', 211, 223–4.

52. Report of meeting in Preston, 28 October 1938, WRVS R10/2, Lancashire County.

53. South East Area, WAC, Executive minutes, 30 December 1941, 19 May 1942, CPA, ARE 9/11/4.

54. West Midlands Women Organisers, minutes, 17 May 1940, CPA, ARE 6/25/1; North West Area, WAC, annual report, 4 June 1940, CPA, ARE 3/11/1; Eastern Area, WAC, minutes, 9 September 1939, 18 January 1940, CPA, ARE 7/11/2; Park Division Conservative Association, annual report, 1941, Sheffield Archives, LD 2210.

55. Stanley ward No. 1, Women Unionists, minutes, 28 September 1939, Lancashire Record Office, LC/5/12/1. They also decided to keep up payments to their usual charities.

56. Shirley ward Women's Conservative Association, minutes, 20 September 1940, 3 November 1941, Southampton Record Office.

57. Redhill Women's Conservative Association, Sussex Record Office, 353/5/6/1; West Bridgeford Conservative Association, minute book, 1937–48, Nottinghamshire Archives, DD.PP2; Park Division Conservative Association, minute book, Sheffield Archives, LD 2210; North West Area, WAC, Reports of Divisional Activities, 24 September 1940, in CPA.

58. Stanley ward No. 1, Women Unionists, minutes, 7 March, 7 October 1940, Lancashire Record Office, LC/5/12/1.

59. WVS, Executive Committee minutes, 27 June 1938, 6 July 1938; Lady Reading, memo dated 23 June 1938, WRVS, V95/38, SJCIWO; Middleton to Home Secretary, 24 June 1938, PRO, HO 45 17580.

60. Fletcher-Moulton to Huxley, 30 October 1939, in WRVS, V/101/38 Conservative Party. There were similar attempts in Leicester: M. E. Walker, report on East Midlands, 22 October 1938, WRVS, R/3.

61. Reading to Walker, 23 November 1938; report by Fletcher-Moulton on Scunthorpe, 2 December 1938, WRVS, R/3 Eastern Regional Office; Fletcher-Moulton to Howat, 25 November 1938, R3/5 Scunthorpe. The mayor was Sir Berkley Sheffield, the 6th baronet, MP for Brigg 1922–29, who owned 40,000 acres.
62. Muriel Borron to Lady Reading, 27 April 1944; Huxley to Boron, 1 May 1944, in WRVS, R/1/2 Darlington.
63. Vera Dart, report on Sunderland, 8 May 1944 and regional administrator's report, 8 February 1945, WRVS, R1/2 Sunderland.
64. WVS General Purposes Committee, minutes, 1 November 1944. Other Tory WVS leaders who experienced a growing incompatibility between their political and social work commitments in the closing months of the war included Lady Lloyd (Brecon), Vachell to Huxley, 15 December 1944, Huxley to Vachell, 18 December 1944, WRVS, R8 Wales; Evelyn Emmet, Worsley to Huxley, 12 December 1944, WRVS, R/12/3 West Sussex; Mrs Weston (Chelmsford), Huxley, report on tour of Region Four, 12 February 1945, WRVS R4 East Anglia.
65. WVS meeting at County Hall, Chichester, 25 May 1945, minutes, WRVS, R/12/3 West Sussex.
66. Iris Davidson to Lady Worsley, 18 July 1945, WRVS, R12/3 West Sussex.
67. Balfour to Reading, 23 November 1945, WRVS, confidential correspondence between Lady Reading and Lady Ruth Balfour.
68. Worsley to Huxley, 7 June 1945, WRVS, R5 Kent.
69. Sybil Howard to Lady Reading, 20 November 1947, WRVS, A1/38. For the panic occasioned by the 1945 Labour victory in one Tory-dominated WVS centre, see Hinton, 'Voluntarism and the Welfare/Warfare State', 293.
70. Chuter Ede to Morrison, 9 February 1951, PRO, CAB 124/914.
71. Reading to Ede, 11 October 1946, PRO, CAB 124/914.
72. Christmas Letter, December 1947, WRVS. On Conservative propaganda, see Ina Zweiniger-Bargielowska, 'Rationing, Austerity and the Conservative Party Recovery after 1945', *Historical Journal*, 37 (1994).
73. Speech at County and County Borough's Organisers Conference, 6 February 1946, WRVS, R6 Regional Office.
74. Sir A. Salisbury MacNalty (ed.), *The Civilian Health and Medical Services, Vol. 1* (London, 1955), 232; Conservative Party Central WAC, minutes, 11 July 1946, CPA; National Federation of Women's Institutes to E. Walker, 8 July 1946, PRO, MAF 102/20.
75. WVS Regional Administrators Conference, 14 February 1947, WRVS.
76. County Borough Organisers Conference, minutes, 11 May 1948, WRVS.
77. Regional Administrators Conference, minutes, 23 September 1949, WRVS.
78. Thursfield to Halpin, 26 August 1946, WRVS, R3 East Midlands. See also Felicity Lane-Fox, cited in B. Campbell, *The Iron Ladies: Why do Women Vote Conservative?* (London, 1987), 85–6.
79. Mrs Daisy Baird to HQ, 16 June 1947, WRVS, R10/2 Blackpool. In the event she remained in charge, obstructing all attempts at revival, until 1951, when her successor, the wife of a leading Tory councillor, took an equally negative view.
80. South East Area, WAC, minutes, 24 February 1949, CPA, ARE 9/11/5.
81. *Lowestoft Journal*, 25 November 1949; *Sevenoaks Chronicle*, 30 September 1949. Lady Hillingdon, who came from a wealthy banking family, had chaired the Conservative Central WAC from 1935 to 1938. During the war she had worked for the WVS as a country organiser and regional administrator for the north Midlands.
82. R. McKibbin, *Classes and Cultures: England 1918–1951* (Oxford, 1998), 62–9; Zweiniger-Bargielowska, 'Rationing, Austerity and the Conservative Party Recovery'; Amy Black and Stephen Brooke, 'The Labour Party, Women, and the Problem of Gender 1951–1966', *Journal of British Studies*, 36 (1997).
83. Miss Evelyn Pilkington (president), North West Conservative WAC, minutes, 20 June 1946, CPA, ARE 3/11/4.
84. South East Area, WAC Executive, minutes, 23 November 1944, CPA, ARE 9/11/4. See also Maxse's views reported in Ad-hoc Committee on Outside Organisations, minutes, 9 October 1945, CPA.
85. South East Area, WAC, minutes, 24 October 1946, CPA, ARE 9/11/4.
86. Eastern Area, WAC, minutes, 21 June 1950, CPA, ARE 7/11/2.

87. Central WAC, minutes, 6 May 1948, CPA; North West Area, WAC, minutes, 8 May 1948, CPA, ARE 3/11/4; Joan Bourne, 'For the Community', *Labour Woman*, February 1948.
88. J. Hinton, 'Militant Housewives: The British Housewives' League and the Attlee Government', *History Workshop Journal*, 38 (1994).
89. Ina Zweiniger-Bargielowska, who has provided valuable documentation of Conservative anti-austerity campaigning, is quite mistaken in asserting that this was effective in shifting women voters disproportionately away from the Labour Party. The polling evidence makes it clear that, while women were indeed significantly more inclined than men to vote Tory throughout the post-war period, there was no significant *change* in the partisan gender gap between 1945 and 1955, apart from a blip in 1950 when it temporarily *narrowed*: I. Zweiniger-Bargielowska, *Austerity in Britain: Rationing, Controls and Consumption 1939–1955* (Oxford, 2000), 253; I. Zweiniger-Bargielowska, 'Explaining the Gender Gap', 201. Class breakdowns of the polling data show that the female swing to Labour in 1950 was exclusively a working-class phenomenon. Middle-class women did indeed respond to the anti-austerity message. Confronting the knee-jerk assumption that 'the women have let us down', Herbert Morrison pointed out at the time that the major cause of Labour's 1950 setback was the desertion of working-class *men*: J. Hinton, 'Women and the Labour Vote 1945–50', *Labour History Review*, 57, 3 (1993). It is ironic that the chauvinist misinformation that Morrison sought to correct should now be in danger of becoming accepted as the conventional wisdom among historians concerned to blame, not women, but a 'masculinist' Labour Party for its failure to accommodate their presumed consumerism: Black and Brooke, 'Labour Party, Women, and the Problem of Gender', 421–3.
90. Eastern Area, WAC, minutes, 21 June 1949, CPA, ARE 7/11/2.
91. South East Area, WAC, minutes, 23 November 1944, CPA, ARE 9/11/4.
92. R. Lewis and A. Maude, *The English Middle Classes* (London, 1953), 230.

7

Echoes in the Wilderness: British Popular Conservatism, 1945–51

PAUL MARTIN

The Conservatism of the masses has been actively cultivated since 1867, when for the first time working men were enfranchised. At this time, Disraeli initiated the Conservative Working Men's Clubs as a means of organising the new and potential Tory vote among these men. Conservative friendly societies and other organisations spread to embrace aspects of working-class culture that most readily lent themselves to the Victorian Conservative domestic principles of financial thrift and general economic self-sufficiency. By the Edwardian era these had been amplified nationally through the appeal to proletarian Conservatism made by Joseph Chamberlain in his tariff reform campaign of 1903–13 in support of punitive tariffs on non-empire imported goods. In the inter-war period, the socio-cultural and economic values and sentiment of working-class Conservatism were retained as many aspirants from blue-collar backgrounds sought entry into the middle classes through lower ranking clerical white-collar jobs. Others sought to escape the inevitability of their class-determined expectations by studying at night school to qualify for entry into a profession such as nursing or teaching.

Many people so educated were considered to be natural Conservative voters before 1945, embracing as they did the Conservative ethos of self-help and aspirant upward mobility. The professions, however, voted Labour in large numbers in 1945 and the governmental dominance of the Conservative Party in the 1920s and 1930s stood in stark contrast to the scale of its defeat in the general election of that year. The shock to Conservative activists and voters alike at the sheer scale of the Labour vote led to a kind of siege mentality compounded by the feeling of betrayal. This radical, nationalising Labour government was perceived by Conservatives at large as a red peril that wished to deprive private citizens of their individuality and freedom to act on their own initiative and to confiscate, through punitive taxation and compulsory purchase order, the material fruits of honest savings and applied business acumen. The defence of Conservative principles at this time was conducted by a minority of the British public who, while they were by no means a mass of any kind, did embrace and invoke the sentiment of mass Conservatism in their rhetoric and opposition to what was popularly termed state interference. Furthermore, they adopted the tactics of mass popular protest. It is an aspect of this period that has received too little attention from both political and social historians in the past and it is with this aspect that this chapter is concerned.[1]

In the wake of Labour's landslide victory in 1945, it has been assumed that middle-class fears of being subsumed into an all-embracing corporate socialist state were exclusively channelled and expressed through the Conservative Party itself and reflected in the success of the recruitment crusades by its chairman, Lord Woolton. An almost exclusive focus on the high politics of Woolton's strategy for the recovery of the Conservative Party has overshadowed the part played by dissent against the 1945–51 Attlee governments by ordinary Conservative (and other) voters. This chapter examines two organisations, the British Housewives League (BHL) and the Vermin Club (VC), which rode the wave of Conservative Party resurgence in the late 1940s.[2] Both organisations were spontaneous and reactive in their formation, and were used as platforms for the articulation of middle-class outrage at the Labour government during the late 1940s. Although organisationally separate from the Conservative Party, both the VC and the BHL carried the support, membership and active involvement of many members of local Conservative associations. As a result they were as much of an embarrassment to the Conservative Party hierarchy as they were an irritant to the Labour Party. Popular Conservatism, at least in these instances, was more prevalent as a reactive, sentimental or emotional grudge than as an expression of adherence to party-political doctrine. Both organisations did, however, privately lobby (indeed sometimes harangue) Woolton's office for public support, because they saw the Conservative Party as a natural ally against statism. However, the re-emergent Conservative Party, unsure about its own position, profile or total support in the country, sought to distance itself from both the BHL and the VC.

There is, of course, a history of political and single-issue pressure groups of the right and the BHL and VC are located within this tradition.[3] Unlike, for example, the Primrose League they were not part of the party machine.[4] Another important difference is that, unlike a good number of previous rightist leagues, both groups were apparently organised by 'ordinary' middle-class, politically inactive Conservative voters rather than disaffected Tory grandees, marginal and maverick MPs, or wealthy party supporters (although there were no doubt some of the latter among their ranks as silent members). Similarly, they can be clearly defined as anti-Labour and pro-Tory, whereas many previous leagues of the right had been set up in order to 'ginger up' the Tories on certain subjects such as tariff reform and empire unity.[5]

I begin by discussing the BHL. In doing so, it is necessary to give some wider context to its concerns and attitudes, and this can be done by looking at another women's organisation in the same period, the National Federation of Women's Institutes (NFWI), which in the late 1940s shared many of the same concerns. However, the NFWI sought to promote women's traditional gender role as part of a wider push for progressive legislation and recognition of the value of women's contribution to society; like other women's organisations that wished to remain politically neutral, it gave the BHL a wide berth, believing it to be little more than a Conservative Party front organisation. The BHL itself was equally active in trying to beat off what it saw as state interference with the gender status quo. This positions the BHL's reactive Conservatism within a wider social discourse on women and the future of Britain at that time.

THE NATIONAL FEDERATION OF WOMEN'S INSTITUTES IN THE LATE 1940s

In the 1930s middle-class women's organisations based on domestic concerns blossomed. The Electrical Women's Association and the Women's Gas Council, for instance, were formed as auxiliaries of the competing gas and electricity industries in order to proselytise to the modern housewife about the advantages of each.

Cookery and other clubs organised by women's magazines and manufacturers of foodstuffs became prolific and the 'practical housekeeping' movement in the inter-war period mushroomed. This was part of a housewife culture that promoted and helped codify traditional women's gender roles. Indeed, a precedent was apparently set for the BHL by the League of Empire Housewives, formed in 1927 probably as an organising and propaganda body for the purpose of promoting 'empire shopping weeks' in which only produce from the UK and the empire would be bought as a mark of patriotic duty and consumer loyalty.[6] This in turn was part of the wider work of the Empire Marketing Board of the late 1920s and early 1930s.[7]

After the Second World War, 'there was much discussion and writing on domesticity'.[8] The National Federation of Women's Institutes, for instance, sought to highlight the economic importance both of women's traditional role, which it felt was being ignored by government measures such as the 'refusal to introduce sick pay for housewives into the National Insurance scheme'.[9] Additionally:

> women who were housewives and those with small children were further alienated from traditional politics by the introduction of double summertime, the stopping of the import of dried eggs to help the balance of payments crisis, the painfully slow improvement of rural water, electricity and sewage supplies, the introduction of bread rationing, the slow removal of the rationing on tea, indeed the whole issue of rationing itself. The letters pages of *Home and Country* [the NFWI journal] in the initial post-war period, were full of women's discontent and disenchantment about all these issues.[10]

Compounding this:

> The expansion of the welfare state and the government in the post-war period brought in the mushrooming of both local and central government experts. Official experts took over a variety of welfare issues which had previously been the sphere and expertise of women in the NFWI and similar organisations.[11]

In the 1940s the NFWI demanded the introduction of a range of progressive legislation including equal pay for women and greater provision of school meals as well as official recognition of the importance of women's contribution as housewives. Maggie

Andrews rightly asserts: 'These issues straddle the perceived boundaries of equal rights and maternal feminism.'[12]

THE BRITISH HOUSEWIVES LEAGUE

The British Housewives League is also an integral part of the wider historical debate around the contested role of women in the immediate post-war years. Although concerned with some of the same issues as the NFWI, however, it was a far more conservative, even reactionary organisation. Thus it saw the provision of school meals as a state imposition on teachers and an undermining of the role of the wife and mother. Indeed it was claimed by one BHL speaker of the period that 'communal feeding was necessary only where the mother was too lazy to cook'.[13] In common with anti-Labour feeling generally, it also regularly accused the Labour government of fostering class hatred.

Far from pressing for legislative recognition of the importance of the job of housewife as part of a wider progressive front for women's rights, the BHL brandished traditional female domesticity as an exclusive weapon wrapped in heavy sentiment which it used to browbeat the Labour government from the right. The self-ascribed title of 'housewife' was at this time still felt to be something to be defended not escaped from. In effect, it was asserted as a form of inverted feminism, the defence of which as a moral obligation it defended against incursions of state managers and officialdom. Newspaper reports and internal Conservative Central Office (CCO) memoranda from branch observers at their meetings confirm this.[14] The BHL was more often to be found allying itself with the food production trade associations such as the Master Bakers and the Butchers Federation, which wanted restrictions lifted. As one Communist Party leaflet noted, 'The British Housewives League does not represent the British housewives. They have poured out money on printed propaganda, booked expensive halls and extensively used loudspeaker vans. It is certainly not the working-class housewife who is supplying the money for this.'[15]

The BHL was formed in 1945 by Mrs Irene Lovelock, who became its president, but its most important office holder was Dorothy Crisp, who arrived on the scene a short while later. For most if its existence the BHL suffered from a split identity in that it publicly asserted its independent non-party status, while privately lobbying a very reluctant Conservative Party to help fund it or at least lend official support to it and its aims. In July 1946, Woolton explicitly denied that there was any connection with the BHL:

> It might save a little time of my political opponents if I were to say publicly that the British Housewives League has no connection with nor is it financed by the Conservative Party ... I have never to the best of my knowledge seen the people who are running that league. I have had no conferences with them of any sort either directly or indirectly. If that is not a complete statement, I do not know what is.[16]

Seven months later, Woolton fended off the urgent pleas of Dorothy Crisp to fund the BHL by reminding her of the public statements which they had both made to the effect that there was no connection between their two organisations. Most tellingly, however, Woolton commented: 'The Conservative Party already has the largest women's organisation in the country, and it would not be to its advantage to be supporting another organisation with similar aims.'[17] In fact, the thinking of the party towards both the BHL and the Vermin Club was that they were pursuing the same ends as the party itself but through the medium of street politics and populist hysteria. The Conservative hierarchy found the BHL distasteful and feared that official association with it would undermine its own recruitment efforts by making it seem preposterous. For Woolton the BHL was superfluous because of the party's women's organisation, although it might be supposed that a good number of its members were in broad agreement with – if not actively supporting – the BHL.

The ironically named Councillor Mrs Welfare claimed that the BHL had some 200 branches throughout the country and that they intended to elect Dorothy Crisp to Parliament on their behalf.[18] It would seem that Dorothy Crisp was something of a thorn in the side of the Conservative Party, continually pestering CCO about funding for the BHL.[19] On one occasion she threatened to resign the chair of the BHL and urge its membership to join the Conservative Party as individuals. Woolton rejected these pressures on the grounds of the repeated public statements of neutrality that both organisations had made.[20]

The British Housewives League in debate

Despite the Tory leadership's lack of enthusiasm for it, the BHL pursued its campaigning through local demonstrations and debates. One instance of note was when the BHL put up a Mrs

Hoyle-Smith to debate the proposition that 'the Labour government has failed the people' with Barbara Castle MP, then
Parliamentary Private Secretary at the Board of Trade on 13 July
1947, at the Co-operative Hall, Downing Street, Manchester. This
seems to have been a very rowdy and vociferous public meeting,
attended overwhelmingly by Labour supporters, in which both
speakers fought to make themselves heard.[21] The BHL's Mrs Hoyle-
Smith:

> described school meals as an imposition on the teachers; and
> said that the state should not do the job of a mother and wife.
> 'Let us have the sanctity of the British home restored', she
> said.[22]

The BHL asserted the traditional role and status of women as
homemakers and nurturers and sought to ring-fence traditional
notions of 'womanliness' as an independent assertion of women's
rights, indeed, an inverted form of feminism.[23] This of course was
not new, in that such cries were heard from both men and women
opposed to the struggle for female enfranchisement in Britain
before the First World War. This is overtly referred to in the report
of the above meeting that described Hoyle-Smith as having 'the
look of the suffragettes about her in her blue costume and navy
straw sailor hat'.[24] It was not lost on Barbara Castle, described as 'a
slim, hatless figure in a grey costume and white silk blouse' who:

> with her right foot advanced, gesticulating, said: 'I am really
> very sorry that you did not give Mrs Hoyle-Smith a fair
> hearing. I do want to suggest to you that we women are on
> trial as to whether or not we can approach these problems
> with constructive minds and reasoning heads. We must be
> impartial however deeply our feelings may run.[25]

Similarly, a Conservative Party observer at a BHL meeting in the
Albert Hall, in which 'a few men dressed in white garments
printed with slogans (about the Health Bill, Food and so on) and
surgeons' masks were walking about the platform', reported that
the chair was taken by 'Miss Adeline Bourne, an old suffragette
with the appropriate style and dramatic manner. She did not speak
into the microphone and was not heard very clearly. Her speech
was not effective.'[26]

The height at which feelings were running and the frustration
felt by those who attended are perhaps illustrated in the following
passage:

Mrs Castle speaking of the government's achievement in house building was interrupted by a tall woman who strode to the platform and planked a newspaper on it. 'Answer that!' she demanded. She was Mrs Thew of Northfield Road, New Moston. The paper contained an editorial on the building position and the eviction of squatters from army huts headed 'Mr Bevan, what is your answer to this?'[27]

The motion when put to the vote was 'heavily defeated'.

The British Housewives League and the Conservative government

The Tories were narrowly returned to office in 1951, partly because of people's frustration with, and resentment of, continued rationing and general material shortages in the immediate post-war reconstruction period. As we have seen, organisations such as the BHL had been utilising such discontent as a weapon with which to resist what they saw as state incursion on domestic sanctity. Even without official approval from the Tory leadership, they had effectively acted as a Conservative propaganda machine over this same period. We find, however, even with a new Conservative government in office, that in 1951 the Huddersfield branch of the BHL met to protest at the 8d meat ration introduced by Webb, the Minister of Food: 'We meet today in order to get meat tomorrow', proclaimed Mrs Winifred M. Sykes, the Huddersfield branch chairman of the BHL to the 300 assembled women. She wrote in a letter to Churchill:

> We would respectfully remind you that our trades unions, the BHL and the Scottish Housewives Association, are strictly non-party and have among their members women of all three political persuasions.[28]

Sykes was presumably either unaware of Dorothy Crisp's overtures to Woolton or was being wilfully coy about them. It is almost certain that the BHL did have women in its membership who were in both the Conservative and Liberal parties if not the Labour Party at that time, which only shows how non-political and how reactive their Conservatism had been.

In 1955 the BHL branch in Rochdale was causing trouble for the local Conservative Association.[29] A number of branch members were also members of the Conservative Party but threatened to resign because of 'being made to look foolish by Mr Butler's Autumn budget'.[30] The local Tory agent, N. E. Finnie, feared that the Rochdale Conservatives would lose members to the Liberals as a result because there seemed to be more support for the BHL in the Liberal Party and a number of Liberal women supported the Housewives League.[31] The desperate pleas of Dorothy Crisp for Conservative Party backing while Labour was in power seem only to have led to disillusion, at least in Rochdale. Finnie, in a letter to an E. C. Bradbury at Conservative Central Office, noted: 'It would appear from certain comments during our discussion that there may be a tendency for them to go over to the Liberal Party as quite a number of the Liberal women support the Housewives League and they are now saying that they have experienced socialism, and under Conservatism prices have continued to rise and that it is time the Liberals were given a chance.' It would seem that, in common with most single-issue campaign groups, the conservatism as noted at the outset was based on popular sentiment rather than on any adhesion to party doctrine. Whilst the issues which the BHL campaigned on were Conservative ones, its members were not themselves Conservative Party functionaries, even if a good many were actually members of the Conservative Party itself. Hence it would appear that the BHL could just as easily direct its ire at a Conservative government, even after the lifting of rationing, as at a socialistic Labour one. Such innate conservatism could be read as human reaction to adverse circumstances, and to the shock of the new which the 1945 Labour government must surely have provided to an older conservative electorate

What was the importance of the British Housewives League?

The BHL represented a reaction to state control of the economy, felt by many middle-class wives and mothers to be an appropriation or undermining of their realm of influence. As such, the Conservatism of their position was reactive in defence of a perceived social and gender role, essentially a sense of self. Such sentiments suggest the possibility of a wider public empathy, which may have appealed across class divides to a greater extent than was represented in the BHL itself. For instance, a public meeting organised by the BHL on 6 July 1947 filled the Albert Hall, although a rally the following day attracted only 1,000 participants.[32] The BHL, in common with the Conservative Party and others, accused Labour of fostering class conflict. The Conservative Party, given its uncertainty as to its own identity at this time, was not in a position to know how to respond to such 'popular Conservatism', other than to distance itself from it for fear of ridicule, even though many local party activists were involved.

For the Vermin Club the position was more ambiguous: internal party memoranda reveal a vacillation between tacit support and complete rejection of its overtures for support.

THE VERMIN CLUB

On the evening of 4 July 1948, Aneurin Bevan, the Labour government's Minister of Health, addressed the annual Labour rally for the north of England at Belle Vue, Manchester, where he made a speech in which he reflected on the poor state of people's health in his youth, offering the opinion:

> That is why no amount of cajolery can eradicate from my heart a deep, burning hatred for the Tory party that inflicted those experiences on me. So far as I am concerned they are lower than vermin. They condemned millions of first-class people to semi-starvation.[33]

This was misreported in the following day's papers as evidence of Bevan's hatred of anyone who had voted Tory in 1945. The *Sunday Despatch* screamed in large type: 'THE MAN WHO HATES 8,093,858 PEOPLE', the total Conservative vote in the 1945 general election.[34] In response to the media-induced hysteria the Vermin Club grew throughout Britain. In the time-honoured tradition of appropriating a pejorative name as a badge of pride, Conservative voters (as opposed to purely party activists, although the club's members inevitably included a good number of Tory activists) decided to call themselves Vermin Clubs, leaders of which were known as 'chief rats' in order to remind the unfortunate Bevan of his gaff at every opportunity. The novelist Dornford Yates even wrote a book, *Lower than Vermin*, about an aristocratic family whose various properties and wealth (Yates himself admired the aristocracy) became increasingly impoverished through socialist taxes, bureaucracy and compulsory appropriation.[35] The cartoonist Strube used his 'Little Man' strip in 'The Man Who Always Pays' to highlight the plight of the lower middle classes as unofficial strikes and government regulations seemed to go entirely against the grain of free enterprise in interfering in the everyday lives of the people.[36]

It was because of this simmering resentment that the Vermin Club was able to grow exponentially, albeit for a short time. For the Tories, the issue of the moment was anti-socialist unity. To this end, an agreement was reached with the Liberals, the Woolton–Teviot Agreement of 1947, which provided for co-operation at constituency level between Liberals and Conservatives. The Conservatives were meanwhile absorbing a number of National Liberal organisations as a strengthening exercise and had absorbed 61 local associations by the 1950 general election. Under these circumstances, Bevan's gaff should have been a godsend to the Tories. However, the relevant files in the Conservative Party Archive indicate that the Tories exercised extreme caution in not capitalising on it, and in disassociating themselves from the Vermin Club, which did.[37]

The development of the Vermin Club

Vermin Clubs seem to have been started independently in response to the national newspaper sensationalisation of Bevan's speech. The earliest reference to them in the CCO files is an advertisement in *The Times* on 28 July 1948, which appeals for 'organisers of Vermin Clubs, now springing up spontaneously all over the country' to contact a box number with a view to national co-ordination.[38] There is then a report in the *Birmingham Evening Despatch*, probably from early August 1948, in which it is stated that 'a local metal-worker has started to manufacture badges and brooches for use by Conservative Party members'.[39] These badges were struck in uncoloured chrome with a picture of a rat and the word 'Vermin' underneath. A letter was sent by an A. E. Titley of Sutton Coldfield to Lord Woolton at Central Office, offering to sell these badges at a discount for distribution among Conservative constituency associations.[40] Colin Mann, Woolton's public relations officer, kindly refused the offer ostensibly to avoid competition with Conservative Party badges.[41] A meeting of 'vermin' was eventually arranged at the Caxton Hall, London, for Friday, 6 August 1948. The report on this meeting states that replies from 47 individual club organisers were received in response to the advert from all over England, Scotland and Wales. The branches of the club were to be called 'nests' (similarly, the branches of the Primrose League were called 'habitations'). Main nests were to approximate to political wards 'with smaller nests in building estates and public houses'.[42]

   It would be a mistake to assume that all of the Vermin Club's 120,000 membership was solely comprised of existing Tories, as the sensationalist nature of the reporting of Bevan's speech evidently touched a nerve in many passive or even floating voters. An observer from Conservative Central Office attested that there were many Liberals in attendance at the Vermin Club's meetings and even some Labour members who wanted to contribute to the charitable work, while not associating themselves with the political end of the club. On the other hand, Bevan's meetings were often now invaded by Vermin Club members, shouting 'Vermin, Vermin'. Bevan was subject to a hate campaign which included packets of excrement being sent to him through the post, while 'Someone daubed across the outside of [his] house at 23 Cliveden Place the inscription in huge black letters 'VERMIN VILLA – HOME OF A LOUD-MOUTHED RAT'.[43]

By April 1949, the Vermin Club seems to have become a fully fledged national organisation. An internal Conservative Central Office memo notes that J. Robson-Armstrong, the Vermin Club chairman, on visiting Colin Mann had informed him that national membership of the Vermin Club stood at 70,000, 'without advertising', and that it was gaining 6,000 members a month.[44] However, the VC's half-yearly report in October 1949 gave the membership as 105,000; it further notes that 'unfortunately a number of members continue to have large amounts outstanding in their name, and it would be appreciated if all members could clear their accounts as quickly as possible'.[45] Nests had been reportedly established throughout the country and 'in each of the white dominions'.[46] Bevan's pejorative phrase was adopted as a symbol of pride by those who felt it had been aimed at them. Life membership was put at 2 shillings. Profits raised from the sale of the club badges designed by Robson-Armstrong were originally intended to be donated to the Conservative Party, but because these would have been subject to '100% purchase tax', it was decided that all the funds raised would be donated to charity (in the event, cancer research)[47] 'and other non-state-aided medical charities'.[48]

An early propaganda leaflet entitled 'How Vile a Vermin are You?' stated: 'Enrol ten more Vermin, and you will become a Vile Vermin. Enrol twenty-five further Vermin, and you will become a Very Vile Vermin. Enrol two hundred Vermin and form a nest.'[49] The officers were stated to be the Earl of Buckinghamshire, president; Lady Deedes and Major-General Sir W. L. O. Twiss, vice-presidents; and J. Robson-Armstrong, chairman. The central office was at Twickenham in Middlesex. It was later reported in the minutes of the half-yearly meeting of 6 October 1949 that the Earl of Buckinghamshire had resigned the presidency in disagreement with a decision to advertise the aims of the club. There were in fact just two principle aims: '1. To organise the anti-socialist electorate,

2. To publicise the danger of socialism', while 4 July was to be proclaimed and celebrated as 'Vermin Day'.[50] The Earl of Buckinghamshire may not have been the only one shy about revealing his membership. The minutes also report that, while membership was currently increasing at the rate of approximately 6,000 per month, several functions, 'whilst socially successful', had fallen short financially because of a lack of attendance.[51]

The Vermin Club was certainly active in publicity terms. Its greatest expenditure was on lapel badges (£3,860), which were initially 'hand-made and until we can see what the response is going to be, the rate of production must be limited'.[52] The rules stated, however, that 'The plastic badge shall be the badge of the club and anyone giving a further 3/6d shall be eligible for a metal badge.'[53] Numerous poster campaigns were also launched. Ties and cufflinks bearing a winged-insect logo were made as were Christmas cards; poster stamps with the bug design and the words 'An Anti-socialist Vermin Helping Cancer Research' were available at 1 shilling per 48.[54] It was reported that, by October 1949, £550 had been donated to the British Empire Cancer Research Fund. The chairman, J. Robson-Armstrong, bombarded Woolton's office with letters, suggesting ideas and joint activities with local Conservative associations. There were pleas for an exchange of speakers and for Conservative agents to advise Vermin Club organisers, but all were rebuffed.

In 1948 a Conservative MP, J. Baker-White, wrote to Woolton, with a suggestion, which he claimed had originated with his constituents, that a Vermin Club should be initiated in every divisional association. It was proposed that membership 'would by no means be open to everybody. It would be open to active party workers, and a new member would have to be proposed either by the branch chairman or the branch secretary.' He also had his own idea for a 'discreet' plastic lapel badge '[being] a tiny beetle worn in the lapel. It would be literally not much larger than an ordinary life-sized ladybird and would be on a pin so that it could be worn in the corner of the buttonhole. It would have a red head, a blue back and white wing covers.'[55] This proposal was duly rejected. The reply from Woolton's office raised concern about possible competition between the two organisations badges and continued:

if we were to adopt a 'vermin' badge and make a sort of joke of it we could hardly at the same time maintain and foster the attitude of shocked indignation which is probably doing us a lot of good among non-party and feeble-party electors. Also there is the danger that we should attach the name 'Vermin Party' to ourselves. Aneurin Bevan would probably be quick to say 'The cap must fit or why do they wear it?' The title of 'Vermin Party' might retain its stigma after its origin was forgotten. Lastly, I think it might help in a way to enhance Aneurin Bevan's prestige and importance and that is surely undesirable.[56]

Tory identity and the impact of the Vermin Club

Clearly, in the absence of a secure idea of its branded image, the Conservative Party feared having something of a farcical name foisted on it in the heat of a passing campaign. In advance of the Vermin Club's half-yearly meeting for 1949 (at which its two principal objectives were proposed and adopted), a circular was sent to the CCO regional agents from Miss Maxse (vice-chairman of the party and key adviser on women's work):

> [the Vermin Club] would appear to be creating yet another organisation with aims partly overlapping with our own, which is unlikely to add any strength to the party and may deflect funds and personal services which would normally come our way. We do not want to issue an official statement disassociating ourselves from the Vermin Club, most if not all of whose members must obviously be drawn from our own supporters. At the same time we do not want to encourage its activities or lend them any countenance, e.g. by supplying speakers, nor should we advise individuals to join.[57]

Therefore, at a period in its history when the Conservative Party was organisationally and publicly asserting its desire for 'anti-socialist unity', it was privately distancing itself from a potential ally even one which was prepared to be a willing tool. The fear of ridicule in taking the Vermin Club seriously led the party to reject this opportunity. Although many in the party nationally disapproved of the Vermin Club, seeing it as an embarrassment, many Conservatives at local level undoubtedly joined it, most especially young Conservatives. Curiously, given Woolton's reticence, Robson-Armstrong claimed that Churchill himself gave permission to allow the branch in his constituency at Woodford to be named the Winston Nest.[58]

Reporting on a letter from Robson-Armstrong to Woolton, CCO public relations officer Colin Mann stated that the Vermin Club was 'already receiving a good deal of help and encouragement from individual constituency agents'.[59] The club itself varied in its position. While it publicly presented a strict 'non-party' line, Robson-Armstrong's letters and memos to CCO described it as 'crypto-conservative' and sought a much closer association with the reluctant Conservative head office. Central Office itself dithered accordingly between encouraging party members to join the club as private individuals and discouraging them from any association with it at all. Certainly Central Office was used to frequent written engagement with the Vermin Club – an internal CCO cover note accompanying a letter from the club simply states: 'Another verminiferous letter.'[60] Another internal memo from the general director at CCO reports that the club had offered its membership records to the party, should they be of any use, while at the same time requesting two or more party speakers for a garden party on 2 July 1949. Central Office's thoughts on the request were in line with those previously described:

> I cannot help feeling that such platforms would be more suitable for either independent MPs, such as Sir Alan Herbert, or for eminent people not necessarily connected with politics. Once we introduce the purely political note with political speeches, the Vermin Clubs, apart from being associated in the public mind with the Conservative Party, would lose the light touch of humour, at present an effective asset to them.[61]

This is all symptomatic of the party's initial uncertainty about its future in a 'socialist' Britain, one which many Labour voters hoped and believed spelled the end of the possibility of another Conservative government.

This now raises the question: did the Vermin Club have any impact on the outcome of the general elections of 1950 and 1951? During both campaigns the Vermin Club worked to keep Bevan's unfortunate words in the public mind at election time. As H. G. Nicholas in *The British General Election of 1950* notes about the West of England, 'It was the West Country which appeared to have the most exuberant "Young Conservatives" and the most animated membership of "The Vermin Clubs" … and the most vehement style of platform oratory.'[62] The 1951 result brought the Tories back into office with a majority of 17. As a useful hectoring device against Labour, the cry of 'Vermin, Vermin' must have had its impact, as no doubt did the printed propaganda. But as an organisation the Vermin Club was probably little more than an irritant. Its importance lies more in giving the historian a different window on post-war consensus politics and in adding another piece to the

jigsaw of the lineage of right-wing pressure groups in the twentieth century.

CONCLUSION

Both the VC and the BHL professed to attract support from the
Liberal and Labour parties, trade unions and other groups as well
as Conservative Party activists, though there is little evidence to
confirm these assertions. Nonetheless, in their appeal they demonstrated that such Conservatism was reactive and issue-specific
rather than party-orientated. Such populist Conservatism was not
necessarily tied to the Conservative Party, but aimed at mass
appeal in its own right. Having said this, such groups served to
keep populist issues in the public eye. At election times this may
well have paid off in terms of votes for the Conservatives, but this
is hard to quantify. However, many Conservative constituency
associations and private individuals wrote to Conservative Central
Office asking for Vermin Club badges in the run up to the 1950
general election, in the belief that they were being distributed from
there.[63] This implies that the Vermin Club was seen as synonymous
with the party if not an actual part of it.

Even though both the BHL and VC were pro-Conservative in
the 1940s, once the Conservative Party came back to power in 1951,
disillusionment, for the BHL at least, seems to have set in quickly.
The Conservatives themselves became the victims of irritants from
the far right (in the shape of A. K. Chesterton's League of Empire
Loyalists from 1954, and which the Euroscepticism of the
Referendum Party and United Kingdom Independence Party
echoed in the 1990s) in the same way that Labour had suffered the
slings and arrows of the Vermin Club and British Housewives
League. Certainly, the period 1945–50 was a unique chapter in
modern British political and social history, one in which the Tories
found themselves uncharacteristically in a significant minority and
on the defensive. In such unusual times, an unusual thing
happened: the respectable Tory-voting middle classes found themselves adopting the street and platform cultures more usually associated with working-class and extremist politics. This in itself
makes the study of these groups worthwhile. In our own time, it
also serves as an interesting mirror to hold against the reappear-
ance on the streets of 'middle England' in opposition to the
Conservative's poll tax in 1990 and the dynamics encapsulated in
the scale and humiliation of the Conservative defeat in the general

election of 1997, when that same popular Conservatism turned on the hand which had fed it since 1979.

NOTES

1. For a fuller account of the BHL (which exists today) and the flamboyant Dorothy Crisp (who was its leading celebrity during the period under discussion), see J. Hinton, 'Militant Housewives: The British Housewives League and the Attlee Government', *History Workshop Journal*, 38 (1994), 128–56. Hinton concludes: 'Housewives were people who coped. They did not take direct action.' While the evidence largely supports him, the BHL like most single issue groups was adept at projecting a larger image of itself through courting media attention. As such, its existence as a populist organisation of the right at this time is important for what it tells us about the resentment felt by the passive middle classes as much as the activists among them who articulated it. As Hinton notes in his introduction, by far the greatest source of information on the BHL that he found was in contemporary newspapers. Dorothy Crisp wrote two self-published autobiographical accounts *A Life For England* (1946), and *A Light In The Night* (1960), the latter of which is an account of her traumatic post-BHL life. Both of these give insight to Crisp's character and life, but do not deal in any detail with her involvement in the BHL. Irene Lovelock, the BHL's founder, also wrote an unpublished and seemingly untitled autobiography, all of which Hinton draws on. He also notes, however, the BHL's refusal to open its archives to him.
2. Some of the material on the Vermin Club first appeared in a longer article, P. Martin, 'The Vermin Club 1948–1951', *History Today*, 47, 6 (June 1997), 17–22.
3. Significant bodies were the Anti-Socialist Union, which overlaps to some extent chronologically with the Vermin Club and would seem to have had some of the same aims, and the obscure Middle-Classes Union, established in 1919 to 'withstand the rapacity of the manual worker and profiteer', *The Times*, 7 March 1919; they point to a legacy of political organisation of such reactionary sentiments. See K. D. Brown, 'The Anti-Socialist Union 1908–1949', in K. D. Brown (ed.), *Essays in Anti-Labour History: Responses to the Rise of Labour in Britain* (London, 1974), 234–62; G. E. Webber, *The Ideology of the British Right 1918–1939* (London, 1986), 17, 29 n. 3, 156.
4. See J. Henderson Robb, *The Primrose League 1883–1906* (New York, 1942); M. Pugh, *The Tories and the People 1880–1935* (Oxford, 1985).
5. For example, the United Empire Party of 1930–31 set up by the press magnates Beaverbrook and Rothermere, Joseph Chamberlain's Tariff Reform League of 1903–13 and its offshoots, such as the Trade Union Tariff Reform League and Henry Page-Croft's National Party of 1917–22. Croft's sister, Lady Pearson, stood as a candidate for the British Union of Fascists in Canterbury.
6. 'The members of the League wear a distinctive badge, which will intimate to a shop-keeper that the wearers wish to buy only home products or empire goods.' 'The League of Empire Housewives', *British Lion*, 25, n.d., cited in J. V. Gottleib, *Feminine Fascism: Women in Britain's Fascist Movement 1923–1945* (London, 2000), 13.
7. S. Constantine, 'Bringing the Empire Alive: The Empire Marketing Board and Imperial Propaganda 1926–33', in J. M. Mackenzie (ed.), *Imperialism and Popular Culture* (Manchester, 1986), 207.
8. M. Andrews, *The Acceptable Face of Feminism: The Women's Institute as a Social Movement* (London, 1997), 147.
9. Ibid.
10. Ibid., 147–8.
11. Ibid., 149.
12. Ibid.
13. *Daily Dispatch*, 14 July 1947, Conservative Party Archive (CPA), Bodleian Library, CCO 3/1/12.
14. Letters to Conservative Central Office (CCO) from British Housewives League (BHL), CPA, CCO 3/3/24; responses to letters from CCO, CPA, CCO 3/1/12; *Huddersfield Daily Examiner*, 22 February 1951.

15. *Don't Be Misled by the Housewives League*, Communist Party leaflet, CPA, CCO 3/1/12; *Huddersfield Daily Examiner*, 22 February 1951.
16. 'Housewives League not Linked with Conservatives', *Western Mail*, 3 July 1947, CPA, CCO 3/1/12.
17. Woolton to Crisp, 3 February 1948, CPA, CCO 3/1/12.
18. Report to CCO by Miss Spencer, observer on behalf of the Conservative Party at the meeting of the BHL at the Albert Hall, Friday 6 June 1947, CPA, CCO 3/1/12.
19. Woolton to Crisp, 3 February 1948, CPA, CCO 3/1/12.
20. Woolton to Crisp, 3 February 1948, CPA, CCO 3/1/12.
21. 'Wives in Uproar at Meeting', *Daily Dispatch*, 14 July 1947, CPA, CCO 3/1/2.
22. *Daily Dispatch*, 14 July 1947.
23. Fascism had previously sought to a far greater extreme to promote traditional female domesticity as a political obligation on women: 'Raising the occupations of mother and housewife to the status of professions in the state was yet another example of the [British Union of Fascists]'s politicisation of domesticity'; Gottlieb, *Feminine Fascism*, 120.
24. *Daily Dispatch*, 14 July 1947. The legacy of women's suffrage activism of the Edwardian period on the right was also most noticeable in British fascism, in both the 1920s and 1930s: see Gottlieb, *Feminine Fascism*, 132–5, 147–77; H. Kean, 'Mary Richardson, Suffragette, Socialist and Fascist', *Women's History Review*, 7, 4 (1998), 475–93.
25. *Daily Dispatch*, 14 July 1947.
26. Report by Spencer on Albert Hall meeting, 6 June 1947, CPA, CCO 3/1/12.
27. *Daily Dispatch*, 14 July 1947.
28. *Huddersfield Daily Examiner*, 22 February 1951.
29. Letter from N. E. Finnie, secretary and agent to Rochdale Conservative and Unionist Association, to E. C. Bradbury, CCO, 24 November 1955, CPA, CCO 3/4/5: 'Since October 1951 we have not heard much about this League, but it would appear that as far as Rochdale is concerned, the officers and some of the members have been meeting fortnightly without publishing the fact.'
30. Ibid.
31. Ibid.
32. Reports from Miss Spencer to CCO, 6 and 7 June 1947, CPA, CCO 3/1/12.
33. M. Foot, *Aneurin Bevan, Vol. 2: 1945–1960* (London, 1973), 238.
34. Ibid., 240.
35. D. Yates, *Lower than Vermin* (London, 1950); A. J. Smithers, *Dornford Yates* (London, 1982); Martin, 'Vermin Club'.
36. Reproduced in Martin, 'Vermin Club', 18.
37. See correspondence in CPA, CCO 3/1/9, CCO 3/3/16, CCO 3/2/29.
38. *The Times*, 28 July 1948, CCO 3/1/9.
39. CCO 3/1/9, with picture of badge; also reproduced in Martin, 'Vermin Club', 20.
40. Titlely to Woolton, 6 August 1948, CPA, CCO 3/1/9.
41. Mann to Titley, 22 August 1948, CPA, CCO 3/1/9.
42. Report on the co-ordination meeting of the Vermin Club, held at Caxton Hall, Westminster, Friday 6 August 1948, 1, para 5, point 2, CPA, CCO 3/1/9.
43. Foot, *Aneurin Bevan, Vol. 2*, 249, 250.
44. Mann to Maxse, 8 April 1949, CPA, CCO 3/2/29.
45. Vermin Club, chairman's half-yearly report, 6 October 1949, points 8 and 9, CPA, CCO 3/2/29.
46. Mann to Maxse, 8 April 1949, CPA, CCO 3/2/29.
47. Report on Vermin Club co-ordination meeting, CCO 3/1/9.
48. *How Vile a Vermin are You?*, Vermin Club leaflet, CPA, CCO 3/2/29.
49. Ibid.
50. Vermin Club Constitution, points 2a (i, ii) and 4c, CPA, CCO 3/2/29.
51. Vermin Club, chairman's half-yearly report, 6 October 1949, points 12 and 13.
52. Ibid., point 10, item 6.
53. Vermin Club Constitution, Rule 4b.
54. Vermin Club, chairman's half-yearly report, 6 October 1949, point 20. Points 18 and 19 also note the production of posters and leaflets for distribution to 'business houses in danger of nationalisation'.
55. Baker-White to Woolton, 16 July 1948, CPA, CCO 3/1/9.

56. Spencer to Chapman-Walker, re Baker-White's letter, 19 July 1948, CPA, CCO 3/1/9.
57. Maxse to CCO area agents, 30 September 1949, CPA, CCO 3/2/29.
58. Mann to Maxse, 8 April 1949, CPA, CCO 3/2/29.
59. Ibid.
60. Mann to Hay, internal CCO memo, 16 August 1948, CPA, CCO 3/1/9.
61. Maxse to general director, CPA, CCO 3/1/9.
62. H. G. Nicholas, *The British General Election of 1950* (London, 1951), 249.
63. For example, V. D. Williams to CCO, 25 September 1951, CPA, CCO 3/3/16: 'Dear Sirs, I am rather anxious, particularly in view of the general election being so near, to obtain two "VERMIN" buttonhole badges. I have tried Birmingham HQs but without success. Can you possibly help me? I will remit the cash immediately I hear from you.'

8

Industrial Relations as 'Human Relations': Conservatism and Trade Unionism, 1945–64[1]

PETER DOREY

Although the relationship between the Conservative Party and the trade unions is generally seen as one characterised by conflict and suspicion,[2] the early post-war period is notable for the extent to which senior Conservatives pursued a much more constructive and conciliatory approach towards organised labour. This derived from a recognition that the Conservative Party needed to respond more positively to the working class in the wake of Labour's landslide election victory in July 1945, even though Conservatives formally downplayed the significance of class as a source of socio-political identity. Not only did the Conservative Party need to persuade ordinary working people that it could be trusted to protect and promote their economic and industrial well-being, it also needed to assuage any anxieties harboured by other sections of British society that the return of a Conservative government would herald a revival of class conflict and industrial strife.

Furthermore, many Conservatives hoped that, by persuading trade unionists and ordinary working people that they had nothing to fear from a Conservative government, the apparent allegiance of much of the working class to the Labour Party might be weakened. In this respect, by linking the advocacy of industrial partnership to a professed commitment to both 'high and stable' levels of employment, and defence of the new welfare state, many Conservatives hoped that trade unionism could be depoliticised, and organised labour's dalliance with socialism diluted.

In this context, Conservative 'progressives' recognised the need for the party to broaden its appeal in the industrial regions of Britain, with Cuthbert Alport tartly observing that while 'I do not suppose that the average voter in Worthing, who is remote from industry, is interested in the problems of industrial relations ... the outcome of the next election will depend on whether we are able to convince the factory worker' that we fully intend to pursue a constructive approach to industrial relations, for it was in 'the industries of Manchester and Birmingham ... urban, industrial areas' that the Conservative Party needed to win support in order to be returned to office.[3]

As part of the Conservatives' attempt at broadening their electoral support following Labour's 1945 victory, the party established the Central Trade Union Advisory Committee in 1947, followed later by the Conservative Trade Unionists. It was hoped that these bodies would facilitate a conduit between the Conservative Party and ordinary industrial workers, whereby Conservative trade unionists in the workplace could simultaneously explain the party's principles and policies to their workmates (thereby countering the arguments of the left), while keeping the party's leadership informed of the grievances and issues with which ordinary working people were concerned. It was also envisaged that Conservative trade unionists would be able to reduce the power and influence of the left by playing a more active role inside the trade unions, through attendance at meetings, and possibly by standing as candidates in trade union elections. However, this was somewhat problematic, given that one of the avowed objectives of these Conservative trade union(ist) bodies was the promotion of 'non-political trade unionism', although a further problem they faced was the instinctive and ideological suspicion or hostility of trade unionism which emanated from the notably petit-bourgeois grass-roots membership of the Conservative Party.[4]

Meanwhile, although a more interventionist approach to the economy, and a conciliatory approach to industrial relations, were primarily intended to secure support for the Conservative Party among both trade unionists and floating voters fearful of a revival of class conflict, there was also a desire among more prescient and progressive Conservatives to appeal to sections of the intelligentsia. This reflected concern in some quarters at the Conservative Party's poor standing with intellectuals, many of whom, it was lamented, had previously 'been singled out by the

Liberals, socialists and communists as being a most important element in the struggle to mould public opinion', while the Conservative Party had 'always underestimated the sort of people known as the intelligentsia'. Yet it was these people, namely 'the professional classes, school and university teachers, writers, scientists, economists', some senior Conservatives believed, who were 'captured by the Fabian Society and who today dominate the Socialist Party'. If the Conservative Party continued to ignore them, then 'they will have no alternative but to gravitate towards the left as they did between the wars.[5]

In order to render the Conservative Party more attractive to sections of the working class especially, there emerged a conscious effort to banish old enmities and animosities, particularly those derived from the 1926 General Strike, the consequent 1927 Trades Disputes Act, and the Great Depression of the 1930s. Many Conservatives viewed the end of the war as a particularly propitious opportunity to seek a fresh start with ordinary working people, while approaching the trade unions in a spirit of considerable conciliation.

To some extent, this entailed revising and rewriting Conservative history, downplaying the attachment to unfettered market forces, and claiming that the party had always recognised a legitimate role for responsible trade unionism. With regard to the former, it was claimed that the Conservative Party 'has never been frightened of using the power of the state to improve social conditions, to organise economic effort, and to provide collective services'.[6] Support for a more interventionist role for the state had been urged by the Tory Reform Committee during the war, for while it was formed, in 1943, primarily to urge acceptance of the previous year's Beveridge Report, it soon 'developed into an organised faction, trying to change Conservative thinking about government management of the economy'.[7] To this end, one of the Tory Reform Committee's founders (and an early chairman), Lord Hinchingbrooke, claimed:

> True Conservative opinion is horrified at the damage done to this country since the last war by 'individualist' businessmen, financiers and speculators ranging freely in a laissez-faire economy and creeping unnoticed into the fold of Conservatism to insult the party with their vote at elections ... and to injure the character of our people. It would wish nothing better than that these men should collect their baggage and depart. True Conservatism has nothing whatever to do with them and their obnoxious policies.[8]

Similar sentiments were expressed by Anthony Eden, when he informed delegates at the Conservatives' 1947 conference that 'We are not a party of unbridled, brutal capitalism, and never have been. Although we believe in personal responsibility, and personal initiative in business, we are not the political children of the laissez-faire school. We opposed them decade after decade.' The same year heard Quintin Hogg (later Lord Hailsham) claim that the Conservative Party had, for a long time, been highly critical of laissez-faire capitalism because it entailed 'an ungodly and rapacious scramble for ill-gotten gains, in the course of which the rich appeared to get richer and the poor poorer'.[9]

In an effort to present the Conservative Party's previous relationship with the trade unions in a more favourable light, it was argued that, from the repeal of the Combination Acts onwards, Conservative administrations had introduced various legislation of benefit to trade unions and ordinary workers, and that the party had long recognised the valuable role of trade unionism in a free society.[10] This attempt at putting a more attractive gloss on the Conservative Party's previous encounters and experiences with organised labour was accompanied by a simultaneous attempt at establishing a more conciliatory and constructive approach towards industrial relations and trade unionism after the war. As such, the period from 1945 to 1964 remains unique for the extent to which the Conservative Party sought to win the trust and co-operation of organised labour, and thereby refused to invoke legislation either to curb the activities of the trade unions, or to regulate industrial relations. While the Conservative Party was willing to countenance an unprecedented degree of government regulation in economic and social affairs after 1945 (even though its rhetoric remained that of freedom and liberty), it was resolute in retaining a laissez-faire stance towards industrial relations and trade unionism, insisting repeatedly that legislative intervention would exacerbate existing problems and yield new ones.

THE GOLDEN AGE OF CONSERVATIVE CONCILIATION, 1945–60

The Industrial Charter

Although many within the Conservative Party had acquired a new respect for the trade unions in the wake of organised labour's role in the war effort, it was the scale of the Labour Party's victory in 1945 which convinced senior Conservatives that they needed to forge a more positive approach towards trade unionism and the industrial working class in Britain. This paralleled their acceptance of a more active, regulatory, role for the state in economic management. According to the party's parliamentary backbench Labour Committee:

> Organised labour has won its place as a full partner in the state to be consulted equally at governmental level … the trade union movement has now firmly established itself as one of the three interests that support our industrial fabric, namely: labour, management and government. The Conservative Party regards the existence of strong and independent trade unionism as an essential safeguard of freedom in an industrial society. It must be the purpose of a Conservative government to strengthen and encourage trade unions.[11]

Elsewhere in the Conservative Party, there was a concern that Labour's emphatic victory might herald a more permanent or substantive shift to the left in British politics and, as such, the Conservatives could not blithely assume that the electoral pendulum would swing back to them at the next election.[12] Thus did Leo Amery warn that there 'can be no permanent revival of Conservatism without a positive alternative policy to the policy of the socialist left … a clear and comprehensive restatement [of Disraeli's principles] in the light of present-day conditions'.[13]

It was in this context that the Conservative Party published *The Industrial Charter* in 1947, variously described thereafter as 'the most important post-war policy document produced by the Conservatives',[14] 'an early milestone' in the Conservative Party's 'adaptation to post-1945 politics',[15] 'a decisive moment in Conservative post-war history',[16] and 'the most memorable concession a free enterprise party ever made to the spirit of Keynesian economics'.[17] The *Industrial Charter* emerged following a demand by delegates at the Conservatives' 1946 conference for a 'statement giving in fuller detail the principles and programme of the party', whereupon an industrial policy committee was established by Winston Churchill, but chaired by Rab Butler. Four other members of the Conservatives' frontbench team sat on the committee (including Harold Macmillan), along with four backbenchers, with one commentator subsequently noting that 'the composition of the committee as a whole ensured that things would move in a progressive direction'.[18]

It was this industrial policy committee which produced the *Industrial Charter*, in which the Conservative Party's traditional belief in a free-market economy was now accompanied by an explicit acknowledgement of 'the need for central direction', and the need to ensure 'security in our social and industrial system'. With regard to organised labour *per se*, the *Industrial Charter* declared that the Conservative Party 'attaches the highest importance to the part to be played by the unions in guiding the national economy'.[19]

However, it was the third and final section of the *Industrial Charter* – entitled 'The Workers' Charter' – that most directly delineated a new Conservative philosophy to workplace industrial relations and the concomitant rights of employees. Declaring that the party's aim was 'to humanise, not nationalise' industry, the 'Workers' Charter' claimed that employees ought to be provided with a reasonable expectation of industrial security (of employment), improved incentives to develop skills and talent, and enhanced status generally. Such measures would constitute 'a series of standards in the field of industrial relations' to which employers would be expected to conform, although the 'Workers' Charter' was adamant that there could be no question of compulsion or legislative prescription. The proposals would only be effective to the extent that they were developed voluntarily and piecemeal, for the 'conditions of industrial life are too varied to be brought within the cramping grip of legislation', which thus meant that 'such a charter cannot be made the subject of an Act of Parliament'.[20]

To its authors and admirers in the Conservative Party, the *Industrial Charter* was 'the pioneer of "the middle way"',[21] a route which Macmillan himself had pointed to on more than one occasion during the inter-war period.[22] Indeed, it was explicitly acknowledged that one of the objectives of the *Industrial Charter* was 'to weld together the Liberal tradition of free enterprise with the … Tory concept of interventionism' and, in so doing, provide the Conservative Party with 'a new Tamworth manifesto'.[23] Some proponents also explicitly cited Disraeli's *Sybil*, and the need to overcome 'two nations' or, in this context, 'two sides' of industry, by promoting a 'united effort in a common cause'.[24] Conservatives subscribing to this perspective were therefore heartened by the evident existence of 'progressives in the party', for they were 'in far greater danger of being sabotaged by our own right wing than of being defeated … by the socialists … held back by these reactionaries on our right'.[25]

Yet, to these 'reactionaries' on the Conservative right, the *Industrial Charter* constituted what backbencher Sir Waldron

Smithers termed, at the party's 1947 conference, 'milk-and-water socialism'. Indeed, he subsequently penned a lengthy missive – entitled *Save England* – replete with portentious ecclesiastical references and biblical quotations, denouncing the *Industrial Charter* for 'its compromises with socialism and communism', and declaring that 'acceptance or rejection of the charter by the party is a matter of life and death for Britain, and therefore the whole world'.[26]

Macmillan's response to such criticisms was characteristically dismissive, declaring that when they claimed that the *Industrial Charter* was not Tory policy, what they really meant was that 'they wish it were not Tory policy'. He added: 'Fortunately, their wishes cannot be granted.'[27] Indeed, the *Industrial Charter* was endorsed by an overwhelming majority at the Conservatives' 1947 conference. Having been so endorsed, the principles enshrined in the *Industrial Charter* were reiterated two years later in the policy document the *Right Road for Britain*, which declared:

> Conservatives believe that the problems of industry are, first of all, human problems, and that continuous attention must be given to the personal relations between management and labour. The key to the proper working of British industry lies in humanising free enterprise, and not in nationalising it. Industrial relations must no longer be thought of in terms of two sides with interests which are permanently opposite and inevitably conflicting. Fundamentally, both management and labour have the same interest in the prosperity of their industry, and to this they must devote their attention in a spirit of co-operation and partnership. The spirit of partnership cannot be enforced by law.[28]

The principles and sentiments enshrined in the *Industrial Charter* and the *Right Road for Britain* thereupon provided the basis of the Conservative Party's approach towards trade unionism throughout the 1950s, while also serving, according to Rab Butler, 'to prove that Conservatives were human'.[29] In fact, Conservative trade union policy during this period comprised four main elements or principles, namely voluntarism, a socio-psychological critique of industrial conflict, advocacy of industrial partnership as an integral part of a human relations approach, and ministerial exhortation over the need for 'responsible' wage bargaining as an alternative to either a formal incomes policy or the abandonment of full employment. Each of these aspects will be considered briefly, before delineating the tensions which developed from the late 1950s onwards, and how these impacted upon the

Conservatives' non-interventionist stance with regard to trade unionism and industrial relations.

Voluntarism

Throughout the 1950s, the Conservative leadership refused to countenance legislation to curb the trade union activities or practices (most notably the closed shop and unofficial strikes) of which the party most disapproved. Instead, the emphasis was on leaving 'the two sides of industry' generally, and the trade unions in particular, to modify their behaviour, or adopt more responsible practices. The prevailing view within the Conservative Party during this period was that 'politics should be kept out of industry',[30] so that the government 'should, as far as it can, keep out of industrial negotiations', thereby enabling 'employers and trade unionists [to] be left to settle these matters through their negotiating machinery or through free bargaining'.[31]

Conservative ministers, especially those at the Ministry of Labour, consistently stated that legislation itself could not procure more harmonious relations in the workplace and, indeed, might actually exacerbate suspicion and distrust among employees, especially if any laws were introduced which appeared to favour employers. A constant refrain of senior Conservatives throughout this period was that 'industrial relations are human relations' and, as such, not amenable to legislative prescription. According to Robert Carr, actively involved in the One Nation Group, for example, 'it is upon voluntary agreement in industry that we must depend for good industrial relations ... good industrial relations cannot be enforced by laws'.[32] Walter Monckton, Minister of Labour from October 1951 to December 1955, explained to his colleagues that the Conservative Party's 'established policy [is] to leave the regulation of their relationships and the determination of terms and conditions of employment to employers and workers, normally acting through their collective organisations', thereby 'supporting the basic principles of industrial self-government'.[33]

What also underpinned ministerial determination to refrain from invoking industrial relations legislation during the 1950s was the recognition that any recourse to the statute book would fatally damage the trust of organised labour which the Conservative Party was painstakingly seeking to foster during this time, and thereby further strengthen the bond between the trade unions and the Labour Party. It was pointed out that 'as a government, we shall have to work with the trade unions ... the more you attack the trade unions, the more wholeheartedly the weight of their organisation will be flung into the next election against us, and this will count for far more than any odd votes you pick up by attacking them'.[34] Or, as Monckton noted, legislative intervention or prescription in relationships between employers and employees was likely to prove 'politically inexpedient and ineffective in practice'.[35] Thus Churchill instructed Monckton, upon appointing him Minister of Labour in 1951, to do his best 'to preserve industrial peace',[36] for he was 'determined that there should be no industrial strikes during his term as Prime Minister'.[37]

Inevitably, there were strikes during the 1950s, and this led certain quarters of the Conservative Party to call for legislation either to curb unofficial stoppages or to require ballots prior to industrial action. However, Iain Macleod, Monckton's successor at the Ministry of Labour from November 1955, refused to accede to such demands, insisting that by their very nature unofficial strikes – which constituted the vast majority of industrial stoppages – were unlikely to be affected by legislation.[38] As for the perennial backbench and annual conference demands for the introduction of statutory strike ballots, Macleod informed delegates at the Conservatives' 1956 conference that there was no evidence that ordinary trade union members were any less militant than their leaders, and therefore he did not accept the premise that ballots would necessarily yield any reduction in strike activity overall.[39] Besides, it was pointed out that there were logistical problems in seeking to invoke statutory ballots prior to strike action, not least of these being the sheer impracticability of fining or imprisoning large numbers of workers who engaged in strike action without having first participated in a ballot.[40]

A further rationale offered by the Conservative leadership for refusing to introduce trade union legislation during the 1950s was that such action might alienate 'moderate' trade unionists, and provide succour to the left. Monckton warned that, unless Conservatives 'carry with us the responsible elements, who are at present in the majority, we run the risk of uniting the whole trade union movement against us'.[41] Another argument invoked by senior Conservatives when seeking to defend voluntarism from perennial backbench or conference demands for trade union legislation, particularly vis-à-vis strike ballots, was to downplay the incidence or impact of industrial action.[42] In 1955 an internal party study even suggested that 'we seem to have got very near to the irreducible number of strikes'; it was suggested that the incidence of strike activity did not 'seem to provide adequate grounds for any widespread review of our policy on industrial relations'.[43]

The socio-psychological critique of industrial conflict

A further reason for ministerial reluctance to invoke legislation, particularly with regard to strikes, was the belief among some senior Conservatives that much industrial conflict was attributable less to 'reds under-the-bed' in the unions than to feelings of alienation among ordinary employees. To the extent that left-wing elements or militants did foment conflict in industry, they were only able to do so because of the existence of such alienation in the first place, which they were able to exploit; 'agitators can hardly make much headway unless they can find latent grievances to work on'.[44] Such alienation, it was suggested, partly derived from the growing size and scale of modern industry and the workplace, for this entailed a widening gulf between management at the top and the employees on the factory floor. At the same time, individual employees found it increasingly difficult to comprehend the significance or value of their particular role or tasks in the overall enterprise, so that a sense of alienation also fuelled a concomitant loss of self-esteem and self-worth. On numerous occasions, Anthony Eden especially lamented the tendency for modern industrial workers to be reduced, in effect, to a mere 'cog in the wheel'.[45] This was deemed to exacerbate the feelings of alienation and low self-worth which many workers now experienced, and which, according to Conservatives subscribing to a human relations approach to industrial relations, often underpinned much of the conflict which occurred between management and labour.

However, it was also recognised that security of employment had an important impact on the attitudes of many workers, to the extent that a Conservative commitment to maintaining high or full employment would itself contribute significantly to improved industrial relations and more positive attitudes on the part of employees. A senior Conservative Research Department official noted that the 'more irregular a man's employment, the greater is the temptation for him to develop irregular habits', whereas 'regular employment and wages tend to develop self-respect and other qualities valuable both to the worker himself and to his employer'. Too often, however, 'the manual worker is picked up and dropped again by industry to suit the circumstances of the moment', and the fact that he is also 'paid by the hour … tends to emphasise the fundamental insecurity of his position'. Such a situation 'does not accord well with our idea of the common interest of workers and management'.[46]

Other Conservative proponents of the human relations

approach also drew attention to this aspect, pointing out: 'Many of the difficulties now being experienced are the result of distrust of the motives of the Conservative Party, and fears of recurrent mass unemployment', a distrust which was 'of long standing', and thus in need of 'patience and persistence' in the application of Conservative principles and policies 'before it can be dispelled'.[47] In this respect, it was acknowledged that 'the memory of unemployment in the inter-war years is a spectre that can only be exorcised with the passage of time', and by 'the strengthening of mutual confidence between management and employees in conditions of at least fairly full employment'.[48]

The advocacy of industrial partnership

Many Conservatives were convinced that one of the most effective means of ameliorating the feelings of alienation and lack of self-worth which many workers experienced, and which sometimes flared up into industrial disputes, was to foster greater partnership in industry and the workplace. This would provide much of the answer to the question of how the contemporary industrial worker was 'to be helped to comprehend the social importance of his job and so of himself'.[49]

Conservative advocacy of industrial partnership certainly did not presuppose any equality between employers and employees – managerial authority remained inviolate – but it did envisage greater communication between management and labour. If there was more frequent and extensive dialogue between the 'two sides of industry', it was envisaged that suspicion would be overcome, sources of anxiety eradicated, and employees themselves would be likely to develop an appreciation both of the value of their own role to the enterprise's success, and of the rationale underpinning various managerial decisions. Robert Carr believed that, where management made a conscious effort to keep the workforce informed about what was happening in the company, smoother and more constructive industrial relations invariably ensued.[50] This view was shared by Churchill's successor as party leader and Prime Minister, Anthony Eden.[51] Throughout the latter half of the 1940s and into the 1950s, senior Conservatives consistently called for an end to 'us and them' attitudes between management and labour; what Eden once referred to as 'the "Maginot line" mentality in industry';[52] or what Sir William Robson Brown termed 'a form of inverse apartheid'.[53]

It was also believed that fostering a spirit of partnership, trust and co-operation between management and labour in the work-place would undermine the malign influence of the left. Harold Watkinson, who was (junior) Minister of Labour from 1952 to 1955, was confident that if employers provided their employees with an honest and straightforward account of the company's financial and commercial situation, they would dispel the false notions about the 'bloated profits of capitalism', which were propagated by communist agitators in the trade unions.[54] At a wider level, it was also envisaged that industrial partnership would provide workers 'with a practical insight into the working of the free enter-prise system'.[55] Either way, it was envisaged that co-partnership schemes would provide 'a very good basis for more harmonious industrial relations', especially when pursued by 'an enlightened management'.[56]

In accordance with the prevailing voluntarist ethos, and the recognition that trust and co-operation could not be enforced by statute, Conservative proponents of industrial partnership insisted on the need for industrial partnership schemes to be developed freely and pragmatically. Co-partnership was 'a plant of delicate growth and not … just a bit of mechanism' and, as such, any hint of compulsion would prove fatal.[57] Consequently, while Conservative Party policy was warmly to welcome industrial part-nership schemes, and to reiterate the general case for them at opportune moments, the emphasis remained on leaving manage-ment and labour 'free to adopt the arrangements best suited to their individual circumstances'.[58]

Meanwhile, to further convince workers that the Conservatives were not merely the party of employers, it was suggested that its leaders and MPs should 'publicly condemn known examples of anti-social behaviour by industrialists, landlords, and wealthy individuals of all kinds, because such people are automatically labelled Conservative'. At the same time, local Conservative asso-ciations were urged not to elect or select officials or local govern-ment candidates 'with bad records as employers, landlords, contractors or traders'. There was also a suggestion that the party should not select too many employers as parliamentary candi-dates, because this 'fosters the idea of the Conservative Party being the bosses' party', although there was also a recognition that, if more working men were adopted as candidates, they were likely 'to be distrusted by [their] fellows'.[59]

Yet enthusiasm for industrial partnership schemes was by no means universal in the Conservative Party, and even some Conservatives normally considered to be on the party's 'progressive' wing, such as Robert Carr, were not entirely convinced about the value of 'co-partnership', which he suspected was of 'limited application'.[60] Other Conservatives also wondered whether the party was placing *too* much emphasis on the alleged virtues of industrial partnership as a means of facilitating more harmonious industrial relations or making employees feel more valued, suggesting that it was 'the amount of money that they can pick up, and not improvement of status, which really interests them'.[61]

Ministerial exhortation over the need for 'responsible' wage bargaining

Just as Conservative ministers were loathe to intervene directly in industrial relations and trade union affairs throughout the 1950s, so too did they refrain from seeking to regulate wages and salaries via incomes policies. Their faith in the potential of education and enlightenment, whereby reasonable men and women would respond positively to rational explanation, extended from industrial relations into the sphere of pay determination. Therefore, the emphasis vis-à-vis wages and salaries was on the maintenance of free collective bargaining, albeit conducted 'responsibly', between employers and trade unions.[62] However, ministers felt obligated to issue warnings about the dangers of inflation and higher unemployment if 'excessive' pay increases were secured.[63] Such ministerial exhortations were not deemed incompatible with the Conservatives' general view: 'The principle of collective bargaining, unfettered from outside, is the foundation of industrial relations, questioned by neither party in industry, nor any party in the state.'[64]

The three possible alternatives to free (but responsible) collective bargaining were deemed to be using legislation to curb trade union activities and powers, permitting a rise in unemployment as a counter to excessive wage increases, and introducing a formal incomes policy. As already explained, legislative curbs on trade unionism were emphatically rejected by a Conservative leadership determined to avoid conflict with organised labour, and unconvinced that legislation would actually eradicate the aspects of trade unionism which the party tended to find most objectionable.

By 1957 Macmillan was acknowledging that there was 'a wide feeling among our own supporters that the thing to do is have a row with the trade unions', yet he dismissed such sentiments as 'merely an instinctive reaction of a class of people who resent the depression of their own standards at the time when the standards of so many people are rising so rapidly'. Certainly, Macmillan insisted, there was 'no object in having a row with the trade unions per se'. Indeed, he ventured to suggest that 'trade union leaders have been very moderate in exploiting their economic opportunities', for many other people 'in similar circumstances would have raised much more the prices of their commodities'.[65] There was increasing impatience in the party with the trade unions in general and the Conservative government's own voluntarist approach in particular. One indication of this was the programme of legislative reform proposed by the Inns of Court Conservative and Unionist Society pamphlet, *A Giant's Strength*, in 1958.

The second option, permitting a rise in unemployment to offset – and effectively punish – 'excessive' pay increases, was also rejected by most of the Conservative leadership, on grounds of both principle and practicability. In terms of principle, the post-1945 Conservative Party was (in accordance with the *Industrial Charter*, and numerous other public pronouncements) committed to maintaining the highest possible level of employment. With regard to the issue of practicability, most of the Conservative leadership – with the notable exception of the Chancellor of the Exchequer, Peter Thorneycroft[66] – rejected the option of abandoning high or full employment because they were persuaded that the level of unemployment required 'to put a really effective stop on wage increases' would be 'politically disastrous', to the extent that 'no government in the UK would be likely to push unemployment as far as this'.[67] This vital consideration was endorsed by the party's own Industrial Research Committee, when it warned the leadership that if unemployment were permitted to rise above three-quarters of a million 'under a Conservative administration … great and lasting harm would be done to the Conservative Party', for such a figure was 'probably a fair estimate of the maximum unemployment the country is prepared to stand'. Anything higher, the committee warned, and 'the Conservative Party is likely to get badly concussed … might indeed sustain a shock from which it would have great difficulty in recovering'.[68] Furthermore, Macleod suggested that, even if the cabinet was prepared to countenance higher unemployment as a response to 'excessive' wage increases, this would probably not, in itself, weaken the power of the trade unions.[69] In any case, it was widely acknowledged that Macmillan was determined to avoid a return to higher unemployment, haunted as he was by memories of the Great Depression when MP for Stockton-on-Tees during the 1930s.[70]

The third option, namely the introduction of a formal incomes policy, was also rejected by Conservative ministers during the 1950s, partly because of the dual commitment to the principles of free collective bargaining and non-intervention in industrial relations, and partly because of doubts about the practicability and enforceability of an incomes policy, particularly because the trade unions themselves were unlikely to agree to such a policy.[71]

Yet none of this is to suggest that Conservative ministers took absolutely no action in the sphere of wage determination during the latter half of the 1950s; on occasion, they did seek to stand firm against pay claims and industrial action in the public sector. The most notable example of this occurred in the summer of 1958, when the government was faced with a strike by London bus drivers in support of a claim for a 25 shillings-per-week pay increase. This time, Conservative ministers – especially the Minister of Labour, Iain Macleod – refused to yield, hoping that by standing firm a clear signal would be sent to other workers, and also envisaging that employers in the private sector would henceforth be heartened enough to take a stronger stance when faced with 'excessive' pay claims.[72] On this occasion, ministerial resistance proved highly successful: after a stoppage of seven weeks, the London bus drivers returned to work without their pay claim being met. It was, according to one commentator, a 'humiliating defeat' for the busmen and their union, the TGWU.[73]

One other innovation of this period was the establishment of a Council on Prices, Productivity and Incomes. More commonly known as the Cohen council, its chairman, Lord Cohen, a judge, was accompanied by two senior economists. Their brief was to consider the impact on full employment and inflation of increases in prices, productivity and pay. Although the council was not vested with any statutory powers, it was hoped that its 'independent authority' would yield 'a useful effect on public opinion', and *inter alia* elicit greater moderation by the trade unions.[74] However, commentators have subsequently concluded that the Cohen council was an ineffective body, merely 'producing a number of hand-wringing and ineffectual reports that exhorted trade unions and workers to restrain their wage demands', which had no discernible effect.[75]

THE HUMAN RELATIONS APPROACH UNDER STRAIN, 1960–64

Although *A Giant's Strength* had indicated a hardening of opinion against the party's constructive and conciliatory approach to trade unionism during the late 1950s, it was during the early 1960s that tensions become more pronounced and the proponents of the human relations approach found themselves increasingly on the defensive. By this time, there was a growing realisation that Britain was experiencing a relative economic decline, with a number of other industrial countries evincing higher rates of productivity and faster rates of growth. Cognisance of this served to fuel Conservative concern about both the incidence of unofficial strikes, and the apparently inflationary impact of 'excessive' wage increases demanded by the unions. In this context, a growing number of Conservatives were persuaded that their party had pursued trade union conciliation and industrial partnership too far for too long, and that 'a new Tory initiative in industrial relations' was needed.[76] Even Harold Macmillan, while still fully determined to secure greater partnership – both within industry, between management and trade unions, and, more generally, between the state and industry – was unable to conceal his despair and frustration with the trade unions on occasions.[77]

Free collective bargaining called into question

By the summer of 1961 the economic situation was deemed serious enough to warrant the imposition of a 'pay pause' for the public sector. This was to last until the following spring, by which time the Macmillan government hoped to have secured agreement on a longer-term pay policy. It was hoped that alongside any economic benefits this pay pause would have a psychological and educative effect, alerting the trade unions to the seriousness of Britain's economic situation, and the concomitant need for much greater moderation and restraint.

Certainly, by the early 1960s, there was a growing recognition that a more explicit or formal pay policy was required if full employment and price stability were to be sustained, although Macmillan remained adamant that any incomes policies would have to be derived from consultation with the trade unions, and thus based on voluntary agreement. Statutory control of pay (or prices) was emphatically ruled out.[78] Pending a longer-term voluntary incomes policy, 1962 witnessed the establishment of two particular economic bodies. Firstly, a National Incomes Commission was created, its role being to consider and comment on pay increases (referred to it by the government) in the context of the 'national interest'. Like the Cohen council, however, it had no powers and was similarly ineffective.

The second institutional innovation of 1962 was the National Economic Development Council (NEDC), a tripartite body in which economic ministers, trade union leaders and employers' representatives would meet to consider, on a regular basis, the performance and problems of the British economy. Although the NEDC was not formally responsible for determining wages or formulating an incomes policy, Conservative ministers clearly envisaged that it would serve to alert trade union leaders to the economic facts of life, and thereby persuade them of the need for wage restraint.[79] In this last respect, the establishment of the NEDC reflected a continued belief in the efficacy of partnership with the trade unions, and the concomitant faith in the power of persuasion and dialogue in securing more responsible behaviour. Genuine discussion, not government diktat, continued to be viewed by senior Conservatives as the most desirable or realistic means of securing more harmonious industrial relations and more moderate pay bargaining.

Indeed, there was an implicit assumption – or hope – that, if such moderation and responsibility could be secured through the type of state–trade union partnership offered by the NEDC, then the backbench and grass-roots pressure for industrial legislation would dissipate. In the meantime, therefore, Conservative ministers continued to promote the voluntarist, human relations approach to industrial relations, and reiterated the argument that punitive or prescriptive legislation would almost certainly prove counterproductive.

A last-ditch defence of voluntarism and human relations

In response to the growing backbench and grass-roots impatience with the trade unions – or, rather, impatience with the party leadership's refusal to invoke legislation against the unions – in May 1962 Rab Butler established an Industrial Relations Committee. Yet, having considered the issues involved, the committee reiterated the practical difficulties which would arise from attempts to ban unofficial strikes or impose statutory ballots prior to strike action (measures routinely demanded by sundry Conservative back-benchers and conference delegates), pointing out that prohibition of strikes had not proved effective during (and immediately after) the Second World War. Furthermore, it was noted that, even if legislation were invoked to ban unofficial strikes, this would mean that only stoppages called by a trade union would be deemed lawful. This would effectively deny non-trade unionists the right to engage in industrial action, or oblige them to join a trade union against their wishes in order to enjoy legal protection. As to the perennial demand that trade union immunities should be reduced by amending the 1906 Trade Disputes Act, it was argued that, if trade unions were rendered liable for the unofficial action of some of their members, this would 'leave the door wide open for a small group of militant extremists to bring about the financial collapse of any trade union – perhaps especially those under moderate control'.

Consequently, the committee concluded that legislation would be 'inappropriate and unenforceable', and thus reiterated the classic voluntarist tenet that 'the state by itself cannot enforce better industrial relations', which therefore meant that 'the surest way to progress is through the encouragement of responsibility within industry itself'.[80] This perspective was endorsed by John Hare, Minister of Labour from July 1960 to October 1963, who continued to espouse the view:

> Legislation would cut across the present policy of trying to bring about a general improvement in industrial relations on a voluntary basis ... it would end the prospect of further progress [and] cause a head-on collision with the trade union movement. It might lead them to withhold their co-operation over the whole field of relations with the government.[81]

Had the cabinet been more inclined to take immediate action, it could have done so in the context of the landmark *Rookes* v. *Barnard* court case of February 1964. This judgement effectively weakened some of the legal immunities that trade unions had enjoyed since 1906, and thus meant that the unions themselves might have proved more amenable to some kind of review at this time.[82] An alternative to immediate legislation canvassed by many in the Conservative Party during the early 1960s was the establishment of an inquiry into trade union law and practices, possibly in the form of a royal commission. However, this was also rejected by the leadership, although some form of review was promised after the next general election. Such a deferment was justified on the grounds that 'the law in relation to trade unions should be reviewed in an atmosphere free from political controversy',[83] an atmosphere which was highly unlikely to pertain with a general election on the horizon.

With the 1964 general election looming, many senior Conservatives doubtless shared the feelings of Macleod, who 'felt frankly schizophrenic' about what the party should do about trade unionism. He was torn between recognition that some kind of action was needed and anxiety about the likely repercussions. Legislation could fuel union hostility towards the Conservative Party, thereby undermining the efforts of the previous ten years to promote conciliation and co-partnership.[84] Such anxiety was evidently shared by Ray Mawby, a former shop steward and president of the Conservative Trade Unionists Advisory Committee, who felt compelled to warn: 'Legislation in the main is negative and deters rather than intitiates action', so that 'a spate of legislation could easily do irreparable damage'.[85] Similarly, the Conservative Parliamentary Labour Committee remained adamant – even in the wake of the *Rookes* v. *Barnard* judgement – that 'the law and its apparatus of injunctions, damages, fines, penal sanctions, etc. has little to contribute to the solution of the problems of industrial relations ... Laws have been found from experience to be almost totally unenforceable and to do more harm than good.'[86]

The Conservative Party therefore contested the 1964 election pledging that 'the law affecting trade unions and employers' associations ... will be the subject of an early inquiry', although there remained a commitment to securing partnership with the trade unions via the NEDC.[87] However, the election defeat ensured that the Conservative Party had to conduct its own review of trade union law in opposition. (The narrowly victorious Labour government itself launched an inquiry into industrial relations and trade unionism via a royal commission chaired by Lord Donovan.) What subsequently emerged from the Conservative Party's own review of trade union law – conducted as part of a much more general and fundamental review of party policies – was a rather more legalistic approach to industrial relations which subsequently yielded the ill-fated 1971 Industrial Relations Act.[88]

The loss of the 1964 general election thus heralded a more conflictual and confrontational stance towards the trade unions by the Conservative Party, an approach which – with the exception of a brief attempt at reconciliation and renewed partnership during 1972–74 – prevailed for the remainder of the twentieth century.[89] Indeed, many of these subsequently became part of the new right. Their ideas and policies acquired greater support and legitimacy in parts of the Conservative Party during the latter half of the 1970s, particularly in the context of accelerating economic decline. Furthermore, these newer Conservatives believed that Britain's economic and industrial problems had been exacerbated by the failure of the 1951–64 Conservative governments to tackle trade union power. These were Conservatives who brooked no criticism of the free market, and who had a visceral hatred of the trade unions. To this new generation of Conservatives, their predecessors' refusal to legislate against the trade unions, and the concomitant advocacy of partnership, was merely a manifestation of craven cowardice and abject appeasement. Subsequent Conservative governments, these new Conservatives reckoned, would have to repair the damage wrought as a consequence of their predecessors' conciliatory stance towards the trade unions. If this meant confrontation and conflict between the Conservatives and the trade unions in the future, then so be it.

CONCLUSION

A major feature of 1951–64 Conservative governments was the extent to which the party leadership sought to avoid clashing with the trade unions. Instead, as we have seen, senior Conservatives were most anxious to win the trust and co-operation of organised labour, and thus to banish old enmities. The scale of the Labour Party's election victory in 1945 was undoubtedly a major factor in obliging the Conservatives to give more careful consideration to broadening the party's appeal. With the Liberal Party having been eclipsed by Labour as the main non-Conservative alternative, and the working class (manual or blue-collar workers) during this period reckoned to be numerically the largest social class in Britain, it was deemed vital that the Conservatives reach out beyond the middle class; simple electoral arithmetic alone made this necessary. In particular, the Conservatives hoped to secure support from skilled workers – the C2s in modern parlance – who would, it was hoped, prove more amenable to the party's advocacy of rewards for individual effort and espousal of social mobility, particularly if they felt anxious about Labour's professed egalitarian principles. The Conservative Party thus found it essential to appeal both to sections of the working class, and to floating voters too for, if either of these groups feared that the return of the Conservatives would unleash a new bout of industrial conflict and class warfare, they would withhold their support from the party, thereby enabling Labour to become 'the natural party of government'.

Certainly, some Conservatives feared that Labour's 1945 election victory signified a clear shift to the left among public opinion, reflected and reinforced by the perceived dominance of left-of-centre ideas among intellectuals (particularly the Fabians), who sought to shape the policy agenda. Prescient Conservatives recognised that, to win the battle of ideas, and regain electoral support from all sections of British society, the party would have to articulate a more 'progressive' alternative of its own.

In the sphere of industrial relations, this entailed a concerted effort at crafting a constructive and conciliatory relationship with the trade unions and organised labour. Hence the switch of emphasis away from advocacy of legislation against the trade unions towards closer partnership with them. Greater communication, not statutory compulsion, was portrayed as the most effective way of ameliorating industrial conflict, particularly in the context of the prevailing human relations perspective, which viewed such strife as socio-pyschological in origin, rather than being politically motivated. Such a perspective insisted that legislative measures against the trade unions would merely exacerbate poor industrial relations, and so the dominant strategy in this context was that of *voluntarism*.

What further underpinned this conciliatory approach to organised labour between 1945 and 1964 was the dominance of so many progressive Conservatives in the higher echelons of the party, as personified by those senior figures who subscribed to the 'one nation' variant of British Conservatism. Butler himself insisted:

> It is the task of the present generation of Conservatives to found our modern faith on the basis of two features of this age, namely the existence of universal adult suffrage and the acceptance by authority of the responsibility for ensuring a certain standard of living, of employment and of security for all.[90]

That the Conservative Party won three successive election victories during the 1950s seemed a clear vindication of this constructive and conciliatory mode of Conservatism; the Conservatives had, it seemed, reconnected with the masses.

NOTES

1. I would like to express my sincere thanks to Martin Maw, formerly Conservative Party archivist at the Bodleian Library, Oxford, and to his successor, Jill Spellman, for their unstinting efficiency and helpfulness in retrieving the documents and files which were consulted for this chapter. I would also like to thank the staff of the Public Record Office, Kew, for their tireless assistance in providing me with requested cabinet papers and ministerial memoranda for the 1951–64 period.
2. For a general overview, see Peter Dorey, *The Conservative Party and the Trade Unions* (London, 1995); Andrew Taylor, 'The Party and the Trade Unions', in Anthony Seldon and Stuart Ball (eds), *Conservative Century: The Conservative Party since 1900* (Oxford,

1994), 499–543.

3. *Conservative Agents' Journal*, 330 (May 1948), 333 (August 1948), Conservative Party Archive (CPA), Bodleian Library.

4. Andrew Rowe, 'Conservatives and Trade Unionists', in Zig Layton-Henry (ed.), *Conservative Party Politics* (Basingstoke, 1980), 216–17.

5. *Conservative Agents' Journal*, 333 (August 1948).

6. Cuthbert Alport, *About Conservative Principles* (London, 1946), 21.

7. Andrew Gamble, *The Conservative Nation* (London, 1974), 33; see also J. D. Hoffman, *The Conservative Party in Opposition, 1945–51* (London, 1964), 40–1.

8. Lord Hinchingbrooke, *Full Speed Ahead: Essays in Tory Reform* (London, 1944).

9. Quintin Hogg, *The Case for Conservatism* (London, 1947), 51.

10. See, for example, 'Notes for Sir Eric Errington at Aldershot', 10 March 1959, 'Draft Notes for the Prime Minister's Speech to TUNAC', 26 February 1959, and 'Notes for Mr Eden – Industrial Relations', 17 March 1954, CPA, Conservative Research Department (CRD) 2/7/6.

11. Parliamentary Labour Committee, 'Report of the Trade Union Problems Sub-committee', 2 May 1951, CPA, ACP 3/1(51)13.

12. Lord Hinchingbrooke, 'The Course of Conservative Politics', *Quarterly Review,* January 1946; Quintin Hogg, 'Too Many Micawbers in the Tory Party', *Daily Mail*, 11 September 1945; Harold Macmillan, 'Strength Through – What?', *Oxford Mail*, 26 January 1946.

13. Leo Amery, *The Conservative Future* (London, 1946), 5.

14. T. F. Lindsay and M. Harrington, *The Conservative Party 1918–1979* (London, 1979), 151.

15. Taylor, 'The Party and the Trade Unions', 513.

16. Ian Gilmour and Mark Garnett, *Whatever Happened to the Tories: The Conservative Party since 1945* (London, 1997), 34.

17. Anthony Howard, *RAB: The Life of R. A. Butler* (London, 1988), 155.

18. John Ramsden, *The Making of Conservative Party Policy* (London, 1980), 109.

19. *The Industrial Charter: A Statement of Conservative Industrial Policy* (Conservative and Unionist Central Office, 1947), 2–4, 21.

20. Ibid., 28–9.

21. Fraser to Clarke, 8 January 1948, CPA, CRD 2/7/1.

22. Harold Macmillan *et al.*, *Industry and the State* (London, 1927); Harold Macmillan, *The Middle Way* (London, 1937).

23. Ramsden, *Making of Conservative Party Policy,* 110.

24. Michael Fraser, 'The Industrial Charter', December 1947, CPA, CRD 2/7/1.

25. Verity to Butler, 24 May 1947, CPA, CRD 2/7/30(1).

26. Smithers to Butler *et al.*, July 1947, CPA, CRD 2/7/29; for similar invective against *The Industrial Charter*, see also Cooke to Butler, 20 May 1947, CPA, CRD 2/7/30(1); Jackson to Butler, June 1947, CPA, CRD 2/7/29; and [name illegible] to Butler, 12 July 1947, Lancaster to Butler, 18 May 1947, Marshall to Butler, 19 May 1947, Morris to Butler, 12 May 1947, all in CPA, CRD 2/7/30(2).

27. Harold Macmillan, *Tides of Fortune 1945–1955* (London, 1969), 306.

28. *The Right Road for Britain* (Conservative and Unionist Central Office, 1949), 23.

29. Advisory Committee on Policy, 19th meeting, 18 June 1954, CPA, ACP (54).

30. 'Industrial Relations – Draft Report', 11 June 1954, CPA, ACP 3 /4(54) 34; see also Douglas to Carr, 30 July 1956, Public Record Office (PRO), LAB 43/280.

31. 'Some Background Facts concerning Industrial Relations', 15 February 1954, CPA, PLC(54) 1.

32. *House of Commons Debates*, 5th series, 568, col. 2127.

33. Memorandum by Minister of Labour, 'Survey of Present Situation', 25 July 1955, PRO, CAB 134/1273, IR(55) 10.

34. Chapman-Walker to Clarke, 4 April 1950, CPA, CRD 2/12/5.

35. Memorandum by Minister of Labour, 'Survey of Present Situation', 25 July 1955; see also Bishop to Macmillan, 17 May 1961, PRO, PREM 11/3570.

36. Quoted in Lord Birkenhead, *Walter Monckton* (London, 1969), 276.

37. Lord Woolton, *Memoirs* (London, 1959), 279–80.

38. *House of Commons Debates*, 5th series, 568, col. 1285. Churchill himself declared that the disadvantages of introducing compulsory strike ballots would greatly outweigh any advantages: ibid., 522, cols. 835–6.

39. See also Advisory Committee on Policy, 33rd meeting, 30 April 1958, CPA, ACP (58).
40. 'Secret Ballots before Strike Action', 2 August 1956, CPA, CRD 2/7/6.
41. Monckton to Eden, 2 June 1955, PRO PREM 11/921.
42. See, for example, ibid.; 'Notes for Mr Eden – Industrial Relations', 17 March 1954, CPA, CRD 2/7/6; 'Some Background Facts concerning Industrial Relations', 15 February 1954, CPA, PLC(54) 1.
43. 'Industrial Relations – A Progress Report', 21 October 1955, CPA, ACP (55) 40; John Hare, 'Industrial Relations – Unofficial Strikes', 28 January 1963, ACP (63) 103. See also 'Some Background Facts concerning Industrial Relations', 15 February 1954, CPA, CRD, PLC(54) 1; 'Draft for Report on the Workers' Charter', 2 May 1951, CPA, PLC(51) 4.
44. 'Report of the Industrial Relations Sub-committee', 9 May 1963. CPA, ACP(63) 105, IRC (62) 33.
45. See, for example, *The Times*, 4 November 1946, 21 March 1947.
46. Michael Fraser, *The Worker in Industry* (London, 1948), 15.
47. Sub-committee on Political Education, 'Report of the Working Party on the Approach to the Industrial Worker', 20 July 1950, CPA, CRD 2/7/6.
48. 'Problems of Social Balance in Industry', 15 November 1955, CPA, CRD 2/7/14, IRC 21.
49. Ibid.
50. *House of Commons Debates*, 5th series, 568, col. 2127.
51. Anthony Eden, *Freedom and Order* (London, 1947), 429–30; see also David Clarke, *The Conservative Faith in the Modern Age* (London, 1947), 29.
52. Quoted in Conservative Research Department, *Notes on Current Politics, 2: Economic and Industrial Affairs* (London, January 1956), 10.
53. *House of Commons Debates*, 5th series, 636, col. 1931, 17 March 1961.
54. *The Times*, 20 October 1950.
55. 'Co-Partnership – 1955', 21 October 1955, CPA, ACP (55) 39.
56. 'Co-Partnership –1952', 10 March 1952, CPA, CRD 2/7/7.
57. Heathcoat-Amory to Fraser, 28 February 1952, CPA, CRD 2/7/7.
58. 'Co-Partnership – 1955', 21 October 1955, CPA, ACP (55) 39.
59. Sub-Committee on Political Education, 'Report of the Working Party on the Approach to the Industrial Worker', 20 July 1950, CPA, CRD 2/7/6.
60. Carr to Fraser, 30 March 1953 and 14 May 1953, CPA, CRD 2/7/7.
61. Bennett to Alport, 22 December 1948, CPA, CRD 2/7/29; see also Sub-committee on Political Education, 'Report of the Working Party on the Approach to the Industrial Worker', 20 July 1950, CPA, CRD 2/7/6.
62. For a full discussion of Conservative approaches to pay determination during this period, see Peter Dorey, *Wage Politics in Britain: The Rise and Fall of Incomes Policies since 1945* (Brighton, 2001), ch. 3.
63. The most notable example being the White Paper, *The Economic Implications of Full Employment*, published in March 1956.
64. 'Draft White Paper on Full Employment and Price Stability', 18 June 1954, PRO, T 227/261.
65. 1 September 1957, PRO, CAB 129/88 C(57) 194; see also Leslie to Gilbert, 23 March 1955, PRO, T 234/91.
66. 7 September 1957, PRO, CAB 129/88 C(57) 195.
67. Hall to Bridges, 19 and 28 November 1951, PRO, T 229/409.
68. 'Wages and Inflation', 2 February 1956, CPA, ACP 3/4 (56) 41.
69. Cabinet Conclusions, 10 September 1957, PRO, CAB 128/31.
70. Harold Macmillan, *Pointing the Way 1959–1961* (Basingstoke, 1972), 218. See also Harold Macmillan quoted in John Ramsden, 'From Churchill to Heath', in Lord Butler (ed.), *The Conservatives* (London, 1977), 448–9; Reginald Maudling, *Memoirs* (London, 1978), 103; Robert Shepherd, *Iain Macleod* (London, 1994), 133.
71. See, for example: Cabinet Conclusions, 8 May 1952, PRO, CAB 128 (52) 51; 'Draft White Paper on Full Employment and Price Stability'; Macleod to Eden, 27 February 1956, PRO, PREM 11/1883.
72. For a detailed account of this episode, see Shepherd, *Iain Macleod*, 134–42.
73. Robert Taylor, *The Trade Union Question in British Politics* (Oxford, 1993), 105–6.
74. Macleod to Macmillan, 27 April 1957, PRO, PREM 11/2878; see also CPA, ACP/57/54.
75. Taylor, *Trade Union Question*, 104–5.

76. 'A Tory Look at Industrial Relations', 29 January 1962, CPA, ACP 3/8(62) 94; 'Report of the Industrial Relations Sub-committee', 8 May 1963, CPA, ACP 3/10(63) 105.
77. Macmillan, *Pointing the Way*, 375; Harold Macmillan, *At the End of the Day 1961–1963* (Basingstoke, 1973), 66.
78. Cabinet Conclusions, 7 December 1961, PRO, CAB 128(61).
79. Macmillan, *End of the Day*, 51.
80. 'Industrial Change: The Human Aspect', 15 July 1963, CPA, CRD 2/7/7.
81. 'Industrial Relations – Unofficial Strikes', 28 January 1963, CPA, ACP 3/10/63/103.
82. Butler to Douglas-Home, 17 February 1964, Douglas-Home to Brooke, 7 February 1964, Godber to Douglas-Home, 14 February 1964 and 29 July 1964, Shawcross to Douglas-Home, 7 February 1964. PRO, PREM 11/4871; Cabinet Conclusions, 13 February and 17 March 1964, PRO, CAB 128/38.
83. 'Trade Unions, Employers Associations and the Law', 19 March 1964, CPA, CRD, PLC(64) 3.
84. Advisory Committee on Policy, 2 May 1962, CPA, ACP 2/2/50.
85. 'Industrial Relations Committee : Notes from Mr Ray Mawby', 6 December 1962, CPA, CRD 2/7/7, IRC 62/16.
86. 'Trade Unions, Employers Associations and the Law'.
87. F. W. S. Craig (ed.), *British General Election Manifestos 1918–1966* (Chichester, 1970), 219.
88. On the Conservative Party's own review of trade union law and practice while in opposition, see CPA, CRD 3/17/19, CRD 3/17/20 and CRD 3/17/21. For a detailed case-study of the development of the 1971 Industrial Relations Act, see Michael Moran, *The Politics of Industrial Relations* (Basingstoke, 1977).
89. For Conservative attitudes and approaches towards trade unionism since 1964, see Peter Dorey, 'Between Pragmatism, Principle and Practicability: The Development of Conservative Trade Union Policy 1974–79', in David Broughton *et al.* (eds), *British Parties and Elections Yearbook 1994* (Ilford, 1994); Peter Dorey, 'No Return to Beer and Sandwiches: Employment and Industrial Relations Policy under John Major', in Peter Dorey (ed.), *The Major Premiership: Politics and Policies under John Major 1990–1997* (Basingstoke, 1999); Peter Dorey, *Wage Politics in Britain: The Rise and Fall of Incomes Policies since 1945* (Brighton, 2001), chs 5 and 7; Peter Dorey, 'Margaret Thatcher's Taming of the Trade Unions', in Iain Dale and Stanislao Pugliese (eds), *The Thatcher Years: The Rebirth of Liberty?* (London, 2002); Andrew Taylor, 'The Conservative Party and the Trade Unions', in John McIlroy, Nina Fishman and Alan Campbell (eds), *British Trade Unions and Industrial Politics, Vol. 2: The High Tide of Trade Unionism 1964–1979* (Aldershot, 1999); Robert Taylor, 'The Heath Government and Industrial Relations: Myth and Reality', in Stuart Ball and Anthony Seldon (eds), *The Heath Government 1970–74: A Reappraisal* (Harlow, 1996).
90. Quoted in *Conservatism 1945–50* (Conservative Political Centre, 1950), 3; see also R. A. Butler, *The Art of the Possible* (London, 1971), 133–4. For a more general overview of Conservative modernisation during the 1945–51 period, see Gamble, *Conservative Nation*, ch. 3, and Hoffman, *Conservative Party in Opposition*.

9

Conservative Party Activists and Immigration Policy from the Late 1940s to the Mid-1970s[1]

N. J. CROWSON

Politically we must not have so tough a policy on immigration that we offend the middle vote, and while strengthening control we must also make a political appeal to the immigrants themselves.[2]

This conclusion of the Conservative shadow cabinet in March 1965 succinctly summarises the difficulties the political establishment was faced with regarding immigration during the period from the late 1940s to the mid-1970s, and even beyond. This was a triple problem: to restrain the volume of new immigration; to ease the assimilation of the existing immigrant population; and at the same time to recognise the electoral potential of Britain's new citizens. The purpose of this chapter is to examine how the Conservative Party responded to the challenge of an immigrant electorate from the late 1940s through to the mid-1970s during which time it became an indigenous minority population. This is an aspect of Conservative strategy that has been overlooked by historians of both the party, and of immigration, in preference to concerns about attitudes to immigration control. In taking this angle of investigation it sheds light upon the evolution of Conservative attitudes to Commonwealth immigration. It demonstrates that there existed a tension within the party between those who recognised the necessity of 'integration' and those disposed to 'control';

a tension that by the mid-1970s and the advent of Margaret Thatcher had still to be resolved.

Analysis of party politics and immigration has been concerned with how Conservative governments sought to restrain the flow of immigrants into Britain. Conservative administrations were responsible for the 1962 Immigration Act, the 1971 Immigrants Act and the 1981 Nationalities Act, all of which in one way or another restricted the ability of immigrants to enter Britain. Zig Layton-Henry and Stephen Brooke have both written in terms of the Conservative leadership legislating for control because of parliamentary pressure, while Ian Spencer has played down the importance of party opinion.[3] Yet, whichever view one subscribes to, it is clear, as John Ramsden has observed, that party policy on Commonwealth immigration 'could not be claimed a success'.[4] The historical orthodoxy is that the party has had a clearly anti-immigrant stance based upon racialism from the beginning, but until the 1960s this was hidden by external concerns about defending the Commonwealth.[5] When the Conservatives returned to government in 1951 migration from the West Indies had already begun. The influx was encouraged by the availability of work and the 1952 decision of the United States to block further West Indian immigration into its own country. By the mid-1950s migrants were also being attracted from the Indian subcontinent. Although only 2,000 migrants entered Britain in 1953 the numbers gaining entry peaked at 136,400 in 1961. In 1968 Kenyan Asians began entering Britain in large numbers, prompting the Labour government to rush through restrictive legislation. Further immigration waves were experienced with the expulsion of the Ugandan Asians in August 1973 and the arrival of Asians from Malawi in February 1976. Consequently, by the late 1960s permanently settled non-white communities had established themselves in many of Britain's major cities. These were concentrated in the large conurbations that were losing population: areas such as Balsall Heath in Birmingham and the Manningham district of Bradford. Whereas in 1961 the Asian and Black population of Britain was only 0.25 per cent of the whole, by the early 1970s their population numbered about 1.2 million and would continue to climb thereafter.

It was the concerns of the local party activists that first drew the issue to the attention of the national leadership, and the platform of the National Union Central Council provided the party's first open debate on Commonwealth coloured immigration in 1955.[6] By a small majority, a resolution was passed proposing that the laws against aliens should be applied against Commonwealth citizens.

However, it is clear that for the 1950s, at least, while the party might be developing a sense of foreboding about immigration it failed to impress its concerns on to government.[7] Nevertheless, activists' anxieties about the immigration issue helped to foster the climate in which the 'race' issue became part of the wider political debate. Stephen Brooke has pointed out that within the Conservative parliamentary party the swing towards restricting immigration was a gradual process that only secured majority support from 1961. Brooke contends that the swell of concern in the constituencies was primarily responsible for altering the stance of the parliamentary party.[8] Equally, when Enoch Powell spoke in 1968 of a white population who 'found themselves strangers in their own country' he went to considerable lengths to justify his anti-immigrant position from the perspective of constituency support by quoting extensively from letters received from constituents.[9] More recently, Randell Hanson has sought to argue that immigrant legislation was never racialist in intention, even if it proved to be in practice.[10]

This chapter intends to show how the immigration issue was used as an electoral asset. This was not purely through the advocacy of 'control' and appealing to 'core' white Conservative voters, but also from an alternative perspective seeking to capture the vote of the new immigrant electorate. It will be argued the party was not necessarily slow to appreciate the significance of the immigrant vote. However, the level of realisation varied between the national organisation and the grass roots. It was often based upon initiatives at the lowest end of the organisation structure rather than directives from Conservative Central Office (CCO) and it was not until 1965 that senior elements within the party were advocating a bold departure suggesting that the party should do more to emphasise what Conservatism could do for the new minority electorate. The desire to appeal direct to the immigrant vote was tempered by concerns that continued immigration threatened Britain's national identity and challenged the very values Conservatism stood to protect. This was a conundrum that the party appeared not to have fully resolved even by the 2001 general election, when the row provoked by comments on race by the retiring MP for Yorkshire East, John Townend, was juxtaposed with party leader William Hague's expectation that the Conservatives could be the first party to have an Asian as leader and prime minister.

This chapter is divided into three sections, which consider the Conservative reaction to the social consequences of immigration, the means by which the party sought to woo the immigrant and the matter of controlling the inward flow of immigrants.

ASSISTING ASSIMILATION?

The influx of Commonwealth immigrants and their tendency to congregate in 'twilight' zones of Britain's major conurbations, such as Brixton in London, Handsworth in Birmingham and Moss Side in Manchester, drew stark attention to the social deprivation experienced by these communities. Yet the problems associated with housing, education and welfare were not new, and it was clear that the presence of the immigrant merely exacerbated existing problems. When seeking to justify their stance of 'closing the door' on immigrants, activists were liable to express concern at the strains being placed upon social and welfare services, of the lawlessness of the immigrants and of the unemployment being experienced.[11] A CCO investigation in 1957 observed that in those cities acting as immigration reception points there were very real housing, social and health issues that were fuelling local white citizens' resentment, something that 'we ignore at our peril'. Yet the considered view of the report was that there was little the party could do except keep warning the government.[12] Perhaps this statement of resignation recognised that from the perspective of government the empirical evidence (collected by the police, local authorities and social services) failed to substantiate these concerns.[13] Yet, as one Bow Group publication proclaimed, it was the party's 'clear duty … to produce a clear and constructive policy to try to prevent the tensions reaching the explosive stage'.[14]

One of the factors intertwined with the immigration debate was the perceived benefit to the economy; certainly this was the stance of the Treasury. One has only to think of the recruitment of West Indian nurses or London Transport's decision in 1956 to liaise with the Barbados Immigrant Service so that migrants would have a job waiting as soon as they arrived. At the grass roots, however, Conservatives were less convinced of the economic benefits; fears about localised unemployment were considerable. It was an oft-repeated observation that should the economy lurch towards recession then immigrant populations would be hit hard, with the resultant unemployment carrying the potential for civil unrest. One solution frequently proposed was that companies who employed immigrants might be encouraged to relocate to areas outside the cities, areas still dominated by the indigenous population. This would ease the burdens on housing and welfare in the inner cities and promote assimilation.

If the fear of future unemployment was one issue of concern about Britain's 'new citizens', then the matter of housing was a very real and immediate problem. It was declared by one meeting of party activists to be 'the major obstacle to reasonably successful integration'.[15] It was a problem exacerbated because, unlike other European countries, Britain had no policy of co-ordinating its strategies for immigration and housing. The burden fell upon local authorities, yet few additional resources were made available by central government to those authorities with special problems caused by the concentration of immigration settlement in particular areas. Activists tended to be strongly opposed to any suggestion that immigrants should be given special assistance, such as priority in allocation of council houses, arguing that this would only provoke more tension than it relieved. This was borne out in practice. For example, Smethwick in July 1961 saw a rent strike begin among 600 white municipal tenants objecting to the admission of a Pakistani immigrant to a council maisonette.[16] There was also disagreement about whether overcrowding could be alleviated by the application of existing legislation, such as the 1961 and 1964 Housing Acts, or whether the structural issue of housing shortages needed to be addressed first.[17] One proposal offered to alleviate the housing issue and promote assimilation was that local authorities should be empowered to prevent localities from having an immigrant population greater than 50 per cent of the total population. For many activists, this was unacceptable because it sought the dispersal of the immigrant community; as the return of pro-control Conservative MPs in Birmingham in 1959 suggested, nimbyism was strong. Although concerns about assimilation existed, the evolution of the party debate in opposition after 1964 illustrated how easiy it was to pander to the control lobby. In 1965, after a speaker scheduled to address the Greater London Conservative Political Centre immigration study group withdrew because of recent comments by Douglas-Home on the subject, Christopher Brocklebank-Fowler implored:

> I suggest that we do all in our power to avoid using immigration control as an incitement to vote Conservative and give a great deal more constructive thought to a national policy for integrating coloured immigrants at every level of our national life.[18]

The return to opposition in 1964 provided an opportunity for

many in the Conservative Party to reflect upon the future direction
of Conservative immigration policy. The change in leadership in
1965, with Heath's election, also gave fresh impetus to the re-
evaluation of policy. The tension between the pro-'control' and
'integrationists' within the party would eventually explode
publicly with Powell's 'rivers of blood' speech. The forum for this
re-evaluation was to be a subcommittee of the Advisory
Committee on Policy. Officially given the title Policy Group 9:
Immigration and formed in January 1965 under the chairmanship
of Selwyn Lloyd, its brief was to 'consider the social problems ...
involved in integrating settled immigrants into the community ...
and to recommend solutions'.[19] However, if Conservatives like
Brocklebank- Fowler hoped that the remit of this group would be
more positive, then they were to be disappointed. At its first
meeting the group decided that although control had not been
explicitly mentioned it 'should not feel inhibited from discussing
the problem in its widest aspects'.[20] Although initially a confidential group, by May 1965 it was considered advantageous 'in
making known that the Conservative Party was active on the
problem of immigration'.[21] When it presented its conclusions in
July 1965, the emphasis was less on social concerns than upon
matters of control. The intended aim was that the numbers
granted entry should not exceed the numbers who returned to
their mother country. Strict controls once within Britain should be
applied, obliging periodic reporting to the authorities. After three
years residency, immigrants would be eligible for citizenship and
the vote, provided they could prove that they were literate, understood English and did not possess a criminal record. Repatriation
should only be voluntary. During its evidence-gathering phase the
group had received proposals from former ministers suggesting
measures to alleviate housing problems and grants to facilitate
integration, but it took its lead from Peter Brooke, and concluded
that the likelihood of integration would be limited:

> There is a great variety of race, religion and culture amongst
> the immigrant groups. Some may be easily assimilated.
> Others may integrate as separate groups within the com-
> munity, retaining their special characteristics. We should not
> necessarily discourage this, providing they conform to
> accepted standards. We recognise, however, that the next
> generation, in such separate groups, will present greater
> problems.

As far as practical measures were concerned these were limited.

The group proposed that local authorities should be encouraged to provide accommodation advice bureaus, but it was anxious that housing should not 'be regarded as a special immigration problem'. In terms of education the group was favourably disposed to distributing immigrant children throughout an educational authority and to creating a core of specialist teachers, with better remuneration, who could be targeted to schools with a high immigration pupil ratio. This echoed the recommendations of a Bow Group pamphlet produced by John Lenton, Nicholas Budgen and Kenneth Clarke.[22] Employers who recruited immigrant labour should be responsible for their housing and the group suggested the provision of training opportunities for second-generation immigrants.[23]

The argument increasingly being made was that until control was introduced it would be impossible to contain social problems. When the Immigration Policy Group, now under the chairmanship of Peter Thorneycroft, reconvened for a weekend conference at Swinton in the autumn of 1965, the discussion was dominated entirely by the issue of control. It concluded:

> There is a general feeling that the psychological attitude of the indigenous population towards immigrants would remain hostile, and positive integration ineffective, so long as it was believed that the government of the day was failing to contain this problem.[24]

Yet, despite this apparent negativity, more positive gestures were being made.

THE IMMIGRANT VOTER

Writing in the late 1970s, Zig Layton-Henry suggested that it was only during the two elections of 1974 that the growing importance of Asian and West Indian voters became apparent to the major political parties.[25] This assessment requires modification. It is clear that from the early 1950s activists were aware of the potential of the immigrant vote, but the remedies necessary were less certain.

Despite suggestions that the new immigrants were disinterested in British politics, fears about the ease with which they could secure the vote were widespread. In April 1957 the party chairman, Oliver Poole, returned from a party meeting in Manchester which had unanimously passed a motion urging the restriction of immigrant entry into Britain. Poole had particular

sympathy with the resolution because Commonwealth immigrants could 'come here without any restrictions at all, obtain the
vote as soon as they can be put on the new register, and often
become a charge to the Health Service, to the local authorities, or
be maintained at our expense in prison'. Furthermore, he
observed, no such reciprocal arrangements would be extended if
the roles were reversed and he visited the immigrants' mother
country.[26] But it was not just the Commonwealth immigrant who
was singled out for attention.[27] The issue of the migrant from Eire
was, if anything, a far more provocative electoral danger to
Conservative eyes. Consistently throughout the 1950s and 1960s
Conservatives at all levels expressed concern that an Irish immigrant was entitled to vote in British elections. For example, in 1953,
the Home Counties Area Council carried a resolution proposed by
Harrow East Association urging that, because Irish citizens living
in Britain were exempt from national service until resident for two
years, a similar residency clause should be applied to the electoral
register.[28] Similarly, as late as 1976 the author of the party's North
West Area report on immigration was surprised at the frequency
with which the Irish were singled out by activists and concluded
that 'dual nationality not only seemed to cause some confusion
over categorisation but to generate resentment owing to the social
security, housing and unemployment situation'.[29] The view articulated was that the Irish were naturally hostile to Conservatism and
the values of the party. The Irish migrants were stereotyped as
Fenians whose only intention was to bring about the downfall of
the British system.[30]

That the immigrant could register to vote suggested to some
that the party needed to develop a strategy to deal with these new
voters. This appears to have become pronounced in advance of the
May 1955 general election. The awareness of the immigrant voter,
particularly the West Indian immigrant, mirrored a noticeable
growth in the net immigration figures. Whereas in 1953, 2,000 West
Indian and 2,000 Indian migrants had entered Britain, the numbers
increased in 1954 to 11,000 for each ethnic group; they would climb
steeply thereafter.[31] The concern of party activists and constituency association officials was directed towards CCO, and especially
the chief organisation officer. The correspondence tended to pose
three questions that reflected hostility towards the immigrant. On
one level concern was expressed about the influx of immigrants.
This concern was given added gravity by the belief that the non-
white immigrant was invariably hostile to Conservatism.
Consequently, this raised the second and third issues of what the

government was going to do about restricting immigration, and what plans the party had for winning the immigrant vote. Perhaps surprisingly, this correspondence was not coming only from areas of immigrant reception.[32] The response of CCO was noncommittal and failed to offer the correspondents any advice, because 'we do not consider that any useful purpose would be served by specific propaganda to colonial immigrants'.[33]

In part the response of CCO was motivated by a belief that it would be a mistake to make immigration a party issue, but also, given the localised nature of immigrant settlement, this was a matter best resolved by the constituency associations whose responsibility it was to mobilise the local vote.[34] In practical terms, local associations did initiate limited contacts with immigrant communities. Coventry reported that it was in contact with local immigrant leaders, but admitted it had been difficult to make progress within these communities. At the 1955 election the Coventry association had engaged the services of a 'friendly' Indian to undertake 'oral propaganda for the party in the vernacular'.[35] In Bradford, upon the initiative of the sitting MP, efforts were made in advance of the 1959 election to hold a series of meetings for Asian voters based upon the rationale that to leave the new electors outside the party system exposed them to the influence of militant leaders. One local councillor even set about learning Urdu, but the contacts were sporadic and tied to self-interest and electoral fortunes.[36] Birmingham Young Conservatives devoted their annual residential conference in 1965 to the matter of Birmingham's 'new citizens', producing a special report of their deliberations. While agreeing that immigration should be restricted to immediate relatives only, they concluded that remedial action was required for the existing population: 'Adopt, Adapt, Improve' was the mantra. Concern was also expressed about the need to recruit immigrant members and to ensure voter registration: 'Because of the inherent prejudice and traditional outlook of older people, it is through the Young Conservatives that this breakthrough must come. [...] and one hopes that by 1970 Young Conservatives who are coloured will be accepted as members rather than treated as novelties.'[37]

The period 1955–57 saw over 40,000 immigrants enter Britain annually. The numbers and their tendency to settle in cities that were electorally vulnerable for the Conservatives obliged the party to take notice. At face value this suggested the party was alert to the political consequences of the immigrant, but the concern was less about how to woo the new electorate than the negative implications of the immigrant on the Conservative electoral machine. In January 1957 a working party of Conservative national and regional officials, under the chairmanship of Barbara Brooke (wife of Financial Secretary to the Treasury, Henry Brooke, who became Home Secretary in 1962), was formed to investigate the consequences of immigration.[38] In its report the Brooke Committee was anxious to emphasise that its recommendations were 'not reached as a result of racial or any other prejudice'; however, immigrant settlement was 'leading to a degree of social and political upheaval ... which could no longer be ignored'. The committee was particularly concerned that the party could ill afford to ignore the resentment of the indigenous white electorate.[39] Submissions to the committee from agents in London, Manchester and Birmingham constituencies observed that very few West Indians and Asians were active electorally, and the committee lamely admitted that 'the party organisation as such could do little to abate this grave problem'.[40] However, it was decided that for the moment this issue was less pressing, given that the Labour Party currently saw little benefit in mobilising the immigrant vote.[41] The recommendation was that a local association, if approached by an immigrant, 'should do their best to be helpful' but because immigrant problems were largely social these could be 'handled on a civic and national basis'. This meant that the party did 'not [need] to devise a political or organisational approach to the immigrants as electors'. The committee was not entirely dismissive of the potential of the immigrant voter and did undertake to monitor the 1957 local elections and the pending Barons Court by-election.[42] The principal 'fear' of the Brooke Committee was that in areas where the immigrants were settling 'the valuable middle-class leadership was being lost through middle-class movement out and away'. This was politically dangerous because it opened the door to 'predatory socialism'; with apoplectic gloom the committee warned that 'before long, Conservatives might expect Birmingham as a whole to be lost to any alternative party allegiance'.[43]

But, how best to woo the immigrant elector? A memorandum sent to the party's General Director in 1957 observed that perhaps in dealing with the West Indian immigrant 'some general principles might be evolved' from those constituencies that had sizeable foreign minorities such as Poles or Cypriots.[44] The party used propaganda material in immigrant languages in both the 1959 and 1964 general elections as well as in a series of by-elections. However, a post-mortem concluded that the 'exercise was of minimal value' not least because electors who cannot understand

English are also illiterate in their own language.[45] Particular concern was expressed that the exercise ran the risk of offending 'English' voters if foreign-language leaflets should be deposited through the wrong letterboxes. A decade later the sentiment was similarly expressed by a pro-control party study group, chaired by George Young and Ivor Stanbrook, which concluded 'there is evidence for believing that Conservative efforts to woo, or appear to woo, the immigrant vote in marginal seats is more likely to lose support among the indigenous voters than gain it among the immigrants'.[46]

Yet, by the early 1970s the size of the Asian and West Indian communities meant that they could not be ignored and left to the Labour Party by default. Central Office responded by creating an ethnic minorities unit: the establishment of Anglo-West Indian and Anglo-Asian Conservative societies were early initiatives of the new unit.[47] Similarly, the decision by the shadow cabinet not to oppose the 1976 Race Relations Act appeared as another positive step. Nevertheless considerable hurdles remained, as a survey by the party's North Western Provincial Area revealed in September 1976.[48] It transpired that the party in the north west had 'few links with the immigrant population'. Although only two associations considered that race relations were bad in their area, over half of the respondents admitted that they had no contact with immigrant communities. Ten associations had representatives serving on community relations councils and 19 associations had the services of a community relations officer. For those associations admitting to contacts these appear to have been rather haphazard – either contacts with leaders of specific groups, such as leaders of the Islamic centre in Crosby, or liaison occurring because of MPs' surgeries. Perhaps not surprisingly, fewer than 15 per cent reported having ethnic activist members. Ashton-under-Lyme reported the assistance of an Asian group in the preparation of a leaflet for the recent local authority elections, but this was 'an isolated incident'. Six associations had tried to persuade immigrants to stand for election in local authority contests, but these were usually professional, well-educated individuals. The report concluded with the observation that in 'constituencies which had a substantial percentage of immigrants [there] was a genuine desire for and working towards social harmony between all races in the area. It was the constituencies on their borders that seemed worried by immigration.' Indeed, this last observation was symptomatic of the response throughout the period under consideration and goes a considerable way to explaining the resurgence of calls for entry controls after February 1976. This was triggered by the perceived failings of the 1971 Immigration Act and the arrival of expelled Asians from Malawi, which would set in motion a renewed debate that would ultimately lead to the 1981 Nationalities Act.

CONTROL: AN ELECTORAL ASSET?

The evolutionary gestation of the party's stance on 'entry control' stretched back to the late 1940s. However, it was the 1958 riots in Notting Hill, Dudley and Nottingham that brought the public debate about immigration to a climax. Unsurprisingly, the issue of control increasingly exercised the minds of Conservative activists and the wider party. The 1959 general election saw a Conservative majority of 100, and the return of a growing band of West Midlands anti-immigrant MPs including the members for Yardley, Sparkbrook and All Saints.[49] It was from this point that local associations (in the shires as well as the boroughs) began debating the matter. During 1960–61 the constituency post-bags of Conservative MPs, from areas as diverse as Bedford, Abingdon, Stratford and Wokingham, began including letters concerning immigration, with the vast majority critical of the 'open door' policy. As one such recipient recorded: 'I realise that this is an exceptionally thorny problem but undoubtedly it is becoming one in which the general public are getting increasingly restive.'[50] Similarly, the deputy area agent for London sought the guidance of CCO about the suitability of scheduling a debate on the 'dynamite' issue of immigration at the area's women's annual conference in 1961. The response was unequivocal: 'avoid adding fuel to the flames of conscientious objection [… in case …] we might create dissatisfaction which we were unable to meet constructively'.[51] In the aftermath of the race rioting, the 1958 annual party conference had passed a resolution urging immigration control, although it had received only six resolutions on the matter. Only seven such resolutions were received for 1960, and no provision was made at the conference for a debate. However, in 1961 the conference agenda was deluged with 39 constituency resolutions demanding entry control, and the 'vigorous' Hayes and Harlington motion was selected for debate.[52] With the statistics showing a continued surge in entry numbers, the government's response was the 1962 Commonwealth Immigration Act.

However, such crude statistical analysis does not reveal the total picture. It is evident that immigration was an issue that caused intra-party strife. Of course this was clearly visible at the level of the parliamentary party with the divisions between the anti-immigrant–Cyril Osborne–Powell school of thought and the more liberally inclined Conservatives (Boyle, Carr, MacLeod). What is less widely appreciated is that these divisions of opinion reflected the debate among activists. For example, in North Wiltshire in June 1963 the Executive Committee, anticipating a forthcoming general election, heard a presentation on the reasons for the party's current unpopularity. After unemployment, the speaker listed the 'colour problem' as the next most significant reason, arguing that Britain was 'exporting good men, importing inferior quality. Urgent need for restrictions.' Yet when the issue was opened to discussion from the floor even the meeting's minutes can barely disguise the objections of a substantial element of the meeting who 'strongly criticised' the speaker's views on race. Earlier in 1960 Birmingham Young Conservatives found themselves divided when faced with a resolution urging stricter entry controls including health checks, assurances of work and powers of deportation. Views were 'strongly expressed' before opponents eventually succeeded in defeating the motion 14 to 13.[53] Other such examples of a divergence of activist opinion can be found throughout the period of the immigration debate.[54] It was apparent that the issue exercised emotions. Yet, if debate could be moved away from purely knee-jerk reaction, there was the emergence of a general consensus.[55]

It is accepted that the 1964 general election marks a watershed. It was the first election in which the 'race' card became an issue. In Birmingham Perry Barr, just days before polling, a leaflet was distributed pronouncing that a Labour victory would mean 300,000 further immigrants with the graphic of a huge arrow pointing down on Birmingham.[56] However, it is a matter of weighting. During the campaign itself, the Conservative leader, Alec Douglas Home, was the only senior politician to address the matter directly, in a speech in Bradford which received only limited media exposure. But at the level of individual constituencies immigration did feature on the agenda. This was most notorious in Smethwick. For some time local Conservatives in that constituency had been agitating against Asian and Black immigrants, and the electoral dividends had been recognised when the party captured control of the local council. During the national campaign the Conservative candidate, Peter Griffiths, openly espoused tough anti-immigrant measures and succeeded in bucking the national swing of 3.4 per cent towards Labour; he secured a 7.5 per cent swing, enabling him to oust the sitting Labour MP, Patrick Gordon Walker. The psephologists have concluded that, in areas with high immigrant populations, the 1962 Act won the Conservatives votes, largely because Labour had violently opposed it at the time. On the other hand, being an advocate of immigrant control did not guarantee holding your seat, as Norman Pannell experienced in Liverpool.[57] Other Conservative candidates deliberately sought to downplay the immigration issue. Edward Boyle, MP for Birmingham Handsworth, told his area chairman: 'We should do better over the immigration issue by letting the differences between Labour and the Conservative policy *emerge* during the course of the campaign – e.g. by our answers at question time – than by making it too explicitly an election issue.'[58] In his post-mortem of the election result, Boyle concluded that his liberal stance on immigration had cost him no more than 500 votes.[59]

The concentration of immigrant communities raised fears among Conservative activists of the strains being placed upon social and welfare services, of the lawlessness of the immigrant and of the unemployment being experienced. Edward Boyle responded to such complaints in mid-1961 by undertaking a tour of his Handsworth constituency. His association's deputy chairman had already indicated that it was 'a matter of very serious concern to a lot of Handsworth people'. Boyle felt able to dismiss the issue, deciding that 'a good many decent Handsworth residents are getting sick of endless talk about this immigration problem'. He warned the constituency's agent that 'our party ought to be very careful not to be too much identified' with those local councillors propagating the race issue.[60] Yet, if Boyle felt able to believe in 1961 that the anti-immigrant stance was confined to a minority of constituents, a Missioners report (a form of party canvassing which also provided data on public opinion) in Handsworth 18 months later appeared to offer a contradictory view. It observed that the 'problem looms large in the minds of the white population of all political parties and constitutes the main topic of political conversation on the doorstep'. Among Conservative supporters, the report identified the usual litany of 'ills' associated with immigration, but also included the belief that those 'who are still out of work after three months should be deported, and that they should not be entitled to claim National Assistance etc. until they have served a qualifying period of resi-dence in the country and contributed towards the national economy'. Threats were also made to transfer voting allegiance to the Liberals.[61] Perhaps it was a sign of frustration with the slow response of national leaders to adopt a pro-control stance that party activists associated themselves with organisations such as the Birmingham Immigration Control Association (established October 1960) and the Southall Residents' Association (founded September 1963).

Powell's very public intervention in the debate in 1968 clearly both polarised and hardened party opinion. The wave of support that Powell received from constituencies after his sacking from the shadow cabinet has been well documented.[62] However, as John Ramsden has pointed out, at the next level upwards in the party's hierarchy – the regional areas, where there was always more loyalty to the leadership – there was a division of opinion. Both the East Midlands and Wessex areas unanimously backed Heath, but the South East was sympathetic to Powell.[63] Again it needs to observed that there were divisions of opinion, such as occurred with Norwood Association in June. On hearing of Powell's dismissal by Heath, local officers sent their leader a telegram criticising his actions. However, when these officials reported their actions to the Executive, they found themselves chastised, with the minutes noting that it was 'clearly felt this [telegram] only reflected views of officers of the association and *not* the wider membership'.[64] Of course, the party could not simply ignore the issue of control. The Labour government was steering through a race relations bill that was deeply unpopular with Conservatives. In fact the party did not shy away from the matter and instead sought to engage with its activists. The Conservative Political Centre was at this time engaged in a consultation exercise with its constituency discussion groups called 'Three-Way Contact'. A briefing document, *Immigration and Race*, was circulated in August, no doubt with the intent of seeking to ameliorate and inform feeling before the annual conference.[65] Four hundred and twelve CPC discussion groups responded to the briefing document and the party leadership can have been left in no doubt as to the likely outcome of any conference debate: 347 groups wanted an end to all immigration, with a further 52 groups prepared to tolerate only the entry of dependants of those immigrants already in Britain. Furthermore, 'it was generally thought, all immigrants must, in the first place, be treated as aliens'.[66] Unsurprisingly, Powell was the darling of the 1968 conference. Under such pressure Heath did revise his stance, accepting that all remaining special privileges would be removed from Commonwealth migrants, reducing them

to alien status, and he also agreed to the need for tighter entry
requirements for dependants. By the following year, conference
was prepared to adopt proposals for repatriation (as Powell had
urged).

With Heath's unexpected return to office in 1970, the new
Conservative administration proceeded to fulfil its policy commitments by introducing the 1971 Immigration Act. The act, which
came into force in January 1973, introduced work permits for immigrants with no rights of permanent residence or entry for dependants and introduced financial assistance for voluntary repatriation.
The viability of the act was almost immediately challenged by the
expulsion of the Ugandan Asians by General Amin, the President of
Uganda, in August. The public showdown proved to be the annual
conference when Enoch Powell, as president of Hackney South and
Shoreditch Conservative Association, moved a critical resolution on
the issue. The moderates within the party, led by David Hunt, the
Young Conservatives' chairman, fought back with an amendment
that congratulated the government for its actions, which they
succeeded in carrying by a large majority. However, while Hunt's
actions might have endeared him to the leadership, Plymouth
Drake Conservative Association was less impressed and immediately sought to deselect him as their prospective candidate.[67]

In the following years, the pro-control lobby regrouped behind
the scenes and the arguments for further legislation in the event of
a return to office were rehearsed. The Conservative Research
Department prepared a briefing document in which it argued that
any attempts to restrict the entry of dependants 'would run
counter to humanitarian principles consistently expressed by
Conservatives'. It concluded with the warning:

> Any restriction which aimed directly at reducing non-white
> rather than total immigration would be discriminatory and
> would undoubtedly antagonise non-white immigrant
> communities, thereby undermining rather than improving
> race relations ... any attempt to use immigration as a high-
> profile, partisan political issue is likely to be counter-
> productive in this respect.[68]

However, in a secret report the Conservative Parliamentary Home
Affairs Committee were less convinced, believing that 'the
Conservative Party has nothing to fear from taking the initiative in
proclaiming a stricter policy on immigration and being prepared to
make changes which, while not dishonouring commitments, will
regulate future immigration from the New Commonwealth so

closely as virtually to bring it to an end'.[69] Within this 40-page report lay the genesis of the 1981 British Nationalities Act.

CONCLUSION

By the early 1970s it was clear that the fabric of British society had been changed irrevocably by Commonwealth immigration. The Asian and Black population now totalled more than 1.2 million and most of Britain's cities and towns now had permanently settled, substantial minorities who were clearly distinguishable by appearance, traditions, customs and practice from the remainder of the population. As one internal party document observed: 'We are not facing tiresome problems called "immigrants" who got here because defective immigration laws let them in but indigenous minority groups which because of racial discrimination and cumulative disadvantage are in some danger of being trapped in a situation of permanent minority.'[70] This presented new problems for those charged with devising future Conservative policy. Control had proved to be to the Conservatives' electoral advantage before, but would it do so in the future? As shown above, the control lobby was still influential, and ultimately it would win the argument. Nevertheless, the 1971 Immigration Act had convinced others within the party that the Conservatives needed to formulate a response that would overcome the ill-will of the ethnic minorities and 'pay more than just lip service to the concept of a multi-racial society based upon equality of opportunity'.[71] When the shadow cabinet decided not to oppose the 1976 Race Relations Act, it appeared for a moment as if the leadership was willing to take a new direction.

NOTES

1. In facilitating my research for this chapter particular thanks must be given to Jill Spellman, archivist of the Conservative Party Archive (CPA), Bodleian Library, and Colin Harris and his team in Reading Room 132. Permission to cite material from the CPA is courtesy of James Walsh, Conservative Political Forum, Conservative Central Office.
2. Minutes of Leader's Consultative Committee (shadow cabinet) 9 March 1965, CPA, LCC(65)29, emphasis added.
3. Z. Layton-Henry, *The Politics of Immigration* (Oxford, 1992); Stephen Brooke, 'The Conservative Party, Immigration and National Identity 1948–1968', in M. Francis and I. Zweiniger-Bargielowska, *The Conservatives and British Society 1880–1990* (Cardiff, 1996); Ian Spencer *British Immigration Policy since 1939* (London, 1997); C. Waters '"Dark Strangers" in our Midst: Discourses of Race and Nation in Britain 1947–63', *Journal of*

British Studies, 36 (1997), 207–38.'

4. J. Ramsden, *Winds of Change: Macmillan to Heath* (London, 1996), 41.
5. For example, D. W. Dean, 'Conservative Governments and the Restriction of Commonwealth Immigration in the 1950s', *Historical Journal*, 35 (1992), 171–94; D. Welsh, 'The Principle of the Thing: The Conservative Government and the Control of Commonwealth Immigration 1957–59', *Contemporary British History*, 12, 2 (1998).
6. J. Ramsden, *Age of Churchill and Eden* (London, 1994), 263.
7. An early example of this activist concern was from the Northern Area Conservative and Unionist Association, July 1952, which wanted the government to act to devise methods of achieving a more rapid and even distribution of the immigrant population. It elicited the reply from that National Union that this was a matter for the Commonwealth: Northumberland Record Office, NRO4137/2.
8. Brooke, 'The Conservative Party', 147–71.
9. In his memoirs, Edward Heath, *The Course of My Life* (London, 1998), 292 suggests that Powell fabricated this evidence.
10. Randall Hansen, *Citizenship and Immigration in Post-war Britain* (Oxford, 2000).
11. For example, see the following discussions: Waterloo Women's Conservative Association (CA), 13 January 1954, Lancashire Record Office, DDX806/2/1; Northern Area Council, 25 February 1961, Northumberland Record Office, NRO3303/4; North Edinburgh CA, 11 December 1961, *Evening News* press cuttings, Edinburgh City Archives; Winchester CA, Women's AGM, 2 March 1968, Hampshire Record Office, 73M86W/8.
12. 'West Indian, Asian and Southern-Irish Immigrants', 7 June 1957, CPA, CCO 4/7/166.
13. This is certainly the view of Spencer and Layton-Henry.
14. J. Lenton, N. Budgen and K. Clarke, *Immigration, Race and Politics: A Birmingham View* (Bow Group, March 1966), 5.
15. Birmingham Young Conservatives, Central Council report on immigration, 7 July 1965, 2, Birmingham Central Library, AQ329.94249CON f. 135.
16. Brooke, 'The Conservative Party', 160.
17. Compare C. Brocklebank-Fowler, C. Bland and T. Farmer, *Commonwealth Immigration* (Bow Group, 1965) 11, with Lenton, Budgen and Clarke, *Immigration, Race and Politics*. The latter considered the 1961 Housing Act 'impracticable and unjustifiable', 24.
18. Christopher Brocklebank-Fowler to David Howell, 9 February 1965, CPA, CRD 3/16/2. Addressing a party meeting in Hampstead on 3 February, Douglas-Home had suggested that illegal immigrants should be repatriated and that a voluntary repatriation system should be introduced; furthermore he urged that dependants must be counted in the immigration statistics.
19. Edward Heath to potential members of the Policy Committee on Immigration, 4 January 1965, CPA, CRD/3/16/2. Membership was to be drawn from both the parliamentary party and from 'experts' in immigration. Selwyn Lloyd (chair), S. Patterson, G. Johnson Smith, Chris Chataway, John Vaughan-Morgan, John Athisayam, Anthony Buck, Edward Taylor, Col. Mathers (secretary).
20. Minutes of Immigration Policy Group, 8 February 1965, CPA, CRD 3/16/1.
21. Minutes of Immigration Policy Group, 7 May 1965, CPA, CRD 3/16/1.
22. Lenton, Budgen and Clarke, *Immigration*, 11–12, 16–17, 19–20.
23. Minutes of Immigration Policy Group, 26 February 1965, Immigration Policy Group Manifesto Points, 5th draft (quote from page 2), CPA, CRD 3/16/1.
24. Memo, 'Weekend Discussion about Policy: Swinton 26–8 November 1965: Immigration', Col. Mathers, 18 January 1966, CPA, CRD 3/16/1.
25. Zig Layton-Henry, 'Immigration', in Z. Layton-Henry (ed.), *Conservative Party Politics* (Basingstoke, 1980), 67.
26. Oliver Poole to Home Secretary, Foreign Secretary and Colonial Secretary, 6 May 1957, CPA, CCO 4/7/166.
27. For example of another immigrant group and the Conservative response but during the 1930s, see N. J. Crowson 'The British Conservative Party and the Jews in the 1930', *Patterns of Prejudice*, 29 (1995). For hostility to the Irish, see Oliver Poole to Iain Macleod, 21 November 1955, reporting on a meeting of the West Midlands Area, CPA, CCO 4/6/151, and E. Sillitoe (on behalf of the West Midlands Conservative Area Trades Union Advisory Committee) to Iain Macleod, 13 December 1961, CPA, CCO 2/6/8.

28. Home Counties Area Council, 14 July 1953, CPA, ARE 8/1/10.
29. 'Report of North West Provincial Area Survey on Immigration' by Morag White, September 1976, CPA, CRD 3/16/3.
30. 'West Indian, Asian and Southern-Irish Immigrants', 7 June 1957, CPA, CCO 4/7/166.
31. Figures taken from Layton-Henry, *Politics of Immigration*, 13.
32. Mrs E. Bevan to Mrs Gray, (Central Office), 7 December 1954; Robert Ryder to John Hare, 20 January 1955; Cmnd. Napier to Conservative Central Office, 26 January 1955, CPA, CCO 4/6/271.
33. Chief organisation officer, Central Office to Cmnd. Napier, 3 February 1955, CPA, CCO 4/6/271.
34. Majorie Turner (South-Eastern Area agent) to Mrs E. Bevan (secretary, Merton and Morden Women's CA), 21 December 1954, CPA, CCO 4/6/271.
35. 'West Indian and Other Immigrants', n.d., CPA, CCO 4/7/166.
36. Ramsden, *Winds of Change*, 43.
37. Birmingham Young Conservatives, 'Report on Immigration and Integration', 7 July 1965, Birmingham Central Reference Library, AQ329.94249CON, ff. 134–40.
38. Membership of the committee comprised Barbara Brooke (chair), Urton (London Area agent), Goldsworthy (deputy Central Office agent), Langstone (agent for Barons Court CA), Greenleas (agent for Brixton CA), Banks (North Western Area agent), Hanlon (chief agent for Liverpool), Galloway (West Midlands Area agent) and Tranter (chief agent for Birmingham).
39. 'West Indian, Asian and Southern-Irish Immigrants', 7 June 1957, CPA, CCO/4/7/166.
40. 'West Indian and Other Immigrants', report on meeting of Brooke Committee, 27 March 1957, CPA, CCO 4/7/299; quotation from 'West Indian, Asian and Southern-Irish Immigrants', 7 June 1957.
41. This assessment is confirmed by the historical analysis of Steven Fielding, 'Brotherhood and the Brothers: Responses to "Coloured" Immigration in the British Labour Party c. 1951–1965', *Journal of Political Ideologies*, 3, 1 (1998), 79–97.
42. 'West Indian and Other Immigrants', 27 March 1957.
43. 'West Indian, Asian and Southern-Irish Immigrants', 7 June 1957.
44. 'Colonial Immigration', 9 January 1957, CPA, CCO 4/7/299.
45. 'Foreign Language Literature for Constituencies', 6 January 1966, CPA, CCO 500/24/236.
46. 'Report of the Study Group on Race Relations and Immigration', June 1976, CPA, CRD 3/16/3.
47. These were formed in January and November 1979 respectively.
48. Responses were received from 61 different constituencies out of a possible 78. 'Report of the North Western Provincial Area Survey on Immigration', White, September 1976.
49. Leonard Seymour (Yardley), Leslie Cleaver (Sparkbrook) and John Hollingworth (All Saints) joined fellow Birmingham MPs who favoured 'control': Harold Gurden (Selly Oak), Geoffrey Lloyd (Sutton Coldfield), Martin Lindsey (Solihull), and Edith Pitt (Edgbaston). Strongly opposed to controls were Edward Boyle (Handsworth) and Audrey Jones (Hall Green).
50. Brooke, 'The Conservative Party', 160. Similar correspondence would erupt in the months after Powell's 'rivers of blood' speech: see James Salt (chairman, Walsall South CA) to Russell Lewis (director, CPC), 8 August 1968 and E. F. Hawkins (Bradford Conservative activist) to Russell Lewis, 6 September 1968, CPA, CCO 150/3/5/1
51. Goldsworthy–Walker correspondence, 31 May–5 June 1961, CPA, CCO 2/6/1.
52. *Programme for 1961 Party Conference, Brighton*, Southampton University Special Collections, Hartley Library, Thorneycroft MSS, MS278/A962/2/4.
53. Birmingham Young Conservatives, Central Council, 7 October 1960, Birmingham Central Reference Library, AQ329.94249CON, ff. 219–20.
54. Other examples would include Reigate CA, 14 July 1961, Surrey Record Office, 353/4/2/1; Shoreham CA, 19 September 1961, 18 June 1968, West Sussex Record Office, CO/1SH/1/1/1.
55. The Greater London Area CPC Immigration Study Group, report by group leader C. Brocklebank-Fowler, n.d. (July 1965), CPA, CCO 150/3/3/2.
56. Birmingham Perry Barr CA election leaflet, October 1964, CPA, CCO 500/24/177. This flyer provoked a political storm when after the election Labour's Lord President of the Council, Herbert Bowden, referred to it in the course of a parliamentary debate, 10 November 1964, CPA, CCO 1/14/352.

57. Interestingly Pannell was asked to consider standing for Edward Boyle's constituency by the chairman of Handsworth CA.
58. Boyle to Sir Charles Burman, 24 August 1964, University of Leeds, Brotherton Library, Boyle MSS, MS 660/20572.
59. Boyle to Cyril Osbourne, 27 October 1964, Boyle MSS, MS 660/24085.
60. F. D. Hall to Boyle, 29 March 1961, Boyle MSS, MS 660/12175; Boyle to H. T. Shires, 11 April 1961, Boyle MSS, MS 669/12178/1–2.
61. Missioners Report 3 from Handsworth, w/e 10 August 1962, Boyle MSS, MS 660/12196/1–2.
62. For example, Harborough CA Executive, 24 April and 24 July 1968, Leicestershire Record Office, DE1170/7.
63. Ramsden, *Winds of Change*, 295.
64. Norwood CA Executive, 7 June 1968, Lambeth Archives, IV/166/1/18.
65. *Immigration and Race: Masterbrief 18* (CPC pamphlet, August 1968), CPA, 22775d.115/413.
66. 'Political Contact Programme: Discussion Paper 18: Immigration and Race Relations', 30 October 1968, Boyle MSS, MS 660/22797/1.
67. Ion Trewin (ed.), *Alan Clark Diaries: Into Politics* (London, 2000), 10.
68. Conservative Research Department memo, 'Immigration into Britain: Some Options for Restrictions', 16 December 1975, CPA, CRD 3/16/3.
69. Report of the Study Group on Race Relations and Immigration of the Conservative Parliamentary Home Affairs Committee, June 1976, CPA, CRD 3/16/3.
70. 'Race Relations White Paper' n.d. (1976), CPA, CCO 4/10/257.
71. 'Race Relations', Chris Gent, n.d., CPA, CCO 4/10/257.

10

The Role of the Conservative Political Centre, 1945–98

PHILIP NORTON[1]

For the first century of its existence, the Conservative Party placed little emphasis on political education within its own ranks or on seeking the views of members on policy. Local associations were largely semi-autonomous entities, existing largely as money-raising bodies and electoral machines to support the party in its quest for electoral victory.[2] The relationship between leaders and led was essentially top down, with supporters expected to be deferential to the leadership, which decided matters of policy.

The position began to change in the 1920s. There was a recognition among some leading party figures, notably J. C. C. Davidson, party chairman 1926–30, and later a rising young politician, R. A. Butler, that some form of political education for members in the country might benefit the party. Greater political awareness would produce a body of local activists better able to respond to the growing challenge of the Labour Party. This awareness produced modest developments. There was the creation of a college, initially near Northampton, and then a larger one at Ashridge, near Berkhampstead, to train agents and to provide short courses for party members. The party also set up a Central Education Department. Its organising committee was chaired by Butler. In 1938 the Education Committee published *A National Faith*, written by 'A Modern Conservative'. The 'Modern Conservative' was a young Conservative and protégé of Butler,

Cuthbert Alport, and the work had an introduction by Butler. The same year, Butler also brought into being a short-lived Conservative Political Circle.[3] Political activity was suspended for the duration of the war. Just before the end of the war, Butler was appointed chairman of the party's Post-war Problems Committee and, with Sir Robert Topping, the general director of the party, set about resuscitating the educational wing of the party. The result was the Conservative Political Centre (CPC), under the directorship of Alport.

In some respects the CPC could be seen as an extension of the pre-war work of the party in political education, but in one crucial respect it was novel. There was some attempt to encourage discussion that would inform the rest of the party, including the party leaders. This was part of the party's post-war process of rejuvenation. The party was seeking to reach out to more people and to give members, especially those not drawn in by other sections of the party, a greater opportunity for participation.

The CPC began life in a semi-basement at 11 Wilton Street, close to Victoria station, 'a house which', Butler later noted, 'subsequently achieved notoriety as the scene of a shooting affray between two Latin American diplomats'.[4] Though funded by Conservative Central Office (CCO), and answerable to the Advisory Committee on Policy and Political Education (which Butler chaired), the CPC achieved – rather like its sister organisation, the Conservative Research Department (CRD) – a semi-independent status within the party. It was described by one former CPC director, drawing on a modern phrase, as 'in the party, but not run by the party'.[5] It was later to be brought under the roof of CCO, both physically and formally, earlier than the Research Department: the CPC became housed in Central Office early in its existence and became an integral part of the party organisation in 1964.

The purpose of this chapter is not to provide a narrative history of the CPC but rather to identify and evaluate the roles of the CPC during its 53-year history, that is, from 1945 until it was succeeded by the Conservative Policy Forum (CPF) in 1998. The roles it has fulfilled have been broader than its formal aims.

The CPC has variously identified its functions in different terms, though the basic tasks have largely remained unchanged. In 1964, its aims were summarised as: 'to encourage people to think about and to discuss politics; to develop understanding of topical and long-term issues; to secure a wider and deeper knowledge of Conservative principles; and to stimulate and give currency to new ideas within the party'.[6] The audiences for such activities were not precisely defined. The 'people' mentioned in the first aim took the audience wider than the party membership. The last aim was directed to the party membership. It is not clear to what extent the other aims were geared to the party or a wider audience.

A clearer guide was embodied in the CPC's functions listed in a booklet published by the CPC in 1967 and revised in 1972.[7] The CPC, it declared, seeks:

- To educate Conservatives about political problems.
- To stimulate thinking about politics throughout the party.
- To disseminate throughout the party new ideas on policy, principles and political action.
- To create a channel for the exchange of views between the party leadership and the party in the constituencies.
- To propagate Conservative views among the general public.

It went on:

> Other parts of the party organisation concern themselves with the necessary tasks of raising funds, locating the voters and getting them to the poll. The CPC seeks victory in the battle of ideas.

The above list identifies more clearly the audience for the work of the CPC. It engaged in the battle of ideas and its principal role was to ensure that the troops were well armed. Nonetheless, it also had an important role in engaging with those who might be sympathetic to the cause. This reaching out to people beyond the party was more important than the formal list of functions suggests.

In practice, the CPC fulfilled essentially four roles, three of them derived from the formal roles listed by the party, the other an informal, but in many respects the most visible, role. Each can be seen in terms of the CPC reaching out to a particular group within the body politic. The first role involved reaching out to a particular group of party activists, the second to party members generally, the third to the politically informed community, and the fourth to a wider public – indeed a national – audience.

The CPC carried out these roles with varying degrees of success. In many respects, the high-point of the CPC in fulfilling the first two functions, and possibly the third as well, was in the mid- to late 1960s. The fourth it fulfilled successfully on a continuing basis.

FACILITATING A DIALOGUE BETWEEN LEADERS
AND PARTY ACTIVISTS

Perhaps the best known and systematic role carried out by the CPC was that of the Contact Programme, originally known as the Two-Way Movement of Ideas, providing for a dialogue between leaders and party members.

Local parties were encouraged to establish CPC groups. These were expected to be kept reasonably small in order to facilitate discussion; constituencies with large numbers of activists could each establish several groups. A contact brief – embodying a topic for discussion, information on the topic, details of relevant literature and asking a series of questions – was sent each month or every other month to local groups. The topic for discussion was chosen by the director of the CPC in consultation with the director of the CRD and the deputy chairman of the party. (For some years, tape recordings of interviews with the relevant minister or front-bencher also accompanied the contact brief.) The groups would meet, discuss the topic, produce a response and despatch it, via area office, to the director of the CPC.

Once he had the reports, the director would aggregate the results and send his summary – including details of any minority views – to the party leader, the party chairman, the executive of the 1922 Committee, the CRD, the Advisory Committee on Policy, and the relevant minister or frontbencher. A reply from that minister or frontbencher, along with the director's summary, would then be circulated to all the discussion groups that sent in a report. The reply would typically be a two- or three-page detailed response.

The number of party members involved in this activity was small. It comprised an elite within the local mass party, though it was essentially a self-selecting elite. The groups tended to be concentrated in the south-east, where the party was strongest. Though the number of groups established initially looked encouraging,[8] by 1954 there were only 214 active CPC discussion groups. The number increased to 525 in 1957 and 1,443 in 1963. The number of party members taking part in discussions in 1963 was about 3,000.[9] This figure showed a modest increase in the latter half of the decade. The number of party members participating in discussions in 1967 regularly exceeded 4,000 – one topic, on 'Education and the Citizen', drew the participation of 5,370 members – and in the next two years the number ranged from just under 3,000 to more than 4,000.[10] A similar range of participants was reported at the beginning of the 1970s; the average number of participants per group was nine or ten.[11] The party reported an increase in participation in the 1970s, the number of participating groups rising to between 500 and 600, and the total number of participants ranging between 4,500 and 6,500.[12] In their study of party members in the early 1990s, Paul Whiteley, Patrick Seyd and Jeremy Richardson found that 1 per cent of the membership belonged to a local CPC group, which equates to approximately 7,500 members.[13]

Too much should not be made of the differences between these figures. A figure of 1 per cent of party members being members of CPC groups does not necessarily equate to 1 per cent taking part in each discussion. What we can conclude from these figures is that somewhere between 3,500 and 7,500 members participated in CPC groups, representing a small percentage of party members but nonetheless a number that showed no decline at a time when party membership was declining. Indeed, as John Ramsden noted of the figures in the 1960s, 'Since expansion took place at a time when party membership almost halved, the increased activity clearly represented a greater permeation of the constituency associations.'[14] The contact programme enabled leaders to enter into a dialogue with what appears to be their most active or at least very committed party members. The fact that it was the most active members can only be inferred and not proved: there is no information on the consistency of activity, or on whether there was much turnover or not in CPC group membership. My perception, derived from limited observation, is that there was considerable continuity in membership.

Facilitating a dialogue between leaders and members was the best known role of the CPC as well as the most criticised. For pluralists, concerned with observable decision making, the CPC did not emerge as an influential body. There was little tangible evidence of the Contact Programme influencing policy making within the party. Reports from the programme were variously circulated and discussed, but there is little to suggest that they impacted substantially or regularly on the consciousness of party leaders. This perception of little or no influence is reinforced by a study of the published memoirs of leading figures in the party's post-war history. A search of the indexes reveals very few references to the CPC and those that exist do not refer to this particular aspect of the CPC's work. The indexes frequently list party conferences, and sometimes the CRD, but references to the CPC are few and far between, even in the memoirs of those who served as party chairmen.

    Yet the impact of the CPC Contact Programme cannot be so
easily dismissed. Three caveats need to be entered. First, there is
some countervailing evidence, or there are at least some countervailing claims, as to the impact of the programme. Butler, though
hardly a disinterested observer, thought that it had some impact in
the early days. As he wrote in his memoirs, 'many scores of discussion groups up and down the country ... were receiving well-
written pamphlets and briefing materials from the CPC, debating
and answering the questions they raised, and enjoying the knowledge that the study and collation of their reports had already
proved a helpful factor in the shaping of the new Conservatism'.[15]
How 'helpful' is difficult if not impossible to ascertain. The potential was certainly there to be helpful, given that the reports were
widely circulated within the party hierarchy. They could help reinforce the position of the leadership, as in 1971 when most CPC
groups supported entry into the European Community.[16] They
could also be less helpful, in that critical reports might have
nudged the leadership into an unwilling policy change. In 1968
most CPC groups favoured a complete ban on immigration and a
month after the report from the groups was published Edward
Heath announced a tougher immigration policy.[17] The political
situation generated by Enoch Powell's 'rivers of blood' speech on
immigration might have produced the same outcome without the
input from the CPC groups; what the group reports did was to
confirm support within the party for Powell's position. As Patrick
Cosgrave has argued, there was also the potential to have an
impact through another route. Some of those engaged in the
discussions later went on to occupy significant positions in the
party, espousing ideas that they may have acquired or refined
through the CPC; Cosgrave cites the case of Powell, who in 1950
took over the chairmanship of the West Midlands CPC.[18] As we
shall see, the director of the CPC was also, at one point, to occupy
an important role in the party's policy-making circle.
    Second, there were also consequences beyond those of inform-
ing debate. The Contact Programme not only offered an opportunity for a dialogue, it also served to socialise and integrate people
into the party. Other party activity could have had the same effect,
but for some it was the opportunity to discuss policy that brought
them in. CPC activity might thus have drawn in people who otherwise would not have become active in or committed to the
Conservative Party. Some might not have wanted to undertake the
mundane but necessary tasks of 'raising funds, locating the voters
and getting them to the poll', being interested only in the 'battle of

ideas'. This, as we shall see, could have contributed to some tension within local associations, but it also served to draw people into debate in a way not provided regularly by other parts of the party organisation. Furthermore, if the figures given do suggest continuity in involvement, CPC meetings may have served to maintain the involvement of members who, arguably, may otherwise have been less committed.

Third, CPC meetings served as a safety valve. Party supporters who wanted to have their say, either regularly or on a particular issue, had a structured outlet for their views. The size of a typical local CPC meeting meant that everyone who wanted to speak usually had an opportunity to do so. Simply attending a CPC meeting and expressing one's opinions on the subject under discussion could fulfil some members' needs to be heard. Reference to those opinions in the subsequent report would be a bonus. It was not uncommon for reports to identify or quote from views expressed by particular groups in addition to aggregating the group responses. CPC groups were also sometimes given the task of drawing up motions for submission to the annual party conference. Helping draft a motion gave one a sense of involvement. Having the motion accepted by the constituency party and then published in the conference handbook was tangible proof of one's input.

A final caveat needs to be entered. The impact being discussed here is solely that of the two-way Contact Programme. As we shall see, the CPC went through an era when it did play a vital role in influencing policy within, and beyond, the Conservative Party.

EDUCATING PARTY MEMBERS

The CPC performed an important educational role. It educated party members – not just those engaged in CPC groups – through a string of publications, summer schools (including, for many years, those at Swinton Conservative College, north Yorkshire),[19] conferences and meetings. The CPC lecture at the party conference was widely recognised as the most important meeting of the party fringe.

The party members most likely to be educated by the CPC were those who were involved in the CPC, but the education seeped out beyond them. The CPC was especially good at the dissemination of pamphlets. For party members wanting to be better informed about politics, then it was the CPC that provided the learning material. The CPC itself was the body through which the material was produced. The pamphlets were not usually written by members of staff of the CPC – the central operation had a small staff – but by politicians, academics and, on a regular basis, by members of the Conservative Research Department. Members of the CRD were frequently young, bright, political high-flyers destined for later political success.

This educative role took different forms. Initially, as Arthur Aughey and I wrote in *Conservatives and Conservatism*, 'probably the most important function of political education was not to raise the political awareness of activists *per se* but to convince them of the justice and correctness of the new direction that Conservative policy had already taken'.[20] The CPC thus provided a conduit through which members could be informed and persuaded. As the minutes of the Advisory Sub-committee on Education of 7 May 1947 make clear, 'one of the objects was to gauge the political knowledge of the party in general and to confirm or otherwise the acceptance by the rank and file of the party of the main trends of party policy'.[21] The reference to 'or otherwise' is instructive, suggesting that a negative reaction could have caused the leadership to pause. There is, though, little to suggest that the 'educating' of party members was anything but successful, both at the level of increasing political awareness generally and in increasing awareness – and acceptance – of party policy.

The CPC, in its educational role, served to counter the perceived anti-intellectual streak within British Conservatism, drawing not only on party leaders in reflective mode but also on a range of scholars. This scholarly streak was reflected not only in those who spoke at CPC meetings and wrote pamphlets but also, on occasion, in the leadership of the CPC itself. Among CPC directors with a scholarly bent were Angus Maude, Peter Goldman, David Howell and Alistair Cooke. This scholarly element is also reflected, substantially and for posterity, in its publications: ranging for example from *Essays in Conservatism* by T. E. Utley in 1949, *The New Conservatism: An Anthology of Post-war Thought 1947–55 in 1955, Some Principles of Conservatism* by Peter Goldman in 1961 through to, more recently, *The Radical Element in the History of the Conservative Party* by Norman Gash in 1989, and *The Seven Voices of Conservatism* by John Vincent in 1991.

This educative role was thus a valuable one to the party. However, its effect should not be exaggerated and it was not without its costs within the party. The number of people who subscribed to the CPC literature service was fewer than 1,000 in the

1950s – the period when it might be assumed to have had its greatest influence in disseminating new ideas – and was still under 2,000 at the beginning of the 1960s.[22] (Sales increased later in the decade.[23]) Sales, however, are not the same as readership. Some associations subscribed to the service and the literature was made available to members.

Countering the anti-intellectual streak within the party was valuable but it involved a delicate two-way operation. It needed to convey a certain impression to a wider audience while, at the same time, not operating in such a way as to feed that very anti-intellectual streak that it sought to counter. As the CPC itself recognised, there were some within the party who were wary of its activities. One investigation into party organisation in 1957 – the Colyton Report – suggested that constituency discussion groups had become isolated from the rest of the party's members. It noted that, as far as political education was concerned, 'there seems to be an enormous amount of it taking place in a closed circuit, and not reaching the general body of members'.[24] Attempts were made, with some success, to increase participation in discussion groups, but the impression of a somewhat detached body appears to have lingered. The CPC booklet *CPC in Action* noted, rather defensively, in 1967: 'There have been times when the CPC has acquired an image of remoteness from the rest of the Conservative Party. Those doing CPC work have been regarded as "intellectuals", living above the real world of canvassing and elections – and the temptation actually exists to foster such an image.'[25] It went on: 'To do so would clearly be wrong', emphasising the need for the activities of the CPC to be linked to other work in the party. By drawing in some who would not otherwise be active in the party, the CPC had to ensure that it did not alienate those who did the necessary legwork for the party but who had no intellectual pretensions themselves. It was not an easy tightrope to walk but, despite various wobbles, it appeared to achieve its principal purpose without pushing members away. After 1945, the development of an intellectual dimension of Conservatism was welcomed by some supporters and at least accepted by the rest.

INFLUENCING THE INTELLECTUAL CLIMATE

Alport and Butler planned to turn the CPC into 'a kind of Conservative Fabian Society which would act as a mouthpiece for our best modern thought and attract that section of the post-war generation who required an intellectual basis for their political faith'.[26] It was designed, in the words of one CPC publication, 'to create a climate of opinion conducive to the election of a Conservative government'.[27] It did this especially through its series of meetings and, most importantly of all, through its publications. The output of CPC pamphlets was substantial.

There are two phases in which the CPC was particularly effective in fulfilling this particular role. The first comprised the early years of the CPC, when there were relatively few competitors. It was the CPC that published the work of the One Nation Group. Iain Macleod had been asked by the CPC to write a pamphlet on the social services. He suggested that it should be a collective effort by the small ginger group of Conservative MPs that was subsequently to call itself the One Nation Group of Tory MPs. *One Nation: A Tory Approach to Social Problems*, edited by Iain Macleod and Angus Maude, was published in 1950; Enoch Powell was among the contributors. Macleod and Powell wrote *The Social Services: Needs and Means*, published in 1952. The group produced two further notable publications. *Change is Our Ally: A Tory Approach to Industrial Relations*, edited by Powell and Maude, appeared in 1954. *The Responsible Society* came out in 1959. A range of other pamphlets appeared, including some by the Expanding Commonwealth Group of MPs, as well as by individuals such as Butler, Quintin Hogg (Lord Hailsham) and Harold Macmillan.

The second effective phase was a short one but probably the most significant. The party suffered a downturn in its fortunes in the early 1960s and then lost the 1964 general election. The need to revitalise the party intellectually was recognised by the party chairman, Lord Blakenham, as well as by Edward Heath. Heath had been appointed by the party leader, Sir Alec Douglas-Home, to initiate and co-ordinate 'the biggest policy review in the party since Rab Butler's in the late 1940s'.[28] A 29-year-old leader writer for the *Daily Telegraph*, David Howell, was appointed director of the CPC and was given the task of generating new ideas.

> Specifically it was indicated to me that the party wanted to hear a lot more about lower taxation, market economics, trade union reform, joining Europe, industrial modernisation and managerial efficiency. I was left in no doubt – by Ted Heath and others – that we were to be the spearhead in opening up these debates.[29]

Howell refocused the energies of the CPC to fulfilling this task. The number of CPC staff employed at area level was reduced and resources devoted instead to promoting policy debate within the party. The CPC commissioned and published a whole new series of pamphlets – under the generic heading of *New Techniques* – by younger Conservative MPs and thinkers. Swinton Conservative College was utilised for policy conferences. Various books, including *The Conservative Opportunity*, were published. The CPC acquired a higher profile at party conferences and, indeed, within the party generally. As we have seen, it was during the period of opposition that the number of party members taking part in CPC discussion groups increased. Howell himself was drawn on to draft the 1966 party manifesto, a responsibility that enhanced the status of the CPC, albeit one that also encountered some resentment on the part of the CRD and others in the party.

This, in many respects, constituted the high point for the work of the CPC. Its director was playing a central role in policy formation. It was increasingly active at the level of the party leadership as well as in the country and it was engaging the interest of more party members. Although the work of the CPC may not have fed directly into party policy, some of the views reported in CPC reports may have served to bolster the neo-liberal approach taken by Howell and supported by the leadership. As early as 1963, CPC groups had reported strong backing for a statutory provision for secret ballots before strikes and for trade unions to be made responsible for damages caused by members.[30] Though there were other groups active in policy debate, including the Bow Group, the CPC achieved a notable status. It could be argued that it played a role in fostering ideas that were to form the basis of Conservative policy when in government in 1970 (until the policy U-turns of 1972) and again in 1979. As we shall, Margaret Thatcher was to use a CPC speech in 1968 to enunciate thoughts that were later to be the basis of her eponymous philosophy.

The CPC continued to produce pamphlets that were powerful contributions to debate. Howell was adopted as a parliamentary candidate and was succeeded as director in 1965 by Russell Lewis. He was succeeded in 1974 by the secretary to the CPC, David Knapp. Knapp was essentially a party functionary rather than a thinker and innovator. His appointment was seen as reflecting a decision to downgrade the role of the CPC. The CPC also had to compete in a more crowded environment. Its output came to be overshadowed by the publications of a range of think-tanks and research bodies. Margaret Thatcher and Sir Keith Joseph founded the Centre for Policy Studies. In the 1980s, Thatcher failed to act on advice, including from David Howell, to make greater use of the

CPC. Even so, the volume of its output remained substantial, though the notice taken of it by media commentators and others tended not to be great. The pamphlets nonetheless served to provide an important outlet for the views and opinions of leading thinkers, and perhaps not-so-leading thinkers, in the party, contributing to debate within and beyond the party. The publications deserved to have a greater audience, and impact, than in fact they did. Even at the end of its existence, the CPC was publishing important and well-argued pamphlets. These included, for example, the pamphlet on devolution, *Strengthening the United Kingdom*, published by the CPC National Policy Group on the Constitution in April 1996.[31] The semi-independent status of the CPC – and the fact that all publications carried a disclaimer that the views were those of the author or authors alone – enabled that policy group to argue a powerful case but without committing the party. This approach enabled the Home Secretary, Michael Howard, to welcome the pamphlet as 'an excellent paper on a crucial area of policy', but without embracing all its recommendations. The CPC thus remained able to contribute to intellectual debate.

This contribution, though, was not without its costs. The semi-independence of the CPC on occasion caused problems. The 'independence' meant that it could put out pamphlets that were not official party pronouncements. The 'semi' meant that it was not totally beyond party control. There were occasions when publication of pamphlets was vetoed by the party leadership. Material prepared by the CPC was checked by the Conservative Research Department. Enoch Powell had a pamphlet blocked in 1967 by the deputy party chairman, Michael Fraser.[32] Plans to publish pamphlets putting both sides of the argument in the debate on membership of the European Community in 1972 were apparently altered to limit or exclude material putting the case against membership.[33] There was also an attempt to prevent publication in 1973 of a pamphlet commemorating a right-wing thinker, Tibor Szamuely.[34] The CPC could seek to influence the intellectual climate, but within limits established by the party leadership.

PLATFORM FOR PARTY LEADERS

The third role, and one far more important than its name might imply, was that of providing a platform for party leaders. This role clearly overlapped with the preceding two but is worth identifying as a separate role. It was not a formally designated role, but it was an important one and it had significant implications for the party.

Offering politicians within the party a platform served to fulfil three benefits. First, it enabled up-and-coming figures to establish themselves in the party. CPC groups invited MPs and parliamentary candidates to come and speak. Margaret Thatcher addressed CPC meetings as an aspiring candidate early in the 1950s. 'At Swinton and at the various Conservative Political Centre meetings in different constituencies, to which I was frequently asked to speak', she wrote, 'I was made to think through the real implications for policy of such widely toted concepts as "One Nation", "the property-owning democracy" and "the safety net".'[35] Enoch Powell, as already mentioned, was very active in the CPC in the West Midlands.

Second, the CPC provided a platform for established figures to cut a reputation as thinkers within the party and to argue a particular point of view. As we have noted, the CPC lecture at the party conference was a prestigious affair. Margaret Thatcher recalled: 'The annual Conservative Political Centre lecture is designed to give some intellectual meat to those attending the Tory party conference. The choice of speaker is generally reserved to the party leader.'[36] In 1957, Lord Hailsham used the occasion – his first speech since being appointed party chairman – to articulate his own views and to rally the party faithful. 'I took particular trouble with the preparation of this speech', wrote Hailsham, 'since I knew that the whole of my future plans depended on its success, and full arrangements were made for television and the immediate publication of the text in pamphlet form under the title *Toryism and the Future.*'[37] The speech 'succeeded beyond my wildest dreams'. In 1968 Margaret Thatcher was invited to give the lecture and chose as her topic 'What's Wrong with Politics?' It allowed her to enunciate views that were later to form a distinct 'ism' in British politics. 'The virtues of hard work and personal responsibility were extolled, greater competition was identified as the means to prevent price rises, and monetarism was foreshadowed.'[38] According to one of her biographers, 'The essence of Thatcherism was there in her words that day: not in the unremarkable policies so much as in her fierce belief in them.'[39] Though not having a major impact at the time, the speech nonetheless had some impact. Thatcher was invited to contribute two articles on political philosophy to *the Daily Telegraph*. It also appeared to have some impact in terms of Thatcher's own philosophical reflections. Reflecting in her memoirs on her comments on incomes and money supply, she wrote: 'In retrospect, it is clear to me that this summed up how far my understanding of these matters had gone – and how far it still needed to go.'[40] Hailsham and Thatcher were but two in a string of leading party figures who used the CPC as a platform to articulate their personal philosophies.

Third, the CPC provided a platform – and this is the central point under this heading – for politicians to reach a much wider audience. Some noteworthy speeches or incidents have occurred at CPC meetings, gaining a national audience and with important consequences for British politics. There are two outstanding examples. One was Hailsham's announcement at the 1963 party conference that he intended to renounce his peerage, thus enabling him to seek the premiership in succession to Macmillan. This occurred in response to the vote of thanks following the CPC lecture. It was a planned announcement. He discussed it with his aide, Dennis Walters, and the party chairman, Oliver Poole.

> Oliver Poole is in favour of 'crossing the Rubicon at the first available opportunity', and suggests the Conservative Political Centre meeting, which is bound to be an emotional occasion, would be the ideal setting. In fact Quintin has already decided to disclaim at the meeting, and we agree on the wording of the disclaimer to be made when he replies to the vote of thanks at the end of his speech.[41]

Hailsham's announcement attracted an enthusiastic ovation, and massive media coverage, but his conduct at the conference dismayed party leaders and might have been the one event that destroyed his chances of succeeding Macmillan.

The other occasion was Enoch Powell's 'rivers of blood' speech, which – it is often overlooked – was given to a CPC meeting. The CPC provided him both with a platform and also with a reason for not issuing his speech through CCO.

> The platform Powell chose for his detonation … was a gathering of the Conservative Political Centre in his native city on 20 April 1968, in a small upstairs room in the Midland Hotel. He put the speech out through the West Midlands Area CPC rather than through Conservative Central Office, which had already circulated three of his tracts in the previous week. This, he maintained, was his normal practice when addressing such a group, and he happened to be its chairman.[42]

A few advance copies were circulated. Its news value was recognised by the regional television company, ATV, and clips were shown on the evening news. Powell's speech caused a furore, cost him his membership of the shadow cabinet and established him as a major figure in British politics.

Had neither Hailsham nor Powell received and accepted invitations from the CPC to speak, the history of the party and, indeed, the country might have been very different. Had Hailsham not accepted the invitation, there is the distinct possibility that he might have gone on to become Prime Minister. Had Powell not spoken at a CPC gathering, he might not have been able to prevent his speech being seen in advance by Heath, who – on such occasions – usually sent William Whitelaw to talk him out of it.[43]

Ironically, the platform offered to party leaders by the CPC might also have served as a means of integrating supporters into the party as much as, if not more than, the Contact Programme. The CPC provided the means by which party members could listen to leading figures in the party and, often, meet informally with them afterwards. The CPC speech at the party conference, for example, was normally well attended and followed by a party. A member of a local party might get to see a leading figure at the annual dinner. Membership of the CPC offered the prospect of listening to other party figures, either in the constituency or possibly at an area or even national CPC meeting.

CONCLUSION

The CPC provided the means to get members more involved and to feel more involved. Only a minority of the party did get involved but these were an important minority – though, drawing purely on the basis of anecdote and observation, an energising minority – contributing a great deal to the party in terms of local leadership. The CPC provided an additional appeal to those already committed to local party politics and an incentive for some who might otherwise not have got involved in politics.

The contribution of the CPC to the Conservative Party, judged solely in terms of the number of participants in CPC activities, may be judged to be modest. However, as John Ramsden has noted, it 'would always be a relatively small group of local activists who wanted to sit round and discuss policy ideas'.[44] The number involved in CPC meetings and Swinton conferences up to the 1960s constituted a greater involvement than that achieved by the Fabian Society, which the CPC had been set up to rival.[45] Its qualitative importance far exceeded the small number of members that took part in discussion groups. It would be difficult to imagine the party without the CPC, or its successor. It did facilitate two-way communication and it did help inform political debate in the UK. It was highly efficient in that, with very limited resources, it delivered a significant benefit to the party.

The CPC thus fulfilled a valuable role. It disappeared, at least in name, in 1998 when it was caught up in a major organisational recasting of the party. The Conservative Party ceased to be the sum of its parts and a national party came into existence. The party leader, William Hague, wanted to make the party more open to its members. They were to have a vote in the choice of future leaders. There was to be a new party gathering in the form of a Convention. Members were also to have a greater say through a new Conservative Policy Forum, designed to feed members' views into policy deliberations. The CPF replaced the CPC. In aspirational terms, the CPF could be described as more ambitious than the CPC. In practice, it has continued many of the activities of the CPC, organising regular conferences and circulating discussion briefs, with summaries prepared for distribution to party leaders. It has had difficulty emulating the continuity offered by directors of the CPC. It had three directors in the first four years of its existence. There is little evidence of it having any more influence on policy development than its predecessor.

The CPC was formed as part of the rejuvenation of the party in post-war years. It disappeared as a result of an attempt to rejuvenate the party following the disastrous general election result of 1997. The CPC marked a notable improvement on what had gone before. There is little evidence that its successor body has done so.

NOTES

1. I am grateful to two former directors of the Conservative Political Centre, David Howell (Lord Howell of Guildford) and Alistair B. Cooke, for reading and making extremely helpful comments on a draft copy of this chapter.
2. See S. Ball, 'Local Conservatism and the Evolution of the Party Organisation', in A. Seldon and S. Ball (eds), *Conservative Century: The Conservative Party since 1900* (Oxford, 1994), 261–73.
3. A. Howard, *RAB: The Life of R. A. Butler* (London, 1987), 82.
4. R. A. Butler, *The Art of the Possible* (London, Penguin edn, 1971), 138.
5. Former director of the CPC in conversation with the author, December 2000.
6. Conservative and Unionist Central Office, *The Party Organisation*, Organisation Series, No. 1 (London, 1964), 15.
7. Conservative Political Centre, *CPC in Action* (London, 1972 edn; originally published 1967), 6.
8. J. Ramsden, *The Making of Conservative Party Policy* (London, 1980), 131.
9. J. Ramsden, *The Winds of Change: Macmillan to Heath 1957–75* (London, 1996), 81.

10. D. Butler and M. Pinto-Duschinsky, *The British General Election of 1970* (London, 1971), 287.
11. P. Norton and A. Aughey, *Conservatives and Conservatism* (London, 1981), 218.
12. Ibid., 218.
13. P. Whiteley, P. Seyd and J. Richardson, *True Blues* (Oxford, 1994), 26.
14. Ramsden, *Winds of Change*, 81.
15. Butler, *Art of the Possible*, 139.
16. S. Ball, 'The Conservative Party and the Heath Government', in S. Ball and A. Seldon (eds), *The Heath Government 1970–1974* (London), 317.
17. Z. Layton-Henry, 'Immigration and the Heath Government', in ibid., 223.
18. P. Cosgrave, *The Lives of Enoch Powell* (London, 1989), 118.
19. Swinton Hall, near Masham, was owned by Lord Swinton (Philip Cunliffe-Lister), and offered regular seminars and conferences to Conservative Party members. It continued in existence until 1973, when it was sold to a trust in order to meet death duties. The director of the college from 1948 was Reginald (from 1961, Sir Reginald) Northam. By 1961, the college had drawn about 27,000 students to its courses: Ramsden, *Winds of Change*, 82.
20. Norton and Aughey, *Conservatives and Conservatism*, 138.
21. Ibid.
22. Ramsden, *Winds of Change*, 81.
23. In 1967/68 the number of subscribers went up by 800: Ramsden, *Winds of Change*, 270.
24. Quoted in Ball, 'Local Conservatism and the Evolution of Party Organisation', in Seldon and Ball (eds), *Conservative Century*, 278.
25. *CPC in Action*, 38.
26. Ramsden, *Making of Conservative Party Policy*, 107.
27. Conservative Political Centre, *CPC in Action* (London, 1983 edn), 3.
28. E. Heath, *The Course of My Life* (London, 1998), 267.
29. David Howell (Lord Howell of Guildford) to author, 21 November 2000.
30. Ramsden, *Winds of Change*, 218.
31. I have to declare an interest as a member of the Policy Group on the Constitution.
32. S. Heffer, *Like the Roman: The Life of Enoch Powell* (London, 1998), 424–5. Fraser was deputy chairman of the Conservative Party at the time.
33. B. Evans and A. Taylor, *From Salisbury to Major* (Manchester, 1996), 196.
34. Evans and Taylor, *From Salisbury to Major*, 174.
35. M. Thatcher, *The Path to Power* (London, 1995), 75.
36. Thatcher, *Path to Power*, 148.
37. Lord Hailsham of St Marylebone, *A Sparrow's Flight* (London, 1990), 320.
38. R. Shepherd, *The Power Brokers* (London, 1991), 176.
39. J. Campbell, *Margaret Thatcher, Vol. 1: The Grocer's Daughter* (London, 2000), 187.
40. Thatcher, *Path to Power*, 149.
41. D. Walters, *Not Always with the Pack* (London, 1989), 124.
42. Heffer, *Like the Roman*, 449.
43. Ibid.
44. Ramsden, *Winds of Change*, 81.
45. Ibid., 82.

11

The Community Affairs Department, 1975–79: A Personal Record

ANDREW ROWE

The Community Affairs Department (CAD) was an element of the Conservative Party organisation, which lasted about five years. It was a product of the concern felt by some of those closest to Edward Heath about the failure of the party to deliver in the two elections of 1974. In particular, Sara Morrison, a vice-chairman of the party, campaigned for major reforms of the party organisation. As Enoch Powell had put it to his constituency annual general meeting in December 1964: 'Let us admit it, we have tolerated … a level of functioning for our party organisation which no management of a business enterprise would tolerate for an instant.'[1] In 1979 *The Times* and the *Guardian* were complimentary about the department's record; but, for Stuart Ball, in *Conservative Century*, the CAD 'had failed to deliver the goods'.[2] This chapter looks at the record and seeks some evaluation of it.

ORIGINS

The Conservative Party's defeat in the spring of 1974 accelerated the cautious attempts of Sara Morrison and Michael Wolff (the recently appointed chief executive of the party) to reshape the organisation. Party membership was at an all-time low, and its fund-raising capacity correspondingly damaged. As Sara Morrison put it in a memo of 15 November 1971, 'the party organisation developed when the chief vehicle for political communication was the political meeting'. This had remained the case despite the changes in the mass media and other forms of communication. She went on to say: 'It is simply not in touch with the new meritocracy or the younger generation at all.'[3] The party had lost, or had never enjoyed, the support of large and influential groups within the population. By 1974 the party was at last beginning to address policy issues which had been largely swept under the carpet. The ideas that Keith Joseph was to publish in *Stranded in the Middle Ground* in 1976 (including his memorable phrase 'the ratchet of socialism'),[4] and the growing belief in the national media that the UK was becoming ungovernable, provided a political backdrop to the proposed reforms to the organisation. Two principal strands in the argument about ungovernability were, first, that the North–South divide had reached unbridgeable proportions and that, unless drastic measures were taken, the country would split in two (*The Economist* even advocated moving Parliament to York), and, second, that the power of the trade unions had run out of control and could not be pinned back. As always, the unions were strongest in the nationalised industries and in the media. Yet the party's links with the unions had atrophied almost to the point of non-existence.

Wolff and Morrison pointed out that the traditional organisation resulted in the weakest local associations being in the areas where seats needed to be won, and they set about trying to change the arrangements. Their modest attempts to centralise authority were strongly resisted. The major constraints on organisational reform were the autonomy of constituency associations, the quality of the professional agents, and fear of change. Because constituencies raised £13 million out of the party's total £20 million they were understandably jealous of their right to determine how 'their' money was spent. As a result, only the richer constituencies could afford to employ a professional agent. In the poorer seats, which the party had to win to secure power, the often dispirited volunteers had little or no professional help. The terms and conditions of service for agents were inadequate. Salaries were low, the training limited and out of date and the definition of the job so wide as to be unworkable. The result was predictable. Most agents were of limited ability, and were employed by amateur committees, who often had little experience of supervising staff. Repeated financial crises had made the central organisation so cautious about spending money that, as late as 1977, the deputy agents at

Conservative Central Office (CCO), who had the key task of moti-
vating the associations in their areas, had never been brought
together for a training course. Furthermore, innovation was
regarded as threatening by most agents. In this view they were
often supported by the National Union, volunteers who had either
achieved their knighthoods or were keen to do so by keeping their
noses as clean as possible. Even under the Hague reforms the
problem remains into the twenty-first century. Until the party can
afford to pay competitive salaries to attract experienced managers,
those few constituencies which can still afford an agent will
continue to employ men and women whose only hope of coping
with their job is to limit its scope to what they personally can control.

A NEW CONTEXT

The 1960s had seen a rapid growth in two distinct but linked
phenomena. First, as the Seebohm Report made clear, community
development and non-governmental organisations (NGOs) were
increasing in importance as deliverers of public policy. All over the
UK, efforts were being made to find ways of helping local communities organise themselves to improve their local conditions. The
Skeffington Committee, the Home Office community development projects and the Craigmillar action group in Edinburgh were
but three of numerous attempts to change the way local people
interacted with their environment and the bureaucracy. Second
was the huge growth in voluntary organisations and single-issue
pressure groups. Many of these had multimillion pound budgets
and attracted as executives the sort of people who, in previous
generations, would have gone into politics. People like Nicholas
Hinton of Save the Children Fund or Elisabeth Hoodless of
Community Service Volunteers believed that they would have
more influence on shaping society as heads of NGOs than they
could ever hope to secure as MPs. This transformation of traditional voluntary organisations into modern NGOs made a striking
impact on the political scene. There was a new constituency for the
party to address and new expertise on which to draw. This was one
reason why, in late 1974, the present writer, who had been a
consultant to the Voluntary Services Unit and had considerable
experience of both community projects and the voluntary sector,
was offered a job at CCO.

The initial brief was to help the party tap into the expertise of
the voluntary sector. There were two main hurdles to overcome.

First was the pervasive interpretation among charities that charitable status meant that no contact could be safely made with political parties. This persists in many organisations even now, no matter how often the point is made that it is both legal and more effective to make contact with all parties. Second, despite the fact that many of the traditional organisations, such as the Women's Royal Voluntary Service, drew heavily on the very people who worked for the Conservative Party,[5] Conservatives tended to regard the entire voluntary sector as irremediably socialist and dangerous to know. That they were more successful at attracting supporters from all parts of society than the Conservative Party and were in effective touch with a much wider spectrum of the electorate was ignored. Today, for example, the Royal Society for the Protection of Birds has a membership that dwarfs that of any political party.

A CCO press release of 6 January 1975 defined his role: 'Mr Rowe will be responsible for maintaining and developing the party's links with community associations, neighbourhood groups, and the rapidly growing host of community-based organisations. His appointment will make it easier for the views and experience of such groups to reach the party's policy makers at an early stage in their deliberations. He will consult widely with constituency associations and all other elements in the party to determine how best achieve this. He will also be strengthening the links already established with national and regional voluntary bodies, particularly those working in the social services.'[6] Rowe amplified this three days later in a memorandum to CCO agents and heads of departments:

> One of the most striking developments in recent years has been the growth of national and local organisations which aim to achieve a political objective but which prefer to operate outside the political parties. At national level comparatively new ones like Shelter or CPAG … have taken the lead in developing techniques for bringing pressure to bear directly on ministers and their departments. And their methods are being increasingly copied by older organisations such as … Age Concern. Many of these organisations are proving very attractive to voluntary workers, especially to the young. They often provide the excitement, responsibility and sense of involvement which it has been difficult for the political parties to generate. Moreover, … they seem to offer a chance of obtaining tangible results more quickly.

Similarly at local level there has been an enormous upsurge of community groups of all sorts and titles, particularly in the cities and housing estates. Many of these fight fierce battles with the local authority or central government depts. And since both are likely to be Labour controlled at the moment the importance of this for local Conservatives seems obvious.

The problem is how to create and maintain the sort of links with all these activities which will be acceptable to them and profitable to the party. Many of these bodies are fiercely independent of party labels and wish to remain so. Indeed, if they were to seek a party affiliation they would choose against the Conservatives. Yet there are very large numbers of Conservatives or would-be Conservative voters involved in these organisations. It is often striking to see how the left-inclined members of them are quite willing to bring their political philosophies to bear in discussions about the policies which should be pursued by their organisation. It is much rarer for the right to do the same. Moreover, these organisations contain not only large reservoirs of experience and information which are invaluable to political policy makers, but also the potential for much greater contributions. I see my job as being to try to help the party at all levels to make useful and acceptable connections with bodies like the ones I have mentioned and both to help them when appropriate and to learn from them.[7]

The election of Margaret Thatcher and the appointment as party chairman of Lord Thorneycroft changed everything. Morrison went, and Michael Wolff was sacked and almost immediately afterwards died of a heart attack. Sir Richard Webster, the chief agent, whose delight at the departure from Conservative Central Office of Wolfe and Morrison was open, overreached himself while Thorneycroft was in hospital; on the chairman's return he was given two hours to clear his desk. His post was abolished and five directorships, directly answerable to the chairman were established. These were: Organisation, Women and Local Government, Communications, Community Affairs, and Research. Under Community Affairs there was placed (in addition to the original brief of voluntary organisations and pressure groups), the youth side of the party, including the Young Conservatives (YCs) and the Federation of Conservative Students (FCS); relations with the ethnic minorities; the Conservative Trade Unionists (CTU), and, once it had been invented, the Small Business Bureau.

TENSIONS AND PRESSURES

The department's ability to function depended throughout its life primarily on the support of the chairman, who defended it on numerous occasions against its critics. These fell into two main kinds: traditionalists and politicians. The traditionalists resented the new department for two main reasons. As professional agents, they felt threatened by an influx of people from outside the party with no experience of working in it, especially when they were working with groups who had hitherto been exclusively the agents' respon-sibility.[8] Also, the new department held meetings and training sessions for its staff to a degree that aroused envy. The other critics were mainly politicians. They believed that the department had a political agenda of its own, which threatened their own political beliefs, and would complain whenever the department's activities inconvenienced them. The chairman was put under pressure, and responded with a minute dated 6 March 1975 in these terms:[9]

> I wish thought to be given to a general organisational policy issue which appears to be much discussed – certainly outside Central Office. A view is widely held that active Conservatives in constituency organisations should concern themselves not simply with recruiting the faithful but in searching out ideas and people in activist groups e.g. meals on wheels, Contact, SCF, ratepayers' and tenants' associations etc. The concept as I understand it, is that these groups should be encouraged to the view that Parliament in general and the Conservative Party in particular has a role in forwarding at least some of their aims and that we will tap a useful source of new ideas which will eventually find its way into our policy-forming activities. A view is, I understand, also held that all this will take up money and valuable time and is not likely at least in the short term to produce many more Conservative voters. I am myself much disposed to favour the activist approach. Mr Rowe was appointed by Mrs Morrison to forward these ideas. I would like Mr Clark to have a talk with him and to suggest ways in which his activities could be incor-porated into our management structure so that his talents can be usefully employed. I recognise that this approach will need to be started on a limited scale in a few areas. It will certainly involve the use of Young Conservatives and it will require as it expands all the help that Sir Richard Webster can secure from the organisation in the country.

Although the support of the chairman was crucial, the finances were in the hands of William Clarke who was especially sceptical. As a result, the new department had to tread warily. The effect was to limit both the salaries that could be paid and the operational freedom on the ground. Almost all the staff were paid very little (around £3,000 per annum) and most were placed in the area offices, reporting on a day-to-day basis to the area agent. Area agents were responsible to the director of organisation, so the Community Affairs Department staff had a difficult structure in which to work. In some areas this worked well; in others, it led to predictable friction and confusion about priorities.

In another respect, the department occupied an unusual position in the structure. Because its remit extended so widely it was responsible to a wide range of political masters. For its trade union work it responded to Jim Prior; on ethnic minorities, it responded to Shadow Home Secretary, William Whitelaw; for the Small Business Bureau, it worked with David Mitchell; and, for youth work and work with voluntary organisations, it worked principally with John Moore – who, as a vice-chairman of the party, took oversight of the whole department. Apart from the main party conference, CCO conference, and the local government and women's conferences, the department ran all the rest. While the director was a separate administrative manager, Chris Patten (the director of research) invited him to his weekly staff meeting and relations between that department and the senior members of the CAD were close.

Many of the techniques employed by the CAD had been employed by good agents over many years. To reach those who had no links with the party, it mounted special interest meetings, sometimes with the assistance of Joan Varley, responsible for the women's section, who was an enthusiast for them. For an organiser the attraction is that hundreds of people, who have no intention of attending, receive an invitation and thus feel included. At times when the government is unpopular, this often leads to new members. Whether or not any notice is taken of the views submitted by those who do attend depends entirely on the prejudices of the policy makers. The tactic is sound because it takes account of the fact that, while most people have no interest at all in politics, they do have an interest in one or two topics close to their hearts and on those they often have a real contribution to make. Except at times of unusual political tension, the British electorate is much readier to attend a meeting that is not explicitly party political than one that is. Yet, if the methods of the department were not always innovative, its goals were often controversial. Fortunately, its staff were mostly untrammelled by considerations of career prospects within the party organisation. People like Wilf Weeks, later founder of the lobbying firm GJW, or Margaret Daly, later an MEP, were among a majority in the department who saw their futures outside the narrow confines of Conservative Central Office.

THE DEPARTMENT'S WORK

It is easy to forget at this distance how different the political scene was in 1975. The received wisdom was that the UK was becoming ungovernable and the North–South divide so unbridgeable that it might split in half. John Moore remembers being spat at and assaulted with bricks when he went to speak at universities; racial tensions were running high in many areas; and the Labour government was soon to extend beyond all bounds the rights of trade unions. So what were the department's goals, apart from the overall remit of attracting into the party people who had hitherto ignored it? Its purpose was to win votes for the party. To do this it had to render the party attractive to people who had either deserted it or had never thought of voting for it. This is the point at which the boundaries between policy and organisation became and remain blurred.

Ethnic minorities

The department was committed to reducing the widespread racism within the party. It presented to the party hierarchy the impeccably correct organisational goal of seeking to win supporters among the Black population, whether originating from the West Indies, the countries of the Asian subcontinent or East Africa. The chairman supported this goal and, as a student, John Moore had marched in anti-segregation demonstrations in the United States. Large numbers of Conservative activists, however, were hostile. Many lived in urban areas from which the large employers had withdrawn, taking with them the skilled and semi-skilled white workforce. Into the decaying streets and ailing small shops had come the Asian immigrants. Not only did they change the culture (and even the smells) of the area, but they were wrongly blamed by the remaining white population for its impoverishment. It took them many years to understand that these incomers were the only improving force in the area. The party also remained acutely aware of the contest at Smethwick in the general election of 1964 in which the Conservative candidate won partly because he refused to disown racist pamphlets.

In 1975 the Conservative activists were elderly. They were the least able to adapt to change, felt the decline of their neighbourhoods most acutely and were understandably inclined to support Enoch Powell and his ally Harvey Proctor in their attacks on 'immigrants'. The staff of the department (with perhaps one exception) were determined to change all this and used the party resources to do so. The section that dealt with the Anglo-Asian and Anglo-Caribbean Conservative societies was run by Mervyn Kohler (now head of policy at Help the Aged), but the Young Conservatives, the Federation of Conservative Students, and some of the Conservative Trade Unionists all helped in the fight. This took many forms: for example, the youth side would run campaigns both within the party and outside it. Central Office was remarkably reluctant to exert serious pressure on the Conservative clubs. These independent drinking clubs had become careless about insisting on party allegiance as a condition of membership, but their name linked them publicly with the Conservative Party, and if they refused to admit non-whites the message given was clear enough. All over the country YC groups and FCS branches would take Black friends to the clubs and seek to shame them into behaving properly. It was a slow process, and often led to tensions between the youth side of the party and the rest.

If the party was to have any serious chance of winning votes among the ethnic minority groups it was essential that members from those groups should feel welcome in it. This was not easy to achieve either organisationally or politically. There was a naive belief that the different groups, especially those from the subcontinent, had 'leaders' who could deliver their followers. All sorts of people put themselves forward in this role. Some of them were excellent people; many others were charlatans. Some had views that were unacceptable in the party; others had only one view – the overriding importance of their own self-advancement. It was never easy to determine whether a constituency was behaving prudently or merely discriminatorily when it rejected the attempts of a non-white person to climb the political ladder. Fortunately, the department had important and effective political allies. MPs like Bernard Weatherill and John Biggs-Davison were tireless in their willingness to visit constituencies and take part in ethnic celebrations. The sensitivities of the time are well shown by the campaign against Weatherill in his own constituency, led by his agent and directed against his sympathy for minority groups. There also came forward important and reliable allies from within the groups themselves. From the Indian population Shreela Flather and Jay Gohel proved invaluable, both because of their courage in facing down racism within the party and because its information about personalities was much better founded than could have been achieved without them.

One of the great difficulties in persuading the minorities that the party was interested in them was that, whenever a shadow cabinet member or other party bigwig paid a visit to a constituency, they naturally met volunteer activists who had worked their way up to be office holders in the party. To single out someone for recognition merely on the grounds of his or her colour was to invite protest. None of the new communities had been here long enough to have thrown up people likely to be holding office in a party area. How could this be overcome? One answer was to create a special ladder within the party and it was helpful that there was a precedent. Members of the Polish community had created an Anglo-Polish Society when they first arrived and, although by now it was unnecessary, it had provided entry to the party for the first arrivals. The department therefore created first an Anglo-Asian Conservative Society (on the inspiration of Narinder Saroop) and an Anglo-Caribbean one. This allowed high-profile visitors to meet members of both communities and to be photographed with them for the local and national press without raising local party hackles. The names were woefully inappropriate, but in a party where innovation is only acceptable if dressed in traditional garb it was better to accept the name than fail to create the mechanism. The Conservative Party Archive contains a list of the aims of the Anglo-West Indian Conservative Society, which begins as follows:

> The Anglo-West Indian Conservative Society exists to provide support for Conservative policies, to assist the UK West Indian communities to participate more fully in the political, social and cultural life of Britain, and to encourage the Conservative sympathies which many West Indians inherently possess.[10]

As always in a political organisation, advances could be jeopardised by high-profile remarks from MPs, and much of the department's work was to try to undo the effect of populist appeals to the anti-immigrant vote. In March 1977, for example, the director minuted the party chairman in the following terms:

The party cannot afford to have candidates talking on race relations with one voice in difficult constituencies and in another elsewhere. In 57 seats the Asian vote alone is bigger than the majority, and it is abundantly clear that the community, whether Asian or Black, will be watching through their specialist press, the performance of candidates everywhere. It will not be enough for Willie Whitelaw to put out the official line in Cumberland while individual candidates are pandering to prejudice in their own seats.

The minute went on to ask for the authority of the leader to be thrown behind appropriate guidance to candidates.[11] In the author's judgement, considerable progress was made between 1975 and 1979 in reducing the racism of the party: the CAD is entitled to claim some of the credit.

The trade unions

Comparable tensions arose in the Conservative Trade Unionists. The party had made sporadic attempts since the 1920s to appeal to Conservatives within the trade union movement, but by 1975 the paid staff had diminished until there were only two elderly men at CCO and a handful of active CTU branches. The voluntary national officers were drawn from people who, in most cases, had retained union membership while being no longer employed in unionised work. Notable exceptions were Tom Ham (a docker from the East End of London), Ron Benson (a railwayman) and Mrs Crum Ewing, about whom more later. The party was divided over having a trade union organisation within it. Mrs Thatcher knew that if the Conservatives were to regain power the unions would have to be taken on. Many of her closest advisers felt that it would jeopardise the purity of the assault on bloated union privilege if, simultaneously, efforts were being made to woo union members into the party. Others – such as Jim Prior, Richard Needham and Peter Bottomley – were in no doubt that it was essential to improve the party's knowledge of union thinking and to appeal to the many trade unionists who felt disenfranchised or oppressed by the closed shop and other excesses of union power.

At the time, trade unions were growing fast and had 1.5 million more members than the total number of voters who had voted Conservative in 1974. The CTU, under John Bowis, began to make useful inroads into the union structures. To the horror of some of Thatcher's team, the department recruited active trade unionists on to its staff. Martin Gillate, who had organised a strike of air traffic controllers, and Margaret Daly, who had organised a strike of City Bank staff, both became full time organisers and, far from being renegades from the cause of true trade unionism, spoke up fiercely for them when they were being attacked unreasonably within the party. Added to this was the decision that as many members of the department staff (and as many MPs and candidates) as possible should join their appropriate union. The CCO members of Association of Scientific, Technical, and Managerial Staffs (ASTMS) attended the annual general meeting of the central banks staff branch and found themselves in a majority, and Mervyn Kohler was duly elected chairman. This had a particular piquancy because this branch also represented Transport House, which at that time also housed the headquarters of the Labour Party! Clive Jenkins speedily found a pretext for disbanding the branch, but it had led to some useful publicity for the CTU and some valuable education for the CAD staff. The importance of involvement in local trade union branches was shown by a survey carried out by the women's section of the party. They found that, while 38 per cent of Tory women belonged to a trade union, 91 per cent never attended a branch meeting. The combination of the department's experience and this statistic added great weight to Margaret Thatcher's often repeated appeals to Conservatives to 'go to your branch meetings and STAY TO THE END!'

By the beginning of 1978 there were already 250 branches of the CTU and Jim Prior was listening to it on many issues. Some of the most useful information came from Scotland, where the CTU organiser, Stephen Young, brought several groups of anxious union members to discuss privately with the team the real issues behind a number of disputes. Many of the people coming were not Conservatives, a further indication of the truth that men and women concerned about their own livelihoods regard party politics as decidedly secondary. It was also an indication of the growing frustration felt by many union members with their government. Another unexpected but valuable source of information on one union's affairs was Mrs Crum Ewing. This aristocratic woman had been the treasurer of the Association of Cinematograph, Television, and Allied Technicians (ACTT) for many years, despite all the efforts of Alan Sapper (the general secretary) to dislodge her. She always claimed that even the left wanted to be sure that its funds were in the hands of someone honest and, while members were happy to let their union's politics be ruled by an extreme left-wing clique, they felt no such happiness about the money.

There were other tensions between the CTU and the party, the clearest of which was racial prejudice. Tom Ham and his Essex and East London colleagues, who had borne the heat of the battle to keep Conservatism alive among the dockers' and allied unions, articulated the traditional hostility felt by their members to the ethnic minorities. It would not be easy to recruit valuable members of the CTU from the Midlands if they were to be insulted in general terms at national CTU meetings. This same Essex clique was later shown to be organising candidate selection in the Essex constituencies with the clear intention of installing extreme right-wing candidates. This was brought to the attention of the party chairman, and the conspiracy largely scotched.

One of the most effective tactics used by the CTU was the creation of a presence at the Trades Union Congress (TUC) conferences. This not only showed the TUC that it had Conservative members, but showed both the media and other trade unionists that the Conservative Party had an organisation capable of articulating their concerns. The climax of this stage of the CAD's involvement with the CTU came at the general election campaign in 1979. In 1977, the director had minuted the party's deputy chairman, Janet Young, with a series of suggestions for the general election campaign. He particularly stressed the value of mounting some high-profile events to attract national media coverage rather than relying on traditional constituency-based campaigning.[12] The principal suggestion was that the department should mount a CTU rally during the campaign to dispel the myth that all trade unionists voted Labour. This was adopted and some 3,000 trade unionists filled Wembley conference centre and captured the top slot on national TV news that night. It was the first time such a display had been tried in British politics, and its impact was considerable.

The youth of the party

The importance of improving the party's standing among young people was greatly sharpened by two factors which had nothing to do with party organisation: the number of teenagers had swelled by over 1 million in the 1960s, and in 1967 the voting age had been lowered from 21 to 18. Within the party, the youth side meanwhile was going from strength to strength. By 1977 the FCS claimed over 200 branches, 16,000 members and political control of more than 50 student unions, including some of the very big ones such as Manchester. These were important gains, not least because the big student unions had sabbatical presidents who could make a most valuable contribution. For the party organisation, the benefits were many. First, it meant that Conservative spokespeople at universities could usually count on considerable support. Second, in student union after student union moderate policies, especially over the right to hold meetings with speakers who were not acceptable to the left, came to be adopted. Third, a whole generation of Conservative students learned campaigning skills that would stand them in good stead later. Their posters were attractive and hard-hitting, and the elections were hard-fought. The CAD, with a youth and community officer in every area, lent as much support as possible while standing at arms length from some of the more outrageous manifestations of Tory enthusiasm. One of the most useful lessons absorbed from the broad left was how to run an effective slate in elections. This was one thing in which CCO could be helpful, and the techniques came to be applied also to trade union elections. Many moderate union officials came to owe their seats to the unacknowledged and carefully unadmitted assistance rendered by CCO.

As usual, the biggest problem for the FCS came from within. In April 1976, Michael Forsyth, a product of St Andrews University, was elected chairman of the federation. His agenda (which, ironically in the light of subsequent events, was strongly pro-Europe) came to include the withdrawal of the FCS from the National Union of Students (NUS) on two grounds. The first was that, however well the FCS performed, it would never be able to take control. The second was that it was wrong in principle for the NUS to be financed out of a compulsory levy. As is so often the case, purism of theory proved disastrous in practice. The director warned the party chairman that, if ever the FCS withdrew from fighting the left, it would turn to internecine war. A few years later the FCS had indeed withdrawn from the NUS and was then disbanded by its own party. While the CAD was responsible for it, FCS became the largest single group in student politics with 20,000 members by 1979.

The Young Conservatives were also growing fast and proved invaluable in many of the contests facing the party – not least, as we have seen, in the fight against racism. In a memo dated 2 March 1978 Rowe reported that the numbers of YCs had increased to its highest level for more than ten years, with an exceptionally high rate of increase for 16–18 year olds.[13] The co-operation between the department and the YCs reached its climax in 1979 when it enabled a youth rally for Europe to be organised successfully in less than four weeks.

The Small Business Bureau

The most enduring element of the CAD has been the Small Business Bureau. David Mitchell MP was fighting to win back the support of small business proprietors and asked for the department's help. The director decided to set up a purpose-built organisation to act as a two-way channel of communication between small businesses and Conservative policy makers. Nothing demonstrated better the lack of imagination in the party organisation. Instead of welcoming a new way to raise funds and influence an important group of the electorate, the local agents complained that they would lose much needed subscriptions to their associations. Since on average there were 1,500 small businesses in every constituency and no constituency could claim as many as 100 among its membership, this was shortsighted in the extreme. The damaging result was that the initial subscription to the bureau had to be set at the ludicrously small figure of £3, which made it financially unviable. Yet, by 1977 it had already attracted more than 1,000 members and over the years has grown to be one of the largest and most influential of the small business organisations. From the beginning it ran its own newspaper and it was interesting to note how many outside investors wanted to take it over. The problem always was that those who wanted to back a commercial product would not accept that it had to carry party material, and several promising backers had to be turned down.

Community affairs

The department did not neglect its original brief. It organised seminars with voluntary organisations and, on one occasion, with directors of social services, to discuss issues of concern to them. One of the most unusual seminars was on vandalism, held at CCO on 19 October 1977. It was attended by the Shadow Home Office team and enlivened by the presence of two young men who had passed much of their life in acts of vandalism. The department also persuaded an astonished CCO to accept that it could apply for a government grant for one employee and six unemployed young people to work on a project designed to get them back into the labour market. Although the grant was given on the strict understanding that no party politics could be preached at the young people, it is notable that one of them later became a Conservative council leader.

CONCLUSION

The aims of the CAD can be summarised under three headings: to make the Conservative Party credible, to reduce the power of the left, and to support the policy makers. In the first of these, it worked to render credible to all the people in its target populations the message that the Conservative Party was interested in them, ready to learn from them and prepared to consider policy proposals which would assist them in their aims, if they were acceptable to the main thrust of Tory philosophy. Perhaps its biggest contribution was to render less alien to party activists people with whom they had hitherto had little contact. The presentation to party conferences of trade unionists, Black speakers and others who were clearly thoughtful and interested in the party did much to break down constituency hostility to them and opened the way to necessary changes. (The organisation of speakers to be called at the different party conferences was an important part of getting the message across.) The second aim to reduce the grip of the left on organisations at every level where they had long enjoyed a free run because Tories had treated them as no-go areas. The third aim was to support the policy makers with better quality information than they had hitherto received. In this, the record was patchy, but an improvement on what had gone before.

In the modern Conservative Party, where the average age of activists is 66 and their numbers have reached a low point, similar outreach strategies need to be employed. The CAD's experience suggests that listening is not enough; tangible support for those opposed to the government is required also, even if at times this proves uncomfortable. In 1977 a CCO agent wrote to ask why YCs and FCS students had taken part in a march against unemployment. Was it not shocking to involve Conservatives in demonstrations, and especially alongside the left? The director replied that it had shown the young that for once the party was as concerned as anyone about the job prospects for their generation; it had rocked the left, who had imagined that it enjoyed sole command of the field, and had won plaudits from the police who had been greatly impressed by the responsible behaviour of the Conservative demonstrators.[14]

It is virtually impossible to work out whether the CAD 'delivered the goods', since party organisations are always overshadowed by the policy changes brought in by the party leaders. Yet some crude measures demonstrate a certain success. In numbers, the Federation of Conservative Students, Young Conservatives

and Conservative Trade Unionists all increased enormously
during the lifetime of the CAD. The ethnic minorities, who had
been viewed by most of the party with grave suspicion and often
dislike, began to find their way into the party hierarchies. The
work of the department was, however, vulnerable always to the
public utterances of the party leaders and it is not surprising that
they did not sign up in large numbers when Mrs Thatcher herself
was not always careful of what she said. It was in such matters that
the internal work of the department, unseen from outside, may
have proved valuable. For example, the director wrote to the
chairman on 6 February 1978:

> Mrs Thatcher's interview has raised an enthusiastic response
> in a number of quarters including the west Midlands. This
> presents the party organisation with some difficulties which
> we should consider urgently before they land the party in
> serious trouble.

After pointing out that there were a number of Conservative
candidates fighting crucial seats in which the ethnic minority vote
was the deciding factor, he went on to say:

> We should stress the crucial distinction between race relations
> and immigration and ensure that everyone who speaks on
> this subject, which will continue to attract media attention,
> gives the reassurances to the ethnic minorities which are
> essential if we are to retain the slightest hope of winning over
> a number of their votes.[15]

As for the links with small business, the election results showed
that the party had re-established itself among them as an important element in its victory. While this was probably a consequence of national policy, it can be fairly claimed that the Small
Business Bureau, which organised hundreds of small business
meetings all over the country, played its part in that turn round.

Probably the lasting message of the CAD is that, in an increasingly diverse and specialised political field, there is merit in
reaching out to sections of the electorate, not through the preferences of the party but through the preferences of the voter. The
new Conservative leadership says that this is what it wants to do,
but it remains to be seen if it has the imagination and sensitivity to
do it. The postscript to the CAD experiment was very disappoint-
ing. After the 1979 election victory the director of the department
left to pursue other avenues, and within a very few months the
department was disbanded and absorbed into the Organisation

Department, where its distinctive approach was lost. Only the Small Business Bureau was allowed to retain a semi-independent role, and therefore remains a major contributor to the party.

NOTES

1. Enoch Powell, December 1964, Conservative Party Archive (CPA), Bodleian Library.
2. S. Ball, 'The National and Regional Party Structure', in A. Seldon and S. Ball (eds), *Conservative Century: The Conservative Party since 1900* (Oxford, 1994), 188.
3. 'The Conservative Party – Communication', memo by Morrison, 15 November 1971, CPA, CCO 20/7/13, in S. Ball (ed.), *The Conservative Party since 1945* (Manchester, 1988), 75–6.
4. K. Joseph, *Stranded in the Middle Ground* (Centre for Policy Studies, 1976).
5. See also Chapter 6 by James Hinton in this volume.
6. Conservative Central Office, press release, 6 January 1975, CPA, Community Affairs Department 1975–78, CCO 4/10/53.
7. Rowe to CCO area agents and heads of departments, 9 January 1975, CPA, Community Affairs Department 1975–78, CCO 4/10/53.
8. 'Sir Richard Webster believed that Mr Rowe was a sinister knight, clothed in the armour of progressivism.' R. Behrens, *The Conservative Party from Heath to Thatcher* (Saxon House, 1980), 50.
9. Lord Thorneycroft to William Clarke, Angus Maude, Alec Todd, Joan Varley and Sir Richard Webster, 'Activist Organisations', 6 March 1975, CPA, Uncatalogued Organisation Department (CCO 500), Community Affairs – general: 1975–80.
10. 'Anglo-West Indian Conservative Society', *c.* April 1978, CPA, Community Affairs Department 1975–78, CCO 4/10/53.
11. Memo, Rowe to Thorneycroft, March 1977, in my possession.
12. Memo, Rowe to Young, in my possession.
13. Rowe to Neave, 2 March 1978, attached to memo Rowe to Garner, 2 March 1978, CPA, Uncatalogued Organisation Department (CCO 500), Community Affairs – general: 1975–80.
14. Papers in my possession.
15. Memo by Rowe, 'Immigration', 6 February 1978, CPA, Uncatalogued Organisation Department (CCO 500), Community Affairs – general: 1975–80.

Thatcherism and
the British People

BRENDAN EVANS

Under the leadership of Margaret Thatcher and John Major, the Conservative Party won four successive general elections and enjoyed 18 years of office from 1979. While the Conservative Party had already acquired the reputation of being the natural party of government, it was this extended period in power which ensured that the twentieth century became the *Conservative Century*.[1] This relationship with the electorate is considered here with reference to a case-study of the Basildon constituency. It is argued that Thatcher failed both to create a populist hegemony and to capture deep and lasting support, so that she and Major secured their victories through the conventional mixture of luck and the manipulation of the opportunities of office to control the electoral cycle. The Basildon case reinforces the view that since the 1970s there has been partisan dealignment in which habitual class-based voting has been replaced by electoral volatility. It can be argued that class voting before the 1970s was the result of institutional structuring rather than the class voting preferences of the electorate; but clearly, since the 1970s, the process of dealignment has encouraged the study of local variations in political behaviour.[2] This diminished the party as the chief instrument of political mobilisation, and emphasised the significance of governmental performance in determining general election outcomes.

Through political folklore Basildon has become an emblematic Thatcherite constituency as a part of the myth of 'Essex man'.

Certain characteristics of the constituency and of the sub-region in which it is located are proposed, although the study also highlights the national situation of an electorally, rather than an ideologically, dominant Conservatism; and even that electoral success was neither smooth nor easy.

The period from February 1975 to September 1992 is examined because while throughout that time Conservatism fluctuated in the opinion polls it retained the capacity to recover politically. From 15 September 1992, however, the date of the infamous 'Black Wednesday' when Britain left the European exchange rate mechanism (ERM), it is apparent that Conservatism declined in popular standing, a position from which it has never recovered. This does not entirely undermine Thatcher's success in her stated mission of changing the Labour Party and destroying socialism. Since New Labour's emergence, and despite its more favourable orientation to the public sector, there are two parties committed to the free enterprise system.[3]

THE DECADE OF DEALIGNMENT

Class-based voting has declined since 1970, as is apparent from general election results and survey evidence. Previously, voters had tended to acquire a psychological attachment to a political party at an early age. These loyalties were reinforced during their lifespan, and voters took cues on specific issues from the party leadership.[4] The number of voters with a lifelong loyalty to any political party has sharply reduced. 'After the 1987 election 64 per cent of voters said they had a lifelong loyalty to the same party.'[5] At the 1983 general election survey evidence suggested that one in five voters were entirely available for conversion.[6] The evidence is that shocks, policy failures and uncontrolled events have disrupted many voters' party allegiances. Polling evidence suggests the view that the 'Winter of Discontent', the Falklands War and a booming economy assisted the Conservatives in 1979, 1982 and 1987 respectively, while the rise in unemployment, the Westland affair and the poll tax controversy in 1980–81, 1986 and 1989–90 respectively damaged them.[7]

Increasing electoral volatility is demonstrated by the comparison between the 1951 election when 96.8 per cent of the voters chose one of the two main parties and 2001 when the comparable statistic was 72.4 per cent. Among Conservative voters, 49 per cent of respondents defined themselves as being 'very strong' in their allegiance in 1964, as against 24 per cent in 1987.[8] Beck argues that it is only the generation that actually experiences a partisan realignment that possesses enduring party loyalties, while its children reveal a declining commitment.[9] The results of general elections demonstrate that instability is now normal politics.[10] The Conservative support that Thatcher secured in 1979 was, therefore, merely a foundation upon which she and her government could erect a durable electoral coalition. Naturally, the party's propaganda machine, together with the local efforts of its activists, have a role to play in promoting the party's appeal to the voters. These efforts would be in vain, however, if their government was not performing in such a way as to satisfy prospective Conservative voters. It was the performance of the Conservative Party in opposition, and more influentially in government, which determined its level of support.

FLUCTUATING CONSERVATIVE POPULARITY, 1979–92

It is apparent that the Conservative governments from 1979 to 1992 enjoyed cyclical periods of popularity, but their popularity coincided with crucial general election years. A leading commentator – influenced by four successive Conservative victories, with margins in the popular vote ranging from 7 to 7.5 per cent in 1979 and 1992 and 11.5 to 14.8 per cent in 1987 and 1983 – argued that there was an emergent one-party system in Britain. He predicted Conservative governments well into the new millennium.[11] The Conservative Party's desire for power and its historic success in winning elections should not be confused, however, with its support from voters on particular issues. Elections are blunt instruments for determining popular preferences on specific issues. Polling evidence suggests that throughout the 13.5 years from Thatcher's victory in 1979 to Black Wednesday the Conservatives did not fully represent widespread views in British society, and there was no evidence of a unique empathy between the government and the people. Only in seven of the 161 months between the 1979 election and Black Wednesday did more people express themselves satisfied than dissatisfied with the Conservative Government.[12]

Thatcher's personal hegemony over British politics is also questioned by the appreciation that in only 15 of the 138 months in which she was Prime Minister did she enjoy a positive rating for leadership. Of the 50 months during which the Conservatives were led by Thatcher in opposition the party enjoyed an opinion-poll lead in 37, although this was a better performance than when she was Prime Minister. Even the polling evidence on voting intention demonstrates that the government was on a roller coaster rather than in a dominating position. During the Thatcher years in government the party was in the lead in 62 but in deficit in 75 months.[13] Black Wednesday finally destroyed any possible view that the Conservatives enjoyed a hegemonic position. In its immediate aftermath, in October 1992, 72 per cent declared themselves hostile to the government, 65 per cent dissatisfied with Major's leadership, and the party slipped into a voting intention deficit of 23 against Labour.[14]

One possible reconciliation of the contradictory trends towards both partisan dealignment and Conservative electoral success in the Thatcher years is that there was a process of differential dealignment in which Labour support was draining away more rapidly than it was for the Conservatives. Yet, while Labour's fall was sharper than the Conservatives' fall from the late 1970s to the early 1990s, support for *both* main parties was lower than in the 1960s. If the Conservative electoral victories represented a fundamental shift to the Conservatives, then the periods when they led in the opinion polls during the Thatcher years would have been enduring. There were three such periods when a shift in popular support towards the Conservatives was apparent (1975–77, 1981–84/85 and 1986–88). Yet none of these periods lasted more than two and a half years; at no stage did the Conservative vote return to the levels of 1969; all were followed by periods of countervailing growth in Labour support.[15]

Some writers suggest a deterministic model, which relates electoral outcomes to economic trends. They trace the 1983 results to suggest that it was the effect of the fall in the value of sterling, which began in 1981, and the consequent rise in output, which led to electoral success in June 1983.[16] They recognise that it is public perceptions about the economic past and expectations about the short-term economic future that impact on electoral outcomes. Their overplayed argument, however, neglects political factors.[17] Their economically deterministic interpretation fails in 1981–84 because it neglects the importance of the Falklands War. This was independently important, but had its greatest impact in reinforcing the electoral potency of Thatcher's resolute style of leadership. It 'dramatically altered public judgements about her competence as Prime Minister, and thereby prompted the development of more sanguine expectations about the future course of the nation's economy under her stewardship'.[18]

It is more convincing to turn to particular explanations for specific general elections. Such explanations range from the Winter of Discontent, taxes, law and order and the mistaken timing of the election by Callaghan in 1979 to Labour strife, the Falklands and the Foot factor in 1983, to peace, prosperity and Kinnock in 1987, and taxes, Kinnock and a fear of inflation in 1992.[19]

The impact of the choice between Thatcher and her rivals was crucial. 'She was simply fortunate that during the crucial middle years of her tenure she was opposed by the opposition leader with the lowest overall public evaluation of any leader since opinion poll data was collected.'[20] The elections of 1983 and 1987 also fell at the optimal time. Thatcher did 'a masterful job of teetering on the volatile balance of public support between the parties, exploiting the opportunities provided by the leadership problems of the Labour Party, public reaction to the Falklands War, the formation of the SDP [Social Democratic Party] and improving economics'.[21]

THE CONSERVATIVE PARTY AND GENERAL ELECTIONS

Harold Macmillan once asserted that the greatest challenge to any government is simply 'events'. From 1975 to May 1979 the Conservative Party in opposition had a slight capacity to influence events, but from May 1979 it could make a notable impact upon events, including the timing of general elections.

The most important component in the Conservative election campaigns was the comparison with its rivals. Images of the quality of leadership and the performance of the economy were crucial. Voters' perceptions of the economy were filtered through three main processes: a retrospective assessment about the state of the national economy and the extent of economic optimism about the future; the pocketbook experiences about recent and future prospects of personal financial well-being for the individual voter; and a perception about the overall competence of the parties at economic management. Conservative Central Office (CCO), together with the efforts of rank-and-file members, made some contribution to the party's success. In 1983, for example, CCO used computers and direct-mail advertising, employed 400 agents, held ticket-only rallies and introduced the use of a 'sincerity' device allowing speakers, particularly Thatcher, 'to read from notes but still appear as if they were looking the audience right in the eye'.[22]

The importance of campaigning by the party is limited in practice, however, by two factors. First, any political party can only market a saleable product. A virtually non-existent party organisation in 1983 would not have prevented a Conservative victory in the post-Falklands atmosphere against an unelectable Labour Party. Equally, a highly efficient Conservative machine could not have prevented the debacle of 1997. Second, Thatcher resorted to her own independent informal advisers to nurture her personal image and to market the party. She relied very heavily upon individuals. These included Gordon Reece, Tim Bell and Harvey Thomas. Reece 'schooled her in television presentation, advising her not to wear fussy clothes' and urging 'a tunic dress with a blouse underneath', and he arranged for her to be taught to lower the pitch of her voice. He also brought the advertising agency Saatchi & Saatchi into her campaigns, most memorably with the 1978 poster 'Labour Isn't Working'.[23] Tim Bell advised on the content and style of the 1987 election campaign.[24] Harvey Thomas organised the campaign rallies by importing the style of the American evangelist Billy Graham, including laser beams and campaign songs.[25] Such techniques helped but only in a context in which government could manipulate events for electoral gain.

A THATCHERITE POPULIST HEGEMONY?

Many commentators suggest that Thatcher had an instinctive relationship with the British people and that she both articulated their attitudes and shaped their values to the point where there was a Thatcherite ideological hegemony. While some commentators claim that her policies and rhetoric struck a chord with the British people, this is a traditional Conservative Party ability. Thatcher is considered to have tapped into populist sentiments, however, in a way that previous leaders would have thought indelicate. In this respect she was assisted by sections of the tabloid press. A case can be advanced that Thatcher consciously exploited submerged popular prejudices, which previous leaders had eschewed. Immigration is an obvious illustration. Enoch Powell welcomed her assertion in January 1978 that many British people feared being 'swamped' by immigrants. He argued that 'however prissily it was expressed, people knew what she meant, and they knew it was the truth. The fear was a real fear. The swamping was a real swamping.'[26] Fringe elements in the party were explicit. John Casey asserted that 'blacks were inferior' and urged that immigrants should be defined as 'guest workers'.[27] Even the official manifesto in 1992 promised 'a strict but fair' policy and pointed to a decline in immigrant numbers since 1979.[28] The *Daily Telegraph* considered that Thatcher had struck a popular position on the issue and asserted that 58 per cent of Labour, 71 per cent of Liberal and 84 per cent of Conservative voters endorsed her view.[29]

Hanging was another issue on which Thatcher took an aggressive stance. In 1983 she provided a parliamentary debate and voted for the restoration of hanging.[30] Her popular appeal in campaigning against welfare scrounging brought dividends in the 1970s. A European Commission survey in 1977 into the attitudes of the European population revealed that 43 per cent in Britain attributed poverty to 'laziness and lack of will power' among the poor, which was a higher proportion than in other countries, where structural rather than agency explanations prevailed. One European commentator asserted that Britain had 'a hard core of social egotism and conservatism of a most reactionary type'. Britain and Thatcher deserved each other.[31] Her exploitation of such values, together with an appeal to the 87 per cent in employment rather than the 13 per cent without work, to material prosperity and to a mood of hedonistic individualism, led to the epigram that 'Thatcher had an immoral majority, not a moral one, at her back.'[32] Thatcher also tapped xenophobic sentiments in her vigorous anti-European sentiments. The forthright expression of such views enhanced her other appeal as a strong leader, and newspapers such as the *Daily Mail* unapologetically emphasised this element asserting that 'more than any other leader since Churchill was baying defiance against the Nazis, she has captured the hearts, the minds and the imagination of the nation'.[33]

Thatcher offered many different versions of leadership. Webster has pointed to the range of feminine styles that she variously deployed: from a 'fishwife' screaming at opponents, to 'compassion' when a major accident occurred, to the 'nanny' hectoring the nation, to a 'feminine sex appeal' to 'Britannia' or the 'Iron lady'.[34] Leaders can offer a multiplicity of identities but ultimately the market decides which prevails.[35]

In reality, the evidence is ambiguous about Thatcher's proclaimed empathy with popular instincts; there is also evidence that attitudes shifted towards a more anti-Thatcherite stance in the 1980s. It is clear that there was no hegemony for Thatcherite views despite the assumption that she had won the battle of ideas. The *British Social Attitudes Survey: 1984* demonstrated that the public was 'sceptical that the government's policies would work. On many issues they were more inclined to believe in the policies the opposition was offering – a large stimulus through increased public spending, particularly on job creation.'[36] In 1986 the taxation-versus-public spending debate revealed the trajectory of popular opinion as demonstrated in Table 12.1.

TABLE 12.1: PUBLIC OPINION ABOUT TAXATION AND SPENDING, 1983–85

	1983 (%)	1984 (%)	1985 (%)
Reduce taxes and spend *less* on health, education and social benefits	9	6	6
Keep taxes and spending on these services *at the same level* as now	54	50	43
Increase taxes and spend more on health, education and social benefits	32	39	45

Source: A Jowell, S. Witherspoon and L. Brook, *British Social Attitudes: The 1986 Report* (Aldershot, 1986), 128.

Furthermore, there is no evidence that Thatcher's leadership style altered the levels of trust or cynicism in political leaders. If the country was demoralised in 1974 with 67 per cent of voters concurring that 'parties are only interested in people's votes, not in their opinions', by 1986 the corresponding figure was 66 per cent.[37] In 1989 the survey concluded that 'in Britain there is scant support for wholesale dismemberment of the welfare state and, indeed, a growing concern about the condition of its most cherished institution, the National Health Service'. Public preferences were close to a defence of the post-war mixed economy.[38] A leading Conservative, Sir Michael Fraser, argued that both 'the radicals of the new right and the new left have failed to capture the intellectual commanding heights' and he predicted that the pendulum would return to the middle ground of politics.[39] It appears that Thatcher was denied the fulfilment of the aspiration she expressed in 1968, that for a party in government, 'it is not enough to have reluctant support'.[40]

Thatcher displayed acute sensitivity about what was 'politically acceptable'.[41] This changed with the shift in her government's strategy after 1987, however, when it seems that she thought that 'the danger from the left had receded at last'.[42] The emphasis upon privatisation led to 11 million people buying shares during the high-water mark of Thatcherism. For a time the Thatcher government was successful in appealing to the new social force of a consumerism of shares, wealth, home ownership, law and order and national glory. She invited voters to conceive of themselves outside groups and to become isolated actors in the 'flourishing market relations of affluent capitalism'.[43] Yet, after 1987 her political antennae failed her, and welfare reforms and the poll tax weakened her appeal at the very time when her court of personal advisers increasingly insulated her from popular opinion.[44]

CONSERVATISM AND ESSEX MAN: THE NOTORIOUS CASE OF BASILDON[45]

For those attracted to the view that Thatcher created a populist hegemony, a myth has arisen that Essex, and particularly the constituency of Basildon, encapsulated the new political territory that she conquered.[46]

The Basildon and 'Essex man' myths have been immortalised in political fiction writing. A Conservative novelist described the phenomenon as men who 'swapped the docks for Fords of Dagenham, and most of them had taken advantage of Mrs Thatcher's right to buy … upwardly mobile, robust patriots to a man, strong believers in law and order … They were the new Tories.'[47] This captures the view that Basildon typified the new political territory that Thatcherite Conservatism is alleged to have conquered; and it implied ultra-Conservative attitudes and a vulgar materialism. 'Essex woman' was also politically important.[48] Thatcher had appealed to the wives of skilled workers in the 1970s, by her appearances on Radio Two's 'Jimmy Young Show', regarded as worth infinitely more than interviews on the television programme 'Panorama'.[49] Basildon sustains the argument that Thatcherism was more a product of dealignment and electoral volatility than the creation of new hegemony. The same applies to Labour's victory in the 1997 general election: a survey in Basildon in 2000 revealed that 'New Labour is failing to capture the enthusiasm of Basildon's voters'.[50] The mood is one of political disengagement.

Basildon has been described as a 'weathercock' constituency and 'a marginal seat in the heartlands of Essex man'.[51] It was set up as a new town development, and its population grew sharply between 1960 and 1980. The overriding socio-economic difference between Basildon and the rest of Britain is that of housing tenure. The 1981 census revealed that 53 per cent of the population resided in local authority or New Town Development Corporation properties as against an English and Welsh proportion of 28.8 per cent.[52]

In the 1992 election, Basildon was the second result declared, in a constituency that Labour had to capture if it was to form a government. The media turned up for the declaration of Labour's first gain largely because of the Basildon myth, although its proximity to London also made it easy for the media to cover. Major had no doubt about the significance of the Basildon declaration:

> The scene at Basildon flashed on the screen. As the candidates filed on to the platform, the cameras panned in on the face of the Conservative David Amess. It was a mask of suppressed emotion. 'He's lost', muttered someone. I looked at his wife. 'No he hasn't. He's won. Look at her.' Moments later the result was announced and David's arms were aloft in triumph. 'That's it, we've won,' I remember saying … 'If we've won Basildon we've won the election,' I told them. And we had.[53]

Basildon emerged from the former South-east Essex constituency. In 1950 it was largely absorbed into the Billericay constituency, which acquired an electorate of 124,215 by the 1970 general election. This was the result of the expansion of Basildon new town. The constituency was described as Basildon after the 1971 Boundary Commission review, although geographically it still included Billericay as well as Basildon new town The Conservatives captured the constituency in 1979, electing a right-wing populist, Harvey Proctor. He campaigned hard on the issue of council house sales by targeting potential beneficiaries in the course of his canvassing. The growth of the new town further increased the electorate by 1979 producing an electoral roll of 103,595. This patently suggested the need for a further redistribution. The 1981 Boundary Commission duly split the seat into Billericay and Basildon respectively.[54] Basildon became a very different and compact new town constituency with only 65,000 voters and Proctor selected the likelier haven of Billericay, creating a vacancy in Basildon. This study focuses on the smaller new-town based constituency of Basildon, which came into existence in 1981, because it was the repeated electoral success of the Conservatives in this more working-class area that requires explanation. Social change was patently affecting the new town by 1981, however, because many council houses had been purchased in the first two years of the Thatcher government. The census returns demonstrate that there was a drop in tenancy from 53 to 51.8 per cent in that period, but the second figure applies to the far lower population residing in the smaller constituency based on the new town. This was the start of a trend because there was a rise in home ownership from 53 per cent in 1981 to 71 per cent in 1996.[55]

Proctor's departure appeared prudent after the boundary change. In the *Almanac of British Politics* Waller predicted that Basildon 'should be a Labour constituency' in the 1983 general election, with a majority, based upon 1979 voting patterns, of 8,000 plus.[56] He neglected the significance of two developments. First, the new Basildon constituency contained marginal wards such as Langdon Hills and Nethermayne with a substantial professional and managerial presence amounting to 15.1 per cent and, second, the impact of the rapid sale of council houses. The popularity of this policy is demonstrated by the 1997 survey in which 36 per cent of voters said it was the best policy the Conservatives had pursued.[57] This preference can be traced back to post-war relocation policies and to the hope of betterment, which the new towns encouraged.

Basildon remained a Conservative constituency from 1979 to 1997, replicating the national political situation. It is likely that the phenomenon it represents is better described as pertaining to south-east Essex or even the entire north Thames corridor. This area has a distinct social mix with a high concentration of C2s and former residents of the East End of London and, in the 1970s and 1980s, a significant proportion of car workers. The swing to the Conservatives in Basildon in 1979 was 13.4 per cent, as against 5.2 per cent in the country at large.[58] The result supports the idea that the north Thames corridor, stretching back into Islington Central, through the East End and along the north bank of the river to Dagenham, was particularly affected by Thatcher's blandishments, since in those ten seats a mean swing of 14.2 per cent was recorded. Basildon was a microcosm of the national political context in that the Labour Party failed to offer the quality of local opposition necessary to recapture the seat. One activist admits to bitter factionalism within the Basildon party, and another asserts that 'the extraordinary thing is how complacent and incredulous Labour activists were in Basildon'.[59]

1983

Basildon Conservatives selected David Amess as their candidate in 1983. He originated from London's East End. It became evident that he was an 'emblematic right-wing Thatcherite' who supported hanging, the poll tax and opposition to sanctions against South Africa. He supported a voluntary identity card system and was opposed to abortion and embryo research; Michael Portillo later appointed him as his parliamentary private secretary.[60] During the campaign, Amess exploited local fears by suggesting that Labour's policy on nuclear disarmament would jeopardise over 5,000 workers' jobs locally in such factories as Marconi and GEC Avionics. Amess claimed a direct appeal to working-class voters and considered that class remained a potent issue in Britain, arguing that the Basildon working class sought the empowerment offered by the opportunity to buy their own homes and retain their own money through tax cuts. He added that they also 'adored' Thatcher, because she appealed both to their self-interest and to their enthusiasm for the 'nation'.[61]

In the years that followed, the epithets of 'Essex man' and 'Mondeo man' were widely used to encapsulate Basildon. The 'Mondeo man'[62] label was potent given that some of the electors were employed at Ford in Dagenham. Skilled workers were becoming secularised and instrumental in their approach to voting behaviour rather than being motivated simply by class or party loyalty. They were portrayed as becoming detached from a solid Labour identity and inclined to vote instrumentally to promote their short-term perceived economic interest.[63] Norman Tebbit recognised the Conservative Party's potential to reach people traditionally regarded as Labour sympathisers: 'I had long believed that most of the values, ethos and policies of Conservatism were strongly supported by working-class voters. Those voters – especially the socio-economic groups C1 and C2 – I saw as natural Conservatives who, nevertheless, saw themselves for tribal reason as Labour.'[64] The tendency for such voters to be footloose is explained by Crewe's differentiation of the working class into the 'old' and 'new'. The new working classes lived in the south, worked in the private sector, were owner-occupiers rather than tenants and tended not to belong to a trade union. Crewe's analysis suggests that 42 per cent of voters in this category in 1983 and 46 per cent in 1987 voted Conservative as against 26 per cent and 28 per cent for Labour.[65] 'Basildon has a higher proportion of skilled workers (C2s) than any other town in Britain.'[66] MORI reported that the 'battleground' in the 1979 election was for the votes of this group, which swung to the Conservatives by almost 12 per cent, twice the rate for the general population. Worcester demonstrates the shift among the voting habits of C2s, with 20 per cent voting Conservative in 1974 as against 40 per cent in both the 1983 and 1987 elections.[67] Many C2 voters in Basildon purchased their council houses; women, in particular, were attracted by the prospect of home ownership.[68] Worcester states that among working-class homeowners nationally the Conservatives led by 11 per cent, while among working-class council tenants Labour led by 38 per cent.[69] Thatcher's 1986 conference speech stressed that it was through property ownership that she could return power to the people.[70]

The general election result in Basildon in June 1983 was surprising, because Labour captured control of the local council in May, despite its left-wing image as a nuclear-free zone. The shift in votes between May and June reflected the national situation. It is apparent that there was a haemorrhage of up to one-fifth of those supporting Labour nationally during the course of the campaign. Yet the uneven distribution of Labour's losses reveals that switching was at its highest in Bradford North and Basildon, at 18 and 16.1 per cent respectively. A common feature was the intervention of a strong SDP/Liberal Alliance candidate.[71] The impact that Sue Slipman had in Basildon requires some reassessment of the cruder Essex man portrayals. Nationally there was a fierce battle between Labour and the SDP/Liberal Alliance for second place. Labour's left-wing upsurge, and the consequent divisions within the party, and the split on the centre-left of British politics between Labour and the Alliance were replicated in Basildon. Labour's candidate selection was 'hard fought and fractious'. The final ballot was a 'head to head' between Bill Hodge supported by the Trotskyite Militant Tendency and a moderate university lecturer, Julian Fulbrook, who was selected. Fulbrook was able, but activists suggest that he was 'ill at ease' with local people. These were favourable circumstances for the SDP/Liberal Alliance candidacy to flourish. The seriousness of the Alliance campaign was evident from the visits of David Owen, David Steel and Shirley Williams. David Owen committed the Alliance to maintaining the policy of council house sales.[72] On this issue it was Labour that was out of touch with many of its erstwhile supporters.

The Times predicted the Conservative victory while Labour activists underestimated Amess, who was 31, as 'a young lightweight on his first outing'.[73] The Basildon result reveals the limits of the Essex man myth. First, even the redrawn constituency boundaries included wards with a substantial middle-class and professional/managerial presence. Clearly the Conservative vote was an amalgam of an established vote in areas of high-quality housing, *traditional* working-class Conservatives and new converts to Thatcherism. Second, the result demonstrates that many former Labour voters defected, not to the Conservatives, but to the SDP. Basildon Conservatives accept that had Slipman been better attuned to the male working-class voters she might have taken more Conservative votes. According to Smith, the election of a right-wing Conservative 'owed much to the strong showing of Sue Slipman, formerly a leading communist, for the SDP'.[74] As an SDP candidate she played better than a Liberal in Labour wards, although she built on existing Liberal support in two wards. Smith's interpretation is apparently upheld because the figures suggest that it was Slipman, assisted by the 'dismal' reputation of the council, who facilitated Amess's victory. This is uncertain, however, because the second preference of Alliance voters is not known. The Alliance possibly provided a safe harbour for Conservative refugees in which case there would still have been a Conservative victory.

TABLE 12.2: BASILDON CONSTITUENCY RESULT, 1983

Candidate	Votes
D. A. Amess (Conservative)	17,516
J. H. Fulbrook (Labour)	16,137
S. Slipman (SDP)	11,634
Conservative majority	*1,379*

1987

By 1987 Labour activists assumed that it was 'a safe bet' that Labour would take the seat, which was fourteenth on Labour's target list. Labour captured 20 seats nationally, so its performance in Basildon was worse than its national standing (see Table 12.3).

Clearly there is a growing regional and neighbourhood variable in voting behaviour. Analysts argue that the dominant party in an area attracts disproportionate support from all classes. Both Amess and Angela Smith argue that, for many former East End families, the process of removal from the solidaristic East End working-class communities to be rehoused in modern accommodation, in a town with vast new shopping malls, redolent of individualised consumption rather than community life, encouraged dealignment. It has been described as 'America in Essex'.[75] Waller refers to

TABLE 12.3: BASILDON CONSTITUENCY RESULT, 1987

Candidate	Votes
D. A. Amess (Conservative)	21,858
J. H. Fulbrook (Labour)	19,209
R. M. Auvray (Liberal)	9,139
Conservative majority	*2,649*

'a long-term swing to the right' in Essex and Hertfordshire new towns.[76] Bodman argues that the neighbourhood effect alters the information flow to the voter, and that if neighbourhood and regional influences are strong then voters with a weakening attachment to party 'will presumably be more susceptible than others with a strong party identification'.[77] There is American evidence that migrants 'do not carry their party loyalty with them but adapt their political opinions towards those which are dominant in the area to which they move'.[78]

As part of the southern region, Basildon experienced prosperity. This was subsidised by the public sector: most defence, military and research laboratory establishments are in the south, as are the majority of the beneficiaries of mortgage tax relief and commuter rail subsidies. In short, the Home Counties is not a place but a 'way of life', separate from a common British identity.[79] Thatcher's support was not geographically representative: 80 per cent of the party's seats were in the south as against 60 per cent from a similar total in 1959.[80]

If influences such as tenancy, local employment prospects, migration, regional impact and socio-economic status assisted Labour defections to the SDP and the Conservatives, there were also political factors. Labour ran poor local campaigns and by 1987 the Basildon Conservatives possessed the advantage of incumbency. Amess was renowned for praising Basildon, and for promoting its interests, in Parliament.[81] Students of constituency campaigning argue that incumbency has an inbuilt advantage owing to the powers of office, the benefits of parliamentary publicity and the record of constituency work.[82] Amess considered that his incumbency bonus was worth 3,000 votes, and Angela Smith asserts that Amess did much 'door knocking'. He claims to have campaigned 'everywhere', 'known the streets' and to have become part of the community.[83]

The tabloid press christened Basildon 'Moscow on Thames' because of the council's anti-Thatcher stance. Smith's interpretation of the relationship between Thatcher and Basildon voters is that by 1987 she 'beguiled enough working-class voters' to thwart Labour, in contrast to Amess's claim that Basildon people 'adored' her.[84] Economic restructuring between 1979 and 1987 had affected Basildon less than the declining parts of Britain and privatisations had enticed some voters into buying shares and becoming participants in a 'people's capitalism'.[85]

1992

The period from 1987 to 1992 for the Conservative Party was dogged by political unpopularity and economic failure, partly induced by the inflationary consequences of the 1988 budget. By 1992 it was no longer credible to blame the recession on the previous Labour government.[86] The 1992 general election was much more of a struggle for the votes of skilled workers because the recession of 1990–92 was damaging the economy of the south-east of England.[87] The omens in Basildon were unclear, however, because the local elections of 1991 had been poor for Labour and the council's image remained negative. This worked to the disadvantage of the Labour candidate in 1992, John Potter, who had been leader of the council for most of the time since 1973. Basildon remained Conservative, symbolising the fact that Labour continued to trail nationally among skilled working-class voters, particularly in the south (see Table 12.4).

The twin issues of Kinnock and taxes explain the Conservative victory of 1992.[88] The *Sun* ridiculed Kinnock, asserting that despite the recession 'it would have been a hell of a lot worse under Kinnock who has never worked for a living and has only been a student'.[89] It described him as 'Taff the Lad' and, under a picture of the shadow cabinet at the prematurely exultant Sheffield rally, referred to the ITV programme 'Stars in their Eyes' in which ordinary people impersonated someone famous for five minutes.[90] On the day before polling day the *Sun* played on the title of a popular Hollywood film, with the headline 'Nightmare on Kinnock Street'.[91] Its election-day front page was a classic of negative political propaganda. Kinnock's head was pictured in a light bulb, and he was described as 'the bald bloke with wispy red hair'. The accompanying message was: 'If Labour wins today, will the last person to leave the country please switch off the lights. See

TABLE 12.4: NORTH–SOUTH DIFFERENCES IN VOTING BEHAVIOUR

	Conservative	Labour	Alliance
New working classes, living in the south:			
1987	46	26	26
1992	38	36	22
Traditional working class, living in *Scotland/northern England:*			
1987	29	57	15
1992	29	56	13

Source: R. Garner and R. Kelly, *British Political Parties Today* (Manchester, 1998), 235.

you at the airport.'[92] The *Sun* inflamed the taxation issue by estimating the additional tax burden for groups such as car workers.[93]
It also reinforced the Conservative exploitation of the immigration
issue by headlining a speech by the Home Secretary, Kenneth
Baker, who predicted neo-Nazi race riots if Labour won because
the immigration floodgates would be opened.[94]

The *Financial Times* correctly analysed the campaign. 'Across
southern England from Bath to Basildon voting will be shaped less
by ideology than by two sets of opposing fears. For many in the
south the present fears over unemployment and bankruptcy are
outweighed by the greater fear that Labour will make things
worse.'[95] A report from Basildon cited the director of the
Cornwallis Business Centre, who asserted that half of the businesses in the centre were doing well and 'the others face difficulties but are determined to be there when the upturn comes'. She
expressed her confidence in the Conservatives and predicted
'things will bounce back'. In analysing the 1992 result it is clear that
Amess skilfully exploited the concerns over Kinnock and taxes.
The conventional wisdom that the press merely reinforces allegiances carries greater force when partisan loyalties are stronger.
In an increasingly secularised and dealigned electorate, the press
reinforces widely held fears and attitudes among electors.

The *Guardian* referred to two different elections, one on television and the other in the tabloid press.[96] Kinnock himself blamed
the tabloids for his defeat, and Baroness Blackstone stated:
'Whatever anyone says about the press being ignored, it has the
effect of a drip on a stone.'[97] Basildon's defeated Labour candidate
was equally adamant. 'I don't remember an election where the
tabloids were so outlandish. It was frightening the pressure on
people not to think.' He claimed a good response to Labour on the
doorsteps, and a fading of the tax and mortgage issues, 'then a

tabloid blitzkrieg in the last days' created a situation in which people 'decided how to vote in the booth based on a subliminal message which came through loud and clear'.[98] Amess informed the *Sun*:

> [It] was your front page that did it. It crystallised all the issues. People in Basildon were so impressed with the *Sun*'s front page that they stuck it up in car windows. Your previous day's issue, which spelled out the nightmare on Kinnock Street, was also highly effective. At the end the voters realised that Kinnock was talking rubbish. They saw that if Kinnock wanted to raise £28 billion he would have to put up taxes. The trouble with Mr K and his shadow cabinet is that they sneer at people who live in Basildon. They wouldn't dream of living there but they expected my constituents to vote for them.[99]

Another commentator mocked Labour's tendency towards 'Chianti swigging, cigar chomping' types who 'sneer at Basildon'. He described Basildon as the 'capital of the Essex man's kingdom' populated by 'six-pack swigging, *Sun* reading, Escort driving, Benidorm holidaying yobbos who don't give a fig for any of the burning issues of the day such as the need to pay more tax and have a Ministry for Women'. People want to look after 'number one'. He eulogised Basildon as 'a township of average, decent people earning a living, wanting a nice car and nice holidays and a say in their children's education, not wanting any of that guff about nuclear free zones'. He concluded that Labour snobs 'hate the sight of Basildon'.[100]

The conundrum symbolised by Basildon was that Labour 'captured the guilty middle class but it had signally failed to make substantial inroads into the C2s and the lower ranks of middle management'.[101] Amess accentuated the themes of the Conservative campaign, aided by visits from Major, Thatcher and Tebbit, who came to 'press the flesh of the Essex men and women whose once unquestionable allegiance has been shaken by the disproportionately vicious effects of the recession in the town'. He was accused of smearing his Labour opponent for 'living in sin'.[102]

The *Guardian* reported that the Basildon result was to be expected in 'archetypal Thatcherite C2 Essex man territory'.[103] A week before it called the Basildon result 'too close to call'. If the explanation is that the Conservatives pulled ahead in the final days, then it is likely that their concentration on Labour's weaknesses, supported by the tabloid press, proved decisive. Many observers testify to press influence – for example, the evidence that

TABLE 12.5: BASILDON CONSTITUENCY RESULT, 1992

Candidate	Votes
D. A. Amess (Conservative)	24,159
J. Potter (Labour)	22,679
G. Williams (Liberal)	6,967
Conservative majority	*1,480*

voters absorb only two political stories when they read a news-paper.[104] Pollsters attest to the electoral importance of the *Sun*.[105] Abercrombie points to a radical oppositional ideology in Britain in the 1980s which was 'often hidden by the weight of dominant ideologies articulated with such power by a privately owned and largely Conservative supporting national press'.[106] Ramsden points to Thatcher's reliance on the press; in 1990, 9 million Conservative supporting papers were sold as against 3.5 million pro-Labour newspapers. He pointed to Murdoch's appeal to the 'new' working class who liked Thatcher's 'populist style and xenophobic politics'.[107] Yet this was 'dangerous' for the Conservatives, because press propaganda is short term and lacks ideological roots. In 1992 it helped reinforce Labour's image in Basildon as the party of 'poverty' and 'failure'.[108]

Despite the boundary changes introduced in 1993, which were adjudged to have enhanced Conservative prospects by 10,000 voters added from the Thurrock wards (including, for example, Stanford le Hope, Corringham and other rural villages), so low was Amess's confidence that he went 'on the chicken run' to Southend. In May 1997 Angela Smith captured Basildon with a 13,280 majority and a 14.7 per cent swing to Labour.

BASILDON: A SUMMARY

Basildon partly sustains the case for a Conservative link to the mass electorate during Thatcher's years. The Conservative capture of Basildon was not based upon a wholesale conversion of the working-class electorate. There is evidence that the 'Thatcher years fostered a sense of individualism and self-improvement and a mistrust of collective action', and this is demonstrated by the fact that a majority of Basildon residents in 2001 do not belong to any club or society. Basildon man 'drinks' or 'goes to the gym' alone.[109] Thatcherism thus finally eroded local civic society and social capital, which had already been weakened by the effects of people decanting to the new town from East End estates. There was some evidence of car workers and new town dwellers moving to the Conservatives but two other factors were important.[110] First, the decanting of former East End dwellers to towns like Basildon assisted the Conservatives because East Enders, exiled East Enders and their children all 'dealigned' together. Hayes and Hudson oversimplify the political circumstances by stressing the uniqueness of Basildon.[111] The new town phenomenon simply exacerbated changes in social structures and political attitudes occurring along the north Thames corridor from central London: 'Thatcherism enjoyed negative success as the corrosive agent which broke down the certainties of old forms of social life.'[112]

Race also played a part in Basildon. Despite the low percentage of New Commonwealth immigrants, some of the white electorate had left the East End to escape its increasingly multicultural character.[113] Of all the issues on which the Basildon Conservative Association could have presented a resolution to annual conference in 1988, it chose race, stating that conference applauds 'the government on the strict control of immigration to the United Kingdom and welcomes the higher price now placed upon British citizenship'.[114]

While the ill-fated Major government, after Black Wednesday in 1992, contributed to the undermining of the appeal of Thatcherite Conservatism, it is notable that Blair was 'received like a pop star in Basildon in 1997'.[115] It is likely that Thatcher's image of competence and determination counted for more than policy. This appeal, more marked in southern than northern England, has been defined as 'statecraft'.[116] In 1992, Labour failed to offer a viable alternative statecraft. Thatcher's statecraft could never provide a basis for a permanent party realignment, and she made Major appear weak by comparison. In short, the Conservatives linked well with sections of a secularising and dealigning electorate, but only ephemerally. If Basildon voters displayed a predisposition towards council house sales, had negative experiences of local Labour government, feared local job losses, possessed a high proportion of skilled workers drawn from a region which was moving Conservative, experienced prosperity, approved of Thatcher's forceful leadership style and was anxious about immigration, this merely represented a heightened intensity of national issues.

A survey of Basildon in 2000 suggests that only 22 per cent of residents identify with Basildon while 73 per cent call themselves working class.[117] It was the combination of an affluent, skilled working class and its geographical location that proved politically salient. It was this socio-economic character which was more influential than the impact of the town. The region in which Basildon is situated mattered, however, as demonstrated by the comment in the local newspaper that the political map of Britain was 'blue in the south and red in the north', revealing 'the gap in feeling between the areas where [Thatcher's] dream of making us a nation of capitalists seems attractive and those where unemployment and poverty dominate'.[118] Basildon represented an evanescent flirtation by some former Labour voters, disaffected with collectivism and attracted to individualism, with a particular leader during an affluent period.

CONCLUSION

The Conservative Party's historic capacity to extend its appeal to those who are not substantial beneficiaries of its policies remained from 1975 to 1992, during which period it managed favourable political and economic circumstances to its own advantage. Yet, while its policies were rooted in some limited elite and mass adherence during the 1970s, their appeal diminished during the 1980s. Thatcher was both the most reviled and respected of post-war prime ministers. Voters do not respond to the qualities of a leader in isolation, but in comparison to the other political leaders on offer. Thatcher was lucky in her opponents. Strong leadership and prosperity temporarily enticed dealigning Labour voters, particularly C2 voters, anxious to buy their houses. There was, however, no Conservative realignment, no differential party dealignment and only limited pro-Conservative issue voting.

NOTES

1.   A. Seldon and S. Ball (eds), *Conservative Century: The Conservative Party since 1900* (Oxford, 1994).
2.   Chris Stevens, 'The Electoral Sociology of Modern Britain Reconsidered', *Contemporary British History*, 13 (1999), 74.
3.   L. Tivey and A. Wright, *Party Ideology in Britain* (London, 1989), 207.
4.   D. Butler and D. Stokes, *Political Change in Modern Britain* (London, 1974).
5.   British Public Opinion, *MORI* (August 1990), 4.
6.   P. Dunleavy and C. Husbands, *Democracy at the Crossroads* (London, 1985) 212.
7.   Gallup, *Gallup Political Index* (1979–92).

8. P. Abramson, 'Of Time and Partisan Stability in Britain', *British Journal of Political Science*, 22 (1992), 385–6.
9. P.A. Beck, 'The Electoral Cycle and Patterns of American Politics', *British Journal of Political Science*, 9 (1979), 125–56.
10. B. Sarlvick and I. Crewe, *Decade of Dealignment: The Conservative Victory of 1979 and Electoral Trends in the 1970s* (Cambridge, 1983); M. Franklin, *The Decline of Class Voting in Britain: Changes in the Basic Electoral Choice 1964–1983* (Oxford, 1985); A. Heath *et al.*, 'Partisan Realignment Revisited', in D. Denver and G. Hands, *Issues and Controversies in British Electoral Behaviour* (Hemel Hempstead, 1992).
11. A. King, *Britain at the Polls* (London, 1992), 246.
12. Gallup, *Political Index* (1979–92).
13. Ibid.
14. Ibid.
15. W. Miller, M. Hoskin and R. Fitzgerald, 'British Parties in the Balance: A Time Series Analysis of Long-term Trends in Conservative and Labour Support', *British Journal of Political Science*, 19 (1989), 217–19.
16. D. Sanders, H. Ward and D. Marsh, 'Government Popularity in the Falklands War: A Reassessment', *British Journal of Political Science*, 17 (1987), 281–313.
17. H. Norpath, 'Guns, Butter and Government Popularity in Britain', *American Political Science Review*, 8 (1987), 947–59; H. Clarke, M. Stewart and C. Zuk, 'Politics, Economics and Party Popularity in Britain 1979–83', *Electoral Studies*, 5 (1986) 123–41.
18. H. Clarke, W. Miller and P. Whiteley, 'Recapturing the Falklands: Model of Conservative Popularity', *British Journal of Political Science*, 26 (1996), 80.
19. See the relevant Nuffield Election Studies volumes by D. Butler and D. Kavanagh, *The British General Election of 1979* (London, 1980), *The British General Election of 1983* (London, 1984), *The British General Election of 1987* (1988) and *The British General Election of 1992* (1992).
20. Miller, Hoskin and Fitzgerald, 'British Parties in the Balance', 230.
21. Ibid., 234.
22. A. J. Davies, *We the Nation: The Conservative Party and the Pursuit of Power* (London, 1995), 196.
23. J. Ranelagh, *Thatcher's People* (London, 1981), 146.
24. Ibid., 217.
25. R. Blake, *The Conservative Party from Peel to Major* (London, 1991), 371.
26. S. Heffer, *Like the Roman: The Life of Enoch Powell* (London, 1998), 860.
27. M. Jones, *Thatcher's Kingdom* (Sydney, 1984), 288.
28. Ibid., 285.
29. *Daily Telegraph*, 23 January 1978.
30. Jones, *Thatcher's Kingdom*, 155.
31. *Daily Telegraph*, 21 July 1977.
32. P. Hennessy and A. Seldon (eds), *Ruling Performance: British Governments from Attlee to Thatcher* (London, 1987), 274.
33. Jones, *Thatcher's Kingdom*, 389.
34. W. Webster, 'Not a Man to Touch Her' (PhD thesis, University of York, 1990).
35. Hennessy and Seldon, *Ruling Performance*, 282.
36. A. Jowell and C. Airey (eds), *British Social Attitudes: The 1984 Report* (Aldershot, 1984), 47.
37. A. Jowell, S. Witherspoon and L. Brook, *British Social Attitudes: The 1987 Report* (Aldershot, 1987), 54.
38. A. Jowell, S. Witherspoon and L. Brook, *British Social Attitudes: The 1989 Report* (Aldershot, 1989), 36–7.
39. Hennessey and Seldon, *Ruling Performance*, 320–2.
40. J. Campbell, *Margaret Thatcher: The Grocer's Daughter* (London, 2000), 186.
41. M. Pirie, *Micropolitics: The Creation of a Successful Politics* (London, 1989), 51.
42. P. Catterall (ed), *Contemporary Britain: An Annual Review* (Oxford, 1990), 30.
43. D. Coates, *Running the Country* (London, 1995), 189.
44. A. Denham and M. Garnett, *British Think Tanks and the Climate of Opinion* (London, 1998), 202.
45. 'Basildon Man, Otherwise Known as the Average Briton', *Guardian*, 20 March 2001.

46. Angela Smith MP and David Amess MP greatly assisted me with this work, as did correspondence with party activists.
47. J. Critchley, *Hung Parliament* (London, 1991), 23.
48 Ibid., 114.
49. Davies, *We, the Nation*, 211.
50. *Guardian*, 20 March 2001.
51. J. Ramsden, *An Appetite for Power* (London, 1998), 453; Blake, *Conservative Party from Peel to Major*, 395.
52. Office of the Population and Census, *1981 Census Report*.
53. J. Major, *An Autobiography* (London, 2000), 305.
54. N. Smith, *Campaigning for Labour in Basildon* (Basildon Labour Party, 2000), 13.
55. D. Hayes and A. Hudson, *Basildon: The Mood of the Nation* (London, 2001), 15.
56. R. Waller, *The Almanac of British Politics* (London, 1983), 10.
57. Hayes and Hudson, *Basildon*, 39.
58. Butler and Kavanagh, *The British General Election of 1979*, 363.
59. Leading local activist in conversation with the author.
60. R. Waller and B. Criddle, *The Almanac of British Politics* (London, 1996), 42; *Basildon Evening Echo*, 16 June 1983.
61. David Amess MP in conversation with me.
62. The 'Mondeo' was Ford's standard saloon car at this time.
63. R. McKenzie and A. Silver, *Angels in Marble* (London, 1968).
64. N. Tebbit, *Upwardly Mobile* (London, 1989), 172.
65. F. Conley, *General Elections Today* (Manchester, 1994), 150.
66. Hayes and Hudson, *Basildon*, 14.
67. R. Worcester, *British Public Opinion: A Guide to the History and Methodology of Political Opinion Polling* (Oxford, 1991), 108.
68. Ibid., 18.
69. Ibid., 109.
70. S. Ball, *The Conservative Party since 1945* (Manchester, 1998), 179.
71. Dunleavy and Husbands, *Democracy at the Crossroads*, 198–9.
72. *Daily Mail*, 14 May 1983,
73. Local activist in conversation with the author.
74. Smith, *Campaigning for Labour in Basildon*, 14.
75. *The Times*, 27 June 1992.
76. Waller and Criddle, *Almanac of British Politics* (1996 edn), 42.
77. A. R. Bodman, 'The Neighbourhood Effect: A Test of the Butler–Stokes Model', *British Journal of Political Science*, 12 (1983), 240.
78. D. Denver and F. Halfacre, 'Inter-constituency Migration and Turnout in the British General Election of 1983', *British Journal of Political Science*, 22 (1992), 572.
79. J. Osmond, *The Divided Kingdom* (London, 1988), 46, 160.
80. Ramsden, *Appetite for Power*, 454.
81. D. Rossiter, R. Johnston and C. Pattie, *The Boundary Commission* (Manchester, 1999), 389; Douglas Hurd, reported in *Guardian*, 2 April 1992.
82. C. Pattie, P. Whiteley, D. Johnston and P. Seyd, 'Measuring Local Campaign Effects: Labour Party Constituency Campaigning at the 1992 General Election', *Political Studies*, 34 (1986), 34.
83. David Amess MP in conversation with me.
84. Smith, *Campaigning for Labour in Basildon*, 13.
85. Coates, *Running the Country*, 175.
86. Ibid., 199.
87. B. Evans, *Thatcherism and British Politics 1975–1999* (London, 1999), 151.
88. *Sun*, 9 April 1992.
89. *Sun*, 3 April 1992.
90. *Sun*, 2 April 1992.
91. *Sun*, 8 April 1992.
92. *Sun*, 9 April 1992.
93. *Sun*, 30 March 1992.
94. *Financial Times*, 7 April 1992.
95. Ibid.

96. *Guardian*, 30 March 1992.
97. *Financial Times*, 11 April 1992.
98. *Guardian*, 18 April 1992.
99. *Sun*, 11 April 1992.
100. *Daily Mail*, 11 May 1992.
101. *Financial Times*, 11 April 1992.
102. *Guardian*, 2 April 1992.
103. *Guardian*, 9 April 1992. In the May 1992 local elections in Basildon the Conservatives captured every seat being contested.
104. *Guardian Extra*, 26 February 2001.
105. *Guardian*, 8 February 2001.
106. N. Abercrombie (ed.), *Dominant Ideologies* (London, 1980), 1–37.
107. Ramsden, *Appetite for Power*, 465.
108. Hayes and Hudson, *Basildon*, 19.
109. Ibid., 42.
110. Butler and Kavanagh, *General Election of 1979*, 397.
111. Hayes and Hudson, *Basildon*, 66.
112. Ibid., 42.
113. Critchley, *Hung Parliament*, 23.
114. *Conservative Party Annual Conference Report* (1988), 41.
115. D. Butler and D. Kavanagh, *The British General Election of 1997* (London, 1998), 218–19.
116. J. Bulpitt, 'The Discipline of the New Democracy: Mrs Thatcher's Statecraft', *Political Studies*, 34 (1986), 19–39.
117. *Guardian*, 20 March 2001.
118. *Basildon Evening Echo*, 12 June 1983.

Notes on Contributors

Stuart Ball is Reader in History at the University of Leicester. He is author of *Baldwin and the Conservative Party: the Crisis of 1929–1931* (1988) and *The Conservative Party and British Politics 1902–1951* (1995); editor of *Parliament and Politics in the Age of Baldwin and MacDonald: The Headlam Diaries 1923–1935* (1992), *Parliament and Politics in the Age of Churchill and Attlee: the Headlam Diaries 1935–1951* (1999), and *The Conservative Party since 1945* (1998); and co-editor of *Conservative Century: The Conservative Party since 1900* (1994) and *The Heath Government 1970–1974: A Reappraisal* (1996).

Catriona Burness has lectured at the Universities of Dundee, Durham, Edinburgh, Glasgow and St Andrews. She now works at the European Parliament in Brussels. Her book *Strange Associations: The Irish Question and the Making of Scottish Unionism 1886–1918* will be published in 2002.

N. J. Crowson is Lecturer in History at the University of Birmingham. He is the author of several articles and of *Facing Fascism: The Conservative Party and the European Dictators 1935–1940* (1997) and the *Longman Companion to the Conservative Party since 1830* (2001). He edited *Fleet Street, Press Barons and Party Politics: The Journals of Collin Brooks 1932–1940* (1998).

Peter Dorey is Senior Lecturer in Politics at Cardiff University. He is author of *The Conservative Party and the Trade Unions* (1995), *British Politics since 1945* (1995), and *Wage Politics in Britain: The Rise and Fall of Incomes Policies since 1945* (2001); and editor of *The Major Premiership* (1999).

Brendan Evans is Professor of Politics and Pro-Vice-Chancellor (academic affairs) at the University of Huddersfield. His previous publications include *The Politics of the Training Market* (1992), *From Salisbury to Major: Continuity and Change in Conservative Politics* (with Andrew Taylor, 1996), and *Thatcherism and British Politics 1975–1997* (1999).

James Hinton is Reader in History at the University of Warwick. His publications include *The First Shop Stewards' Movement* (1973), *Labour and Socialism: A History of the British Labour Movement 1867–1974* (1983), *Shop Floor Citizens: Engineering Democracy in 1940s Britain* (1994), and *Continuities of Class: Women and Social Leadership in Mid-Twentieth Century England* (2002).

Ian Holliday is Professor of Policy Studies and Head of the Department of Public and Social Administration, City University of Hong Kong. His publications include *The British Cabinet System* (co-authored, 1996), *Fundamentals in British Politics* (co-edited, 1999), *Developments in British Politics 4, 5 and 6* (co-edited, 1993, 1997, 2000) and articles on British politics and policy.

Nicholas Mansfield has been Director of the National Museum of Labour History since 1989 and is a Research Fellow in the Department of History at Manchester University. His recent publications include *English Farmworkers and Local Patriotism 1900–1930* (2001).

Paul Martin teaches postgraduate courses in public history (the first of this kind in Britain) at Ruskin College, Oxford, and museum studies at the University of Leicester. He has written books on material culture studies and articles on twentieth-century historical subjects as diverse as popular music and French resistance war memorials.

Kevin Morgan is Senior Lecturer in Government at the University of Manchester. He is author of *Against Fascism and War: Ruptures and Continuities in British Communist Politics 1935–1941* (1989) and *Harry Pollitt* (1993), and is editor of the journal *Socialist History*. He is currently completing a study of the Webbs and Soviet Communism.

Lord Norton of Louth is Professor of Government and Director of the Centre for Legislative Studies at the University of Hull. His many publications include *Dissension in the House of Commons 1945–1974* (1975), *Conservative Dissidents: Dissent within the Parliamentary Conservative Party 1970–1974* (1978), *Dissension in the House of Commons 1974–1979* (1980), *The Commons in Perspective* (1981), *The Constitution in Flux* (1982), *The British Polity* (4th edn., 2001), and *Does Parliament Matter?* (1993). He is co-author of *Conservatives and Conservatism* (1981) and *Back from Westminster?* (1993). He is editor of *The Conservative Party* (1996) and, among many other works, a three-volume series on *Parliaments in Western Europe* (1998–2002).

Andrew Rowe was a Lecturer at Edinburgh University, before serving as Director of the Community Affairs Department at Conservative Central Office from 1975 to 1979. From 1983 to 2001 he was Conservative MP for Mid-Kent.

Andrew Taylor was formerly Professor of Politics at the University of Huddersfield and is currently Reader in Politics at the University of Sheffield. He has written widely on the role of trade unions in British politics and the Conservative Party, and is author of *From Salisbury to Major: Continuity and Change in Conservative Politics* (with Brendan Evans, 1996). His latest book is *The National Union of Mineworkers and British Politics, 1944–1968* (2002); the second volume, covering 1969–95, will be published in 2003.

Index